THE

FILM-MAKER'S

ART

THE
FILM-MAKER'S
ART

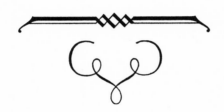

HAIG P. MANOOGIAN

BASIC BOOKS, INC. / PUBLISHERS

NEW YORK   LONDON

PN
1995
.9
.P7
M3

© 1966 by Haig P. Manoogian

Library of Congress Catalog Card Number: 66–16372

Manufactured in the United States of America

Designed by Vincent Torre

TO BETZI

The greatest thing a human soul ever does in this world is to see something, and tell what it saw in a plain way. Hundreds of people can talk for one who can think but thousands can think for one who can see. To see clearly is poetry, prophecy and religion, all in one.

JOHN RUSKIN

CONTENTS

CONTENTS

THE
FILM-MAKER'S
ART

1

THE FILM-MAKER'S PERSPECTIVE

Michel de Montaigne, the sixteenth-century French philosopher, wrote that "arts and sciences are not cast in a mold, but are formed and perfected by degrees, by frequent handling and polishing, as bears leisurely lick their cubs into form." Certainly, he did not have the art and science of film-making in mind, but his statement is more than applicable to the demanding task of uniting in a finished film creative spirit and technical skill. Vast labor and knowledge as well as talent are required, for the blending of technology with form and substance is neither simple nor straightforward. The point at which content leaves off and technique begins is blurred, and yet they are so interdependent that one is impossible without the other. Above all, then, the film-maker must not only be fully aware of both art and technique, but of technology as well. Film-making is a twentieth-century art born of science.

No one can create a film, much less do the work called for, unless he understands the technology. Far more than in other arts, the artistic results depend on familiarity with science and machinery. Engineering has provided so many tools, devices, and processes that film-making today is like a gadgeteer's dream come true. Consider ultrasensitive high-speed film that allows picture-taking under seemingly impossible light conditions, or transistors that make feasible vest-pocket synchronous units that record actual sound and speech almost anywhere.

Such developments, which make possible so much more, may at times be an obstacle, because the temptation is so great, and so subtle, to concentrate on mastery of the techniques. In the heady excitement of achieving an effect or of bringing off a difficult technical tour de force, it is easy to find a pseudoartistic satisfaction that blinds one to the demands of a fully artistic piece of work.

Film-making usually appeals to sensitive people who have artistic ability coupled with manual dexterity. Because they are less familiar and more specific, the mechanics of film-making have been given a great deal of attention in courses and textbooks from many film-making countries. However, just as no typist, no matter how speedy or accurate, can create a work of art on the typewriter by mere technical facility, so no film-maker, however clever with the camera, can produce an artistic film without transcending his technological knowledge. This book is written to whet the artistic imagination, to stir up the aesthetic sensibilities. The film-maker, of course, must understand his tools and make them work for him; but if this interest in mechanics becomes an end in itself, his films will probably be slick, but not necessarily artistically worthwhile.

THE COMPONENTS OF ART

In 1879, murals were discovered on the walls of a cave in Altamira, Spain, drawn by men of the Paleolithic period. As far back in time as one can go, man has tried to say something about himself and the world he lives in. It is probably safe to assume that, no sooner were these murals completed by some members of the tribe, than other members came forward to learn how and why they had been done. So long as there have been artists, there have been audiences and critics who have struggled to understand in what way the artist's work echoes his thoughts and feelings. To express the nature of art, the words *substance, content, form,* and *craft* are used.

Substance is thought and feeling that stems from the artist drawing inspiration from himself, his fellow man, or his universe. He can be fired by a complex thought having its roots in moral, philosophical, religious, or social conviction; or may be driven to express a fleeting passion, a delicate attitude. There is no limitation, for the range is as varied as life.

Content is the subject matter itself, and can be used to express much or little substance of varied kinds. It guides the direction and defines the broad limits within which the artist can present his thoughts and feelings. A measure of the artist's talent lies in his ability to fuse *content* and substance in the discipline of *form.*

Form is both a physical and a relative concept. In a piece of sculpture, it is the shape, outline, and juxtaposition of the parts; in a painting, it is the size and shape of the canvas as well as the composition of the elements within those boundaries. In music, form is achieved by the arrangement of notes and measures. In the drama also, form is not only expressed in the physical confines of the stage, but in the relationship to one another of the various parts of each particular work. Outward form is obvious, but there is also inner form, providing subtle arrangements, refinements, and delineations that give each piece an individuality and variety of its own, even though it may not be consciously perceived by the untrained eye or ear.

The success with which the artist blends these elements is dependent on his *craft,* which has come to mean not only the

3

skill and dexterity with which he uses his materials, but the manner by which he achieves his effects. Obviously, a fine craftsman is not necessarily a good artist, for he may have superb form but weak content and no substance at all. Nor is a great artist necessarily the best craftsman, for his work may have strong content and rich substance, but no ascertainable form. But it is through craft that the way is paved for creative study of the arts. The would-be artist learns his craft and practices to perfect the means by which his ideas can be recognized and understood.

The problem for the film-maker, once he has grasped these principles, is to recognize them in the film, and then to study them for their development and relationship in creating the whole. If but one craft and one form were involved in film-making, the task would be relatively simple. Almost unmanageable complexity is introduced, however, because more than any other art, film-making borrows from all the arts. And, as if this were not enough, it boldly takes these elements from the older arts and blends them with disciplines of its own. The art of film-making, in short, is the most tantalizing and tortuous area of expression yet devised, complete with blind alleys, traps, and pitfalls.

FILM: THE DEBTOR ART

In the wide range of film-making, constant use is made of the imaginative elements of the older arts. More than this, the film in many ways is given freely to wholesale borrowing, from music, painting, dance, and drama as well.

From music the film secures rhythmic arrangements, and at times develops these to the point of being characterized by a musical form. From painting comes compositional arrangements and the subtle intricacies of design. From dance comes the ebb and flow of movement, the refinement of communication through physical gesture and relationship. And from the theater comes both the playwright, an original and creative artist, and the stage director, an interpretive artist who fuses the written play idea with the craft and form of his direction, thus heightening the substance of the content through his staging. Also from the theater come those interpretive artists and designers responsible for scenery, costumes, and lighting, as well as the make-up artists, animators, film cutters, and editors.

Film-making, then, is a debtor art not so much because the film-maker gets his ideas from drama and literature—although there is wide and obvious use of such sources—but because he works constantly with the principles of the older arts, plus writing and direction, and blends all of them with whatever craft and art might lie in the use of the camera and editing. No source material is beyond the camera's grasp. The film borrows freely from actual life, the novel, short story, essay, poem, and play. The areas of film-making—writing, direction, camera, and editing—are not clear-cut and compartmentalized, with each area developed to its fullest in every film; nevertheless, a good working knowledge of each is required. The film-maker must fully realize the scope and limitations of all these areas and the manner in which they relate to one another.

Because the film borrows so freely from other arts and adds a dimension of its own, it has an extremely broad range. The interaction between writing, direction, camera work, and editing, and the many possible variations of emphasis on these elements, have led to a spate of film classifications—sometimes in terms of content, sometimes in terms of technique, but usually more semantically convenient than artistically edifying. The significant point is that the nature of the film's substance governs the relationship of the writing, the direction, the use of the camera, and the editing.

COMMON DISTINCTIONS

Terms used to classify films are: theatrical, nontheatrical, art film, documentary, lyrical, avant-garde, experimental, industrial, and educational. Each defines a category of film in such a broad stroke that it serves essentially as a superficial explanation rather than as a clarification of the true nature of the film. Many of these classifications have been devised by film distributors, necessarily for the express purpose of facilitating their business activity. Yet some have been introduced by serious film-makers in an effort to describe inherent film characteristics, or to set a specific type of film apart in order to give it distinction and class. All this might be well and good if each film fit neatly into its proper pigeonhole; but because of all the elements involved, the very flexibility of the medium ensures that these tidy distinctions will usually be blurred. Certainly, they are hardly sufficient to provide the beginning film-maker with a clear insight into and understanding of the film's make-up.

Still, it might be best to break down these film classifications according to their accepted or colloquial definitions. The broadest distinction is between the theatrical and nontheatrical film. Usually "theatrical" refers to the Hollywood or foreign narrative feature film, and "nontheatrical" takes in just about all other kinds of films made anywhere by anyone. The theatrical film is shown in a commercial moviehouse to the general public, while the nontheatrical film is shown everywhere else. This distinction implies that the feature (theatrical) film invariably deals with *story*, while the nontheatrical category includes every kind of film that does not contain a story in the traditional pattern. It is also often assumed that each group works with a different gauge film. The wide gauge (35mm) stock, or anything wider, is used for films released for showing in commercial theaters throughout the country. Narrow gauge (16mm) stock is more often used for films made to be shown to schools, churches, social and institutional organizations. Although these distinctions usually hold true, there are too many exceptions to the rule for such a classification to be of any real value. Although it is true that the actual screening prints are of these gauges, it happens more often that the so-called nontheatrical producer will shoot on 35mm stock with a 16mm reduction print struck from it for release. There are a number of technical reasons for such a procedure, including ease in working and improved quality. Reversing this procedure, that is, shooting in the narrow gauge and going to the wider gauge in printing, is not an accepted practice because it is costly and quality is sacrificed.

The documentary film, a part of the nontheatrical field, is usually considered distinct from the nuts-and-bolts (or industrial) film. Most commonly, the documentary is described as social or lyrical. "Social" implies that the film deals with some true-to-life aspect of human society, religious, political, ethical, or economic; that it gets its impact from visual appeal; and that this visual appeal is achieved by artistry, without loss of the real-life quality. "Lyrical" refers to films that lean heavily toward artistic interpretation, having a core of film poetry (a term certainly calling for some kind of explanation), subject matter usually concerning the forces of nature, and great emphasis on the distinguishing quality of the photography. Nevertheless, exceptions come readily to mind. *The City* (1939) by Willard Van Dyke is a social commentary dealing with the need for planned housing, but lyrical in its approach. Harry Watt's *Night Mail* (1936), Basil Wright's *Song of Ceylon* (1934), and Robert Flaherty's *Nanook of the North* (1922) and *Man of Aran* (1934), all classics of their time, span the definitions and take on uniqueness, each in its own individualized way.

The educational film, one that has the express object of teaching, covers an extremely wide range of sins from overproduction, on the one hand, to idiotic oversimplification, on the other. Experimentation is rare, not only because there exists a strong reactionary group, but because it takes a very special experience and know-how to meet the demands of both good teaching and good film-making. Such film-makers are unfortunately too few at present, and one often finds one aspect of the film sacrificed to the other.

The terms "avant-garde" and "experimental" are applied to those films that have any sort of "off-beat" quality or do not fit into the standard categories. Experimentation runs rampant in these films, and anything goes—from impressionistic arrangements of colors or shapes to cacophonous sounds made with anything but musical instruments.

The term "art film" may refer to specific subject matter, such as painting or sculpture. It may also refer to pretentiousness; that is to say, it may be used to categorize a film that is overloaded with camera and editing tricks. Critics, although enthusiastic about Orson Welles's *Citizen Kane* (1941), cite such artiness as a weakness.

The industrial film is one that is sponsored by an industry, and it may range from an "how-we-make-it" film to a film of good-will advertising. Initially, Flaherty's *Nanook of the North* was such a film, for it was sponsored by the furriers Revillon Frères. The film, however, is not a story of fur trapping; it is a social documentary on Eskimo life.

There are still more kinds of films: religious, for example, which range from Bible stories to family issues having a foundation in morality. And within groups there are further subdivisions, some based on content differences, others on the methods by which the films have been put together.

This brief outline should be enough to show that film analysis and understanding cannot come simply through definitions of genre; to distinguish a lyrical documentary from an institutional film by definition only is too superficial a distinction to be of value. Indeed, it could lead to the unnecessary acceptance of preconceived limitations that would serve only to the film world's loss. Most important, the pursuit of such a seemingly simple problem as the connection between narration and picture in the documentary can lead to an emotional and intellectual digestion of but one of film-making's complexities. Yet once grasped, this understanding allows the film-maker to utilize his tools to the fullest in expressing himself.

LINKING THE ARTS

Whether the film is an art form or merely a device to provide mass entertainment has been discussed, argued, and written about since a short time after it turned to narrative storytelling. Some groups likened the film to a technical gadget, and although they marveled at the illusion of movement on a big screen, to them essentially it was a novelty. Others distinguished "good" films from "bad" ones, placing one in the category of art and the other in entertainment, never daring to define either art or entertainment, but admitting that the two were not mutually exclusive. Avid film enthusiasts have insisted that films are a peculiar form, unlike older arts, and require independent rules and laws.

In 1919, Germany's Robert Wiene provided the film world with *The Cabinet of Dr. Caligari,* a melodramatic, expressionistically set story as seen through a madman's eyes, and it attracted the attention of intellectuals, critics, and serious artists. Film historians have pointed out that this film was subsequently instrumental in bringing about application of the words *art* and *art form* to film. Since that time, innumerable films have been produced that have been classified as works of art, yet the nature of this art has not been completely clear. The variety of films produced between 1900 and the present time prove that giving name-tags to the film—novelty, mass entertainment, commercial—although they fit in countless cases, does not in any way alter the fact that it links up with the older arts to introduce a unique medium for artistic expression. The film, as previously stated, has borrowed from drama, dance, music, and painting; but this does not mean simply that elements of these older arts may appear in the film from time to time. Rather, it means that, to a considerable degree, all of these older arts are an integral part of the film.

The correlation between drama and film is obvious; the simple dictionary definition of the word "drama" supports both: "a composition arranged for enactment . . . and intended to portray life or character, or to tell a story by actions and usually dialogue, tending toward some result based upon them." This does not mean that film and theater are alike, but that they draw their basic inspiration from a common source. In spite of the wide gulf that separates the film from the theater, the film-maker relates himself to the life about him much in the way of the theater's artist-playwright. The parallel is not in method, but in intent.

Dance finds its roots in movement arranged to a rhythmic pattern, and on the higher level it can create a heady effect. The grace of the performer, seeming to violate the laws of gravity, embraces an audience and enables it to break with reality. Like the image of a beautiful bird in soaring flight, the sight of the dancer often gives the audience a sense of physical release. Dancing is free, flowing, impetuous, and often violent. This fluid quality is to be had in many films, and lies in the way the individual shots are arranged and how they are related to subject matter. It is most evident when the subject moves and the camera moves, accordingly or in counterpoint, and when units such as these are juxtaposed and caused to flow freely one into the other.

The basis of music is rhythm: as there are a given number of beats to a measure, there are a number of beats to a filmed sequence. These beats are introduced at those points where the picture changes, commonly called "cuts." Generally, the faster the picture changes, the quicker the recurring accent and the faster the tempo; conversely, the longer it takes for the picture to change, the slower the accent, the slower the tempo. Effects seen on the screen where one picture seems to disappear into the next, commonly called "dissolves," provide a slow accent or elongated beat. These, too, can be lengthened or shortened. And, as in music, where sounds (which might be likened to subject matter) are arranged rhythmically, so in the film a relationship exists between the subject and the tempo of the cuts. For example, the Sergei Eisenstein production of *The Battleship Potemkin* (1925) is structured in three major movements, as in a symphony. A more recent example is the Stanley Kramer production, *High Noon* (1952), particularly during the few moments before twelve o'clock. The camera repeatedly photographs a swinging clock pendulum, coming closer, making the angle more severe, and building the tempo as each cut correlates completely with the background music. The film-maker, in this respect, relates himself to his material as a symphonic conductor relates himself to his musicians.

Those aspects of painting dealing with composition—emphasis, balance, stability, and sequence—are an integral part of film-making. Each shot or individual picture cannot of itself have the commanding power of an oil or water color, for film pictures are fleeting illusions that must communicate a single idea to the audience immediately. Obviously, then, a shot cannot be taken any-which-way, but must be carefully selected and arranged with others so that they can be seen and grasped easily. For each shot unit to be so, design principles invariably have to be observed. In addition, the use of color has a similar value in film as in painting, and this includes black-and-white as well as color films. The color of paint and its power to evoke an emotional response find its counterpart in film in lighting, despite the fact that so much film is in black and white. The delicate shades, tones, variations, highs and lows have to be handled with as much taste and selection as the pigments in a painting. The

11

opening scene of Ingmar Bergman's *The Seventh Seal* (1956), for example, well illustrates this point: a huge black bird of prey is seen against a bleak sky, symbolizing death's presence over all. The entire scene is given to these harsh contrasts and blended with subtle shades of gray. The use of actual color film, of course, adds another dimension, but it is basically the use of light that assists the creation of mood through tone.

Perhaps the nature of film art, as of other art, will never be completely clear, but several points are definite: the film-maker must have a good understanding of dramatic elements; a strong feeling for movement and its meaning in terms of flow and change; a first-rate ear for rhythm and its changes in variation and tempo; and a keen eye for those elements of design that can present each single thought pictorially.

FILM BEGINNINGS

In the infant days of motion pictures, photographed scenes of the surf, the street, or the park enthralled audiences. Initially, the camera took one shot and all movement was contained in it. Lewis Jacobs, in *The Rise of the American Film*, captures the spirit and excitement of the period as he relates how audiences "were spellbound by the jerky shadows that mysteriously evolved into a scene of a foreign land, shouted with genuine fear as the screen showed a train hurtling toward them, and were speechless at the sight of President McKinley's inauguration."[1] One of the early pictures, *The Execution of Mary Queen of Scots* (1893–94), shows the headsman bringing Mary to the chopping block. Unseen, a dummy is substituted for Mary's live form. The picture is concluded with the axe coming down and wadded material, signifying blood, coming from the cavity. In

---

[1] Lewis Jacobs, *The Rise of the American Film* (New York: Harcourt, Brace and Company, 1939), p. 6.

another film, *Washday Troubles* (1895), a woman is scrubbing clothes in front of her house while a mischievous young boy scampers in and out of the scene. Eventually he upsets the wash basin, and the film is completed. These films, as did those that depicted actual street scenes, mostly used realistic backgrounds.

At about the same time, Georges Méliès, a magician and artist who had become fascinated by the new medium, staged highly theatrical scenes, used well-known stories for source material, and photographed them in tableaux. In his *A Trip to the Moon* (1902), based on a Jules Verne story, he stumbled onto ways to extend or condense time and space relationships by stop-motion photography. By fixing the camera in a static position in relation to the tableau, he could stop photographing at a certain point, change the subject matter around (add a new actor or remove an established prop), and then resume shooting, thus making it appear that someone or something had mysteriously appeared or disappeared in the scene. He thus became the first to explore the "magic" of the motion-picture camera. He was imaginative, inventive, satiric, and original, and recognition of his genius unfortunately came much too late.

In these developments the film's potential is apparent, as both theatricality and actuality are handled. Even more apparent today is that the multiple ways of camera use require a highly refined taste for stylistic consistency, with life's reality serving as the springboard.

In Edwin S. Porter's film classic, *The Great Train Robbery* (1903), some scenes are set against a realistic background while others use painted scenery, all of which is readily apparent in the film. More important, Porter moved his camera from vantage point to vantage point, not only to tell his story better, but to create suspense as well. Some modern viewers, surfeited by a steady diet of television Westerns, are inclined to dismiss this, the first Western, because of its banal story content; the outlaws tie up the train dispatcher, the train is held up, the dispatcher's daughter finds her father in the nick of time, the alarm is given, a posse is organized, and the outlaws are caught. However, this film's value is not in its story, but rather in the camera's use of selected pieces of scenes to produce continuity and suspense, thus instituting a unique way of storytelling. Porter was not fully aware of the importance of his discovery, for in later pictures he went back to the static scene. But other men picked up Porter's ideas and turned out films that told their stories through the presentation of successive selected shots.

At that time no one thought about art or art form in relation to the film. Only a dozen or so years later, when David Wark Griffith made *The Birth of a Nation* (1915) and *Intolerance* (1916), did it become clear that Porter's crude findings had led to a technique for guiding the audience through a story, aware of incident, action, reaction, and meaning. Whether or not it was art is a moot question. Griffith revealed that not only did a film-maker have to arrange his shots to get his story across, but that the selection of shots within the order intensified the content. Here, then, was a craft that could be developed to artistic proportions because it could be interpretive.

The Germans, Russians, French, Swedes, and Americans began turning out an array of artistic story films. Notable among these is *The Last Laugh* (1924), directed by F. W. Murnau and written by Carl Mayer, in which the camera shifts its point of view constantly, creates an objective world one moment and a world as seen through the character's eyes the next, and moves restlessly and relentlessly to tell the story of a man destroyed by pride; Mauritz Stiller's *The Story of Gösta Berling* (1924), made from the Selma Lagerlöf novel, in which plot is secondary to character, continuity linkages are emotional rather than mechanical, and the sea and the landscape serve to punctuate the psychological drives of the characters; Carl-Theodor Dreyer's *The Passion of Joan of Arc* (1928), an intense, brooding story gaining tremendous power through the constant use of the close-up; Erich von Stroheim's *Greed* (1924), overdone and cliché-ridden in many respects, but still introducing a realism overpowering in its effect; and, of course, Sergei Eisenstein's *Potemkin* (1925), which introduced a method of cutting that brought the word "montage" into film-making. Each of these men displayed a personal style, the artist's mark, as well as a keen awareness of the camera and the editing process.

Also in the 1920's, Robert J. Flaherty, pioneer and explorer, made *Nanook of the North* (1922) under commercial aegis, starting a seemingly new approach, the documentary. *Nanook* is the simple story, told naturally, of an Eskimo's day-to-day fight for survival in his natural habitat. Here was an untheatrical realism that probed beyond its documentary implications and became as deep an artistic expression as could be found in the story film.

This brief look at a few of the significant films of the past points up the numerous ways in which film content, realistic or theatrical, can be organized, and shows the importance of presenting this content so that it can be understood—with all its subtle meanings—as intended by the individual film-maker. Equally important, it reveals that the content can be heightened by the manner in which the camera is used, and that the material photographed can be arranged and rearranged according to the desired meaning.

THE RANGE OF FILM

Film is extremely flexible, and it is this flexibility that makes film-making so difficult for the beginner, or even for the individual who has had stage directing experience. For example, film is used by the medical profession, to photograph a delicate surgical operation. The camera may be brought in close to the working area, held rigidly, and the entire operation recorded from one angle. The camera is governed by the nature of the activity to give a record of the operation, and obviously there cannot be room or time for takes and retakes. There is no need for more than a combination of simple recording techniques. As inartistic as this static production may be, it is still a film.

Conversely, *Ballet Mécanique* (1924), made by the French cubist painter Fernand Léger, is an abstract film made up of moving objects presented in a definite rhythmic pattern. Plates, ladles, tureens, and cut-out Arabic numerals are seen repeatedly as the film is given to design and pattern. Mood, rhythm, tempo —rise, fall, build, rise, fall—are achieved primarily through the length of the shots, the moving compositional arrangements as they affect each other, the light and dark within the composition, and the cumulative quality of all these elements as they act and interact.

Of these two films, one places all its emphasis on subject matter, while the other places its emphasis on technique, the subject matter being no more than a way for the technique to be explored. These extremes represent the range of film flexibility and suggest the infinite possibilities for all films.

The more the film-maker develops his story according to the various forms of literature, whether play, novel, short story, or whatever, the more he is restricted in the use of film technique. The more he frees his story from traditional forms, lessening their demands, the closer he gets to pure technique. Many stage plays transferred to the screen remain essentially stage plays, except for a slight change or two of scene; the camera is used primarily to record the action, and the content is presented through the actors' speeches and actions. Here is recorded dramatic art, in its own way separate from filmic interpretation. Films that create visual interest and excitement through the interpretive qualities of the camera dwell on nonverbal expression and attempt to secure articulation and depth through the probing camera. Dialogue is not a primary vehicle, but a factor used to delineate and refine the picture. Although in both cases the structure comes from literature, it is to a different degree. The moment content breaks with literature completely, giving full expression to camera technique per se, the film is forced into the abstract. Thus, the relationship between film technique and literary form is never constant and always depends on the extent to which each separate art is developed. What is curious is that both cannot be fully developed; rather, one or the other must give way, the degree varying in accordance with the specific effects.

Abstract and experimental films achieve their rhythmic quality primarily through editing, while traditional story films have their editing largely dictated by the action and speeches of the actors. A film-maker may rove over an entire city with his camera, taking shots of people, automobiles, traffic signs, sidewalk vendors, tall buildings, revolving doors, eating places. He has no script, but simply an idea; most likely he is motivated by a special attitude toward his subject matter. When he sits in his cutting room, taking pieces from here and there, he does his writing with scissors and splicer. All of the content he wishes to communicate is completely molded by his knowledge of filmic arrangement. In contrast, the film-maker or editor who has a written script dealing with exposition, rising action, complication, climax, and denouement, and progressing in terms of prescribed action and dialogue, cannot exercise the same filmic freedom—the script itself, dependent on its structural rigidity, calls the turn. Most of the better story films combine the best elements of both writing and cinematic arrangement. However, good filmic sense can support and enhance the story, or lack of it can be ruinous.

Examples of strong filmic editing are the oft-mentioned drunk scene of the revelers in *The Last Laugh* (1924), and the exciting battle sequences of Laurence Olivier's *Henry V* (1946); but each unit is only a part of the bigger assembly that is controlled by the literary structure.

Content, and the way in which it is seen by the film-maker, is the controlling element. Any one type of film technique cannot arbitrarily be superimposed on all material. Nor can one be sure of producing a highly interpretive film. Such interpretation depends on an innate sense, a feeling for the individual shot, and for the ways in which thoughts, feelings, and emotions can be projected through their arrangement. This sense is intricately woven into the film-maker's approach to content; and it is this approach alone that shapes and governs the technique. No specific combination of craft and content produces the best or purest film art. The many first-rate films made lean in one direction or another. It is more important for the film-maker to understand what he wants to say and to choose the best technique to convey it. Craft and content are inextricably tied together.

Film novelty may be confused with artistic expression. The phrase "very artistic" is sometimes applied to a film that contains unusual angles, severe perspectives, extreme close-ups, and rapid cuts. If they are used arbitrarily, in that they fail to explore or illuminate the content, the result is a tour de force, not art, regardless of the amount of discussion generated. Film art must be judged by the same standards as the older arts. Leo Tolstoy wrote that "art is a human activity having for its purpose the transmission to others of the highest and best feelings to which men have risen." The late Alexander Dean, Associate Professor of Play Directing at Yale University, said that "art is man's interpretation of life expressed in a way that can be universally recognized and understood."[2] In both statements, a work is considered art through the value of what is being said plus the way it is said.

In summary, it must be remembered that the camera is a dead thing, and as is often said, no more effective than the man who uses it. It can be used to photograph multiple streams of light in an abstract pattern, or a well-developed dramatic story, high in literary appeal. Film is superbly flexible; and the

---

[2] Alexander Dean and Lawrence Carra, *Fundamentals of Play Direction* (New York: Holt, Rinehart, & Winston, 1965), p. 3.

way in which its content is handled in terms of its purpose determines its success as work of art, educational tool, or piece of institutional promotion.

THE MEANING OF ACTION

The idea that the motion picture is essentially an action medium often leads to connecting the word "action" with physical deeds. This is not so much wrong as it is restricting, creating the false impression that good film invariably calls for blood, guts, and thunder, seeking to fulfill the common taste for escape and amusement, rather than providing a true picture of film potential. The motion picture, initially regarded as a novelty, arrived at a time when the economy and the social structure were marked by limited sources of low-cost entertainment and by strong class distinctions. The immigrant, the laborer, and the factory worker, all with limited education or unfamiliar with the New World, and all hard pressed for funds, found that the film offered the best type of diversion one could get for the grand sum of five cents. Therefore, the early films were given to Pollyanna themes, with stories stressing physical action. Such films reflected the code of a specific group in readily understood terms. The so-called "action film" of later years evolved from this beginning.

Nevertheless, the action film cannot be associated only with poor or uneducated people; it satisfies that inner curiosity in all of us that makes us perk up our ears at the sound of the fire engines racing by, and chase after them to catch a glimpse of flames roaring out the windows of a burning building. Perhaps this kind of excitement is necessary, however infantile. It is tied directly to escape fare, and can be had free today, on television.

Violent action, or action for action's sake, is not peculiar to the film, but simply more in evidence. Innumerable plays have had just such an emphasis, and the same can be said of radio in its heyday, when Westerns and detective thrillers made up a good part of its programing. Today, of course, television has usurped the title of the action medium.

Action itself is not to be disparaged; indeed it is absolutely essential to all film, as to all dramatic presentations. But action need not mean only bashing skulls, searing flesh with 45's, or searching the Badlands for water. It can be of three kinds: physical, emotional, and intellectual. All dramatic film, factual or fictional, makes the same demand—that each scene move forward through at least one or any combination of the three. On this basis, action is the film's lifeblood, for it means going ahead, moving from point to point progressively on all levels, exactly as in other forms of literature.

Of the three kinds of action, the subtler are emotional and intellectual. Emotional action is revealed mostly through character and character relationships. In Josef von Sternberg's production *The Blue Angel* (1930), with Emil Jannings and Marlene Dietrich, the professor visits the cabaret singer, Lola, to chasten her for her effect on his students, only to find her an intriguing, captivating creature. As the scene progresses, the two engage in a bit of well-directed byplay revealing their attitudes, desires, and emotions. Such a scene contains action. Fritz Lang's *Metropolis* (1926), although ponderous and given to overstatement and melodrama, still contains scenes involving the ruler and the ruled, elements of the management versus labor struggle. These scenes were motivated primarily by idea. Orson Welles's *The Trial* (1963) and Joseph Strick's production of the Jean Genet play *The Balcony* (1963), adapted by Ben Maddow—success or failure notwithstanding—are essentially allegorical films, with the story constantly forging ahead through its intellectual implications. In these latter cases the entire film is motivated by action of idea, a most difficult but worthwhile story value.

A SENSE FOR VISUALIZATION

As a visual art the film requires that each individual shot have meaning of its own and in relation to the whole. A series of shots so presented result in a flow of images building dramatic ideas. This thought has been expressed in different ways many times, but the phrase "flow of images" is vague and unsatisfactory. "Visual appeal" is high sounding but just as inadequate. If the film is unique because it can tell a story through a series of pictures, there must be a concrete explanation.

A visually effective shot is one in which content and technique are blended by the sensitivity of the film-maker to present or support a specific point of view. It must be satisfying in terms of composition, light and shade, perspective, tempo, relationship to other shots, and emotional impact. Further, it must make known one or more of the following: the physical action that is occurring, the emotional action or reaction, and any specific thoughts or ideas.

To illustrate visual appeal in terms of a simple medium close-up, take a shot of a young girl walking. That is the sum of what is going on physically, but where is she going? How? Reluctantly or happily? Under what circumstances? A shot from the back, against a somber, bleakly lit setting, with the girl moving slowly away, will tell a far different story from a shot in which she runs head-on into the camera, face up and smiling, brightly lit, with summer flowers in the background. If the first shot is followed by a cut to her entering a dim, low-ceilinged room, to be confronted by a grim, angry woman, a mood is built up. The second shot, followed by one in which she splashes into a pool of water, would also have built to a climax, but a totally different one.

Each shot, then, has a central point to convey, but that point must be supported by every element at the film-maker's com-

21

mand. Stated in the simplest terms, a picture that lacks visual appeal conveys nothing, because it lacks mood, flavor, and/or action, and may be so general that by attempting to convey a thousand-and-one different things to any one person, it renders itself obscure.

This does not mean that each shot calls for a multiplicity of information. Although the basic unit of the film is the individual shot, the shot is fleeting; it moves along on the screen at the rate of twenty-four individual pictures (frames) every second. Therefore, it cannot have the design complexity, say, of a painting that hangs in a gallery for observers to study, react to, and digest. Each shot is related to the preceding and following shot, and must have one basic idea to transmit. To have visual wealth, that idea must be supported by as much detail as can be given within the framework of the shot. Every aspect and element of that shot must add up to and heighten that central idea. This means that the film-maker must determine the physical, emotional, and intellectual crux of each shot. Then he must include only those other values that enrich the central idea. Thus, only one value comes through, quickly and directly; but strongly fortified by subtle reinforcement, it has impact. This technique is similar to the way in which the playwright presents his characters. He chooses the characteristic most representative of the entire person: selfishness, altruism, sentimentality, callousness, etc. He then selects a series of lesser characteristics that blend with or support the impression he wishes to give. He carefully selects and arranges his character's words and actions within the main framework of his play to be consistent with those characteristics, thus drawing a full character by implication. Like an iceberg, of which only one-third is visible above water, the well-drawn character must be presented so that the audience assumes the presence of a whole (or real) being. Unlike the novelist, who can devote page after page to character delineation, the playwright must make his character come alive by choosing every word and act for its supporting value, as well as for its contribution to moving the plot along. In the same way, depending on the film-maker's ability, a shot can merely move the plot along or can be rich in implication. A shot with visual power and vitality requires the film-maker to exercise his imagination to explore his material, use logic and observation, probe for feeling and thought, and arrange what he finds in correct proportion. Choice of camera angle and position is fully significant.

Such shot development does not apply only to films using professional actors in a dramatic story. That it applies to films using real people in a real situation is thoroughly proved by Robert Flaherty's *Man of Aran* (1934), in which he mounts shot after shot encompassing various levels of meaning. In one such shot he shows a mother and boy standing on a cliff, looking out to sea, concerned over the men in an open boat who are fighting to make it to shore before a storm sets in. The basic idea is the physical struggle of the men, but also conveyed are the closely knit family and the concern each member has for the others; the awesomeness of nature's elements, which they must constantly battle, and the fortitude that these people (and by implication man) show in the face of danger. Such a series of shots, enriched with meaning, provides a sweeping flood of images that reach out to embrace the viewer in an intoxicating experience. And there is no trick, no mystery to it. It all depends on how well the man behind the camera can see, can observe, and can select.

FILM AND SOUND

Although many technical innovations had been introduced by the late 1920's and film technique had begun to flower, the advent of sound produced a temporary setback. The lack of microphone and camera mobility (cameras were placed in hotboxes so that

their whirring sound would not be picked up) prevented the
film-makers from handling the camera with ease, as they had
done previously. Sound itself lacked today's refinements, of
course, and ways and means of handling it, mechanically speaking, were in the try-it-and-see-how-you-make-out stage. As the
emphasis on dialogue increased, the scenes became stagier and,
understandably, static. The main reason for this was technical.
The use of sound more than doubled the complexities facing
the film-maker, and editing became equally difficult because it
called for simultaneous handling of picture and sound. But
historians writing about the period point out that the artistic
need of the directors, coupled with the inventiveness of the technical men, released the film from sound's strangle hold in
roughly two years. Interestingly, there were purists then who
felt that sound destroyed the film art, that the film's value was
in visual arrangement solely, and that sound was an intruder.
Even today this idea has not been completely dissipated.

The argument, of course, is based in part on the idea that the
spoken word has a rhythmic arrangement all its own, and is
separate and distinct from the rhythm of picture arrangement.
But such an argument does not explore all of film's possibilities
and concentrates solely on its eye appeal. Conversely, arguments
have been introduced to justify sound on the basis that the films
required it from the very beginning. The early piano accompani-
ments are offered as proof. Carrying the point a step further,
it is said that film very definitely contains a time factor, shot by
shot, because it contains movement, and that time in art cannot
exist without sound.

The question that does not seem to have been answered, however, has to do with the oft-quoted expression that "one picture
is worth ten thousand words." As glib as the quote is, it involves
an important question. Can the fine feelings and attitudes of an
individual be communicated purely through picture, or is language basically man's most effective way of expressing himself? The picture deals mainly with the world of tangibles. The

camera photographs a face, a body, an action, or a view, and, depending on how well the face is delineated, for example, the camera can reveal the inner world up to a point. But how much of that world can it explore? When it comes to very fine shadings, the unveiling of man's innermost hurts or joys, the separation of a qualm from a compunction, the camera's revelations fall short and another dimension is called for: language. Though a picture may be carefully designed in depth, and may be subjective in its approach, it remains limited because it can only depict a generalization of thought and feeling. How quickly did the film-makers of the silent days fall on the title insert to round out their pictures! How superficial the theme in so many of the silent pictures that grossly exaggerated action in order to communicate! How laughable and pedestrian were those early efforts! Of all the silents, perhaps Murnau's *The Last Laugh* (1924) and Eisenstein's *Potemkin* (1925) show the silent film at its greatest power. But even in them, character and idea are generalizations.

In Laurence Olivier's filmed production of *Hamlet* (1948), the prince is discovered on the castle parapet shortly after speaking with his ghost-father. The grimness of the walls, the heaviness of the fog, and the expression on Hamlet's face all reveal the oppressive, troublesome nature of the scene. But as fine as the physical aspects are, the camera is unable to penetrate the gossamerlike differences between life and death that Hamlet is contemplating. It is the sound track that provides us with "whether 'tis nobler in the mind to suffer the slings and arrows of outrageous fortune, or to take arms against a sea of troubles. . . ."

So, the use and value of the spoken word in film are apparent. The camera shapes, defines, and interprets the world about us, while sound elucidates its subtleties and refinements. Dialogue in film should never be used to tell an audience what it has already seen. This is repetition and the mark of the poor craftsman and artist. Rather, the dialogue should complement the picture, each functioning as part of the whole in interpreting and exploring life. So, too, with sound effects. No useful purpose is served by including all noises that repeat the idea already contained in the picture. Sound effects are most effective if they elaborate on the theme or character and thereby carry the story further. It is just such use that separates the technician from the artist. The former strives for reality for its own sake, while the latter is motivated by what he has to say.

Music is to sound what lighting is to picture. Both assist the scene's tonality, and when used efficiently enable the viewer to get to the crux of the shot's content and to understand it quickly. Great selection and care are required in the use of music, because it is not simply a question of appropriate mood music to fill in a background, but of kind, amount, placement, and function.

Dialogue, sound effects, and music are as important to film-making as the pictures. Each is part of the whole and must complement the others to bring out the meaning. For this reason the film-maker must consider all aspects of the film while in the initial stages of planning. Correct use of sound calls for as much creativity and imagination as go into the making of a meaning-ful shot.

THE POINT OF VIEW

A good creative piece of work bears the mark of its creator. It has an identity of its own because it has purpose and carries the conviction of the author. The complete searching out of the subject matter, and the blending of it perfectly with form and technique, provide the work with dignity, give it stature, and stamp it as a genuinely artistic work. From its beginning the motion picture, like other artistic media, has often been sorely lacking in these qualities. For every film with the slightest amount of distinction, hundreds have been made up of pure drivel; with stories written primarily to reflect life, not to interpret it, self-righteous themes, and plots of violence for its own sake. The truth in Darwin's statement that the work of a scientist engaged in "physiological experiment on animals is justifiable for real investigation, but not for mere damnable and detestable curiosity" can also be applied to the artist: he should investigate life for purpose, truth, and beauty, not merely out of sentimentality or a desire to leave a record. Even the better films of the past, revered by film scholars, are often lacking in artistic stature. In a short time they have gathered sufficient dust to lend enchantment and to cloak their awkward failings both in content and technique; but their value is primarily historical—they are to be studied but not to be accepted as the ultimate in film presentation.

A number of reasons have been advanced to explain away the film's frequent pedestrian quality. One is that business is involved, with its host of economic requirements; another is that film production uses many persons and not just one creator. Still another is that film is a popular art serving a mass audience and must, therefore, appeal to the lowest common denominator.

We will consider one point at a time. To begin with, it has never been proven that art and box office are incompatible. A look at Shakespeare's England tells us that while the bulls and bears were being baited on one side of the street, *Hamlet* was drawing the crowds on the other. Second, as far as large numbers of production personnel are concerned, the theater has always been beset by this problem too, yet has managed to hold on to creative identity and to present a point of view. As for the last point, there is really no such thing as one mass audience, but rather a wide span of provincial audiences; and even if it were desirable to appeal to the lowest common denominator, there is no guarantee that the same factor will be "lowest" in every group. Indeed, it would seem that if Shakespeare's appeal through the ages and over the world indicates one of the nearest approaches to true universality, the whole argument is turned upside down. Those very works that strive for the widest possible audience by the elimination of challenge are the soonest forgotten by most people.

These arguments, however, are too involved and complex to be settled here. But whether they are true or not, it is apparent that today television has taken over the production of high-quantity, low-quality material, and has stolen the bulk of the film audience. The film industry, thus, has been forced to alter its appeal. Some film-makers are attempting to hold their ground through blunderbuss production—the ten-million-dollar Bible epics. Others have resorted to extremely low-grade mystery thrillers and pointless sex stories appealing primarily to hoodlumism. But some are emphasizing honest works with serious content value. This latter group provides the key to the film's future and shows that, in spite of film production's complexity, its further development lies in individual expression.

No film decade has been as fruitful as the period between 1950 and 1960, and the present decade appears as if it will outstrip the last. From Japan, Italy, France, and Sweden, as well as the United States and England, have come a good number of inspiring and authentic pieces of work. Interestingly enough, the outstanding quality of these works is the individual mark of the artist. Most representative of these artists is Sweden's Ingmar Bergman. All of these outstanding films—Kurosawa's *Rashomon* (1951), Bergman's *Wild Strawberries* (1957), Antonioni's *The Outcry* (1957), Ray's *Pather Panchali* (1955), Clayton's *Room at the Top* (1958), Fellini's *Nights of Cabiria* (1957), Truffaut's *The 400 Blows* (1958), to name but a few—have this striking characteristic of a personalized theme, as opposed to just another well-made story turned out in technical perfection by a host of people.

Even the work of the outstanding film directors of the 1930's, who rose above the so-called demands of the box office to present films more true to their personalities, did not achieve the strength evidenced in films today. These early film-makers placed the focus on direction; it was generally recognized that the film was a medium for directors, whereas in the theater, the playwright remained supreme. This emphasis has done more to cloud the essence of film-making art than to clarify it. It arose because directors had basically weak and saccharine scripts forced on them. Through his use of the camera, the director did his best to "milk" each scene for its positive values and to eliminate the poorer aspects. When he was successful, the director's mark on the film was clearer than that of the writer. Today, of course, the director's purpose remains the same, but there is a marked increase in stronger scripts. Often the director and the writer are the same person or are very close collaborators, and this gives much greater integrity and impact to the finished product.

Although technological advances and refinements of technique will continue, the future of the film does not rest on these. Whether because of the economic changes brought about by television, the growing sophistication of the population, or the natural maturing of our film artists, good films are beginning to present a point of view. It is notable that many of the newly arrived film-makers are writer-directors or writer-producers. Their reputations are not built on taking a hackneyed script and dressing it up with technique to overpower an audience, but on feeling deeply about a subject and seeking to express this feeling by fusing it with craft and form into a motion picture.

Considering the age in which we live, film-making will always be beset with economic problems. But the strangle hold that kept films as a commodity-product of the large studio is at present beyond the loosening stage. Individuality and genuine artistry, strange as it seems, are the industry's lifeblood today. The film-maker now must concern himself about his own development, his maturity, his power to see, to think, and to feel. The motion picture today is really a new-found art.

2

THE FILM
STRUCTURE

Plot is the working out of the story of a film, comprising a causally connected series of motivated incidents; structure refers to the way in which the events of the plot are ordered and integrated. The two, therefore, are not quite synonymous; yet depending on whether the film is narrative or documentary, the word "plot" is used to describe the story arrangement of the former, and the word "structure" to describe the idea arrangement of the latter. Most important, the essence of structure is the arrangement of the various story or idea units so that the whole can be effectively understood. Structure is the blueprint, the skeleton, the design, that binds a film together and represents the thought progression of the film-maker. It is found universally in all artistic works, whether it be the physical armature under a modeling, or the progression of movements in a sonata. In the case of the film, it is the skewer that pierces and binds the actions and the ideas into a coherent unit.

Good structure is simple, yet infinitely varied. The main factors governing the artist's selection and organization of his material are the very same ones taught school children learning to think and write effectively: unity, coherence, emphasis, and interest.

Unity is the element of oneness; all parts must be related to the central subject and be an integral part of it so that the whole, in turn, will be apparent and meaningful. Coherence deals with the relationship of one unit to the next, so that there is not only a logical connection among them, but also a "build." That is, the units must be progressive and lead to a conclusion. Coherence depends on cause, effect, and probability, and concerns itself with development, thus leading to understanding. Emphasis has to do with the positioning of the major and minor units, as well as the order of individual shots. Included here are proportion and repetition to provide relative value and weight to the various elements. Emphasis introduces subordination so that points of significance are readily recognized. Interest is maintained by proper choice of content presented with due regard for unity, coherence, and emphasis.

Essentially, discussions of this kind remain academic because they are abstract. When specifics are mentioned actual story units must be dealt with, as each story must be developed in terms of itself. Still there remain some rather obvious arrangements, or structures, which can be discussed in a general way.

Simplest is the structure dealing with direct physical continuity: the child was born, he lived as a man, he died. In essence, such a story is said to begin at the beginning, make its way through the middle, and go on to an end. Variations of the structure of physical continuity can begin in the middle, imply the beginning, and go on to an end; or can start at the end, flash back to the beginning, and proceed further with the end, only implying the middle. On the other hand, a story can be framed within a kind of prologue and epilogue; or it can be interwoven in a complex manner with one unit serving as a main thread while subordinate units make their way in and out of the plot, coming together at the end to weave a coherent whole. These are but a

3 1

few types of structure. What they have in common and what is significant is that they are all based on literary usage. The word "story" and the words "beginning" and "end," of course, imply a narrative. Substituting the word "idea" for "story" in a piece of nonfiction still brings to mind a kind of development that is organized within the literary convention.

Of late this literary convention is assuming a lessening role. Where previously stories were conceived and shots were introduced to illustrate them (this in spite of established use of film technique in early pedestrian efforts), now shots and stories are developed as one in a dynamic interplay between the literary convention and the cinematic shot arrangements.

The pioneer film-makers, whose major efforts appeared between 1900 and 1920, made significant strides in the development of the narrative film. When Georges Méliès introduced stories into film and devised "artificially arranged scenes,"[1] as he called them, into a progressive and cumulative scenario, he was structuring his films according to accepted literary rules. His camera remained fixed, his scenes were tableaux, and their arrangement followed the conventional story pattern; but they were the first significant stride in the development of narrative film. Edwin S. Porter, and later D. W. Griffith, provided the second significant stride. By moving the camera about, thus getting a number of shots, and then editing those shots so as to communicate the story far more dramatically and in terms peculiar to the film, they introduced the whole film craft, as it came to be known, although their film skeletons were still literary ones.

Without discounting further advances made since Griffith's time, in recent years there has been yet another development, by no means true of all films, but arousing great interest. The cinematic arrangement of the shots is not only dynamically connected, but is an integral part of the basic structure, always as important and sometimes more so than the literary framework.

---

[1] Jacobs, *op. cit.*, p. 24.

Such use of the camera and editing principles does not appear to be in conflict with the old traditions but to blend in and support or heighten, thereby changing the whole effect. It is also possible to remain within a narrative framework and yet to move away from conventional storytelling structures to those, say, of music, where rhythm, tempo, and mood mainly supply the order and progression.

Often in films referred to as avant-garde or experimental, where the subject matter is an abstraction, the structure of music as opposed to that of literature may provide the sole framework. In films dealing with tangible things, such as the operation of a printing press, the shots may be arranged according to beats, and the musical background may provide the unifying framework. Now, however, abstractions or tangibles notwithstanding, the film-makers, through daring shot manipulation, have moved storytelling far beyond conventional patterns. In storytelling films like Alan Resnais's *Hiroshima Mon Amour* (1959), for example, the cinematic arrangement of the shots is blended with and heightened by a unique and unusually complex structure that provides a compelling exploration of both character and theme.

Borrowing from the other arts, yet always imposing its own artistic demands, film is an elusive and challenging medium. The film-maker would do well to keep in mind that the gamut of film structures provides far greater flexibility than do the rules of the older arts, and that wider knowledge and more complex skills are needed to capitalize artistically on the opportunities thus offered.

EXTERNAL STRUCTURE: SHOT,
SCENE SEQUENCE, TOTALITY

Down through the ages, whether there have been five acts in a play or three, and whether a novel has had ten chapters or twenty-five, there has always been an arbitrarily imposed convention, helpful to the author in providing an over-all structure and to the audience as landmarks along the way. Apart from the acts or chapters, however, it has been the content of the work that has produced the complex, intricate, and individual internal structure. The motion picture does not *appear* to have such an outer and inner structure. It is not divided into acts or into specifically demarcated scenes. Still, from the earliest drama, it is evident that acts and scenes are essential groupings that give the playwright control over his material and provide him with an over-all framework. Convention or not, the maker of a narrative film must also have his anchor points, his main units, his acts. The motion picture does have these, although they go by other names and do not fall into the prescribed patterns of the novel or the play, because in film the content has a much greater effect on external structure than in other forms of storytelling.

The smallest complex unit in a film is the shot, best described as an uninterrupted strip of film recording some part of an action. It is made up of a series of individual pictures or frames. Each unit (shot) begins when the camera begins to operate and comes to an end when the camera ceases. Should the camera start again, a new shot would be in the making.[2] A shot, therefore, can be quite short or extremely long. It can also be static, in that the camera has not moved in any way on its own axis; or it can be flowing, in that the camera has been tilted up or down or turned to the right or left. A shot can also combine both static and flowing features by having its tripod mounted on a rolling device, such as a dolly or a truck. In that case, the camera itself can remain static while its mount is rolled, pushed, or pulled.

---

[2] In some circles, the words "shot" and "scene" are used synonymously and both words are used as defined above. In others, a shot is referred to only as an uninterrupted strip of film recording an action in one composition. As soon as the camera moves within that strip of film to include more than one composition, it is called a scene. Neither of these definitions is used in this book. Such an arbitrary and loose interpretation can only bring confusion to the beginning film-maker and cause him to lose control over his subject matter.

3 4

But in each case, a new shot is created only when the camera itself has ceased to operate and then is started up again.

A meaningful arrangement of shots, leading toward the completion of a minor premise, is called a "scene." A scene can occur in one locale or twenty; it can include static or moving shots or a combination of both; and it can be made up of any number of shots. It is the smallest unit of a film that is complete in itself and that communicates a whole action and/or thought. It has a beginning, middle, and end and is called both a scene or a minor premise. As it is supported by a series of shots, so a series of scenes in turn support a major premise, or a sequence. Any number of scenes may form a sequence, and any number of sequences may form the totality. Simply enough, the totality is the dominant value emerging from the whole film—its theme. The external structure could be expressed diagrammatically as in Diagram No. 1, bearing in mind that the number of shots, scenes, and sequences is limitless and determined by content.

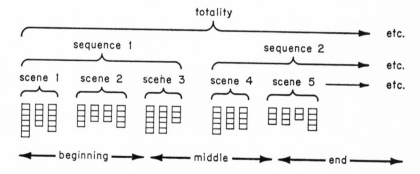

For instance, let us say that scene 1 concerns a young boy who has been scolded and sent to his room. The boy sulks, feels sorry for himself, and out of his self-pity grows anger. He then decides to run away from home, packs a few of his effects, and leaves through a window. This is a scene because within the greater context of the whole film it is a minor premise, has a beginning, middle, and end, and completes a whole action.

This scene can be portrayed in five, fifteen, or fifty shots, depending on the film-maker's interpretation of it and the way in which he manipulates his camera to achieve his interpretation. Not only the number of shots, but the quality and content of each shot support or undermine the film-maker's purpose in that scene. Through his choice of shots the film-maker can reinforce the original values in a scene as written, or quite significantly reinterpret them through his use of the camera. In turn, an editor can rearrange the shots in such a way that the film-maker's basic intent is considerably altered. This has been known to happen—so much so that the film-maker never recognized the original scene he thought he had filmed. Generally, however, the editor improves, focuses, sharpens, and defines the scene, and often introduces more meaningful values into it by arrangement and rearrangement of the shots. The effectiveness of the scene, therefore, is directly related to the manner in which the film-maker has organized, photographed, arranged, and edited the individual shots. He thus gains the element of control. Either he is careful that each shot contributes full measure to the value of the scene, thus assuring impact, or he accepts the obvious and winds up with an uninspired scene. For no film can be greater than the cumulative effect of its individual shots.

The sequence in a film is roughly comparable to an act in a play, in that it deals with a major premise or a large segment of the story and is made up of a number of scenes. There the likeness ends, however. A film may contain any number of sequences, according to the dictates of the content, and they are not always obviously recognizable, although, like scenes, they have a beginning, middle, and end that include some major progression of the action. In the early days of film-making, the word "sequence" was used in a highly limited sense to mean an episode without any interruption caused by time lapse or a break in the action. Since many early films were stories of physical action, the sequence described essentially a number of scenes in direct continuity. Modern usage, however, has come to indicate a group of scenes that communicate enough information to make a complete unit, but at the same time serve as a major signpost leading to the next premise.

Although the breadth and scope of film break down the restriction of the act in a play, in one sense the sequence can be equated with the act because it performs a similar function. But much beyond this the shot, scene, and sequence parts of a film enable the film-maker to work with small, individual units to achieve the whole, thus gaining control over his film.

SHOT ARRANGEMENT AND STRUCTURE

One can diagram the shot arrangement quite apart from the structure it supports, but the separation is purely academic. Each contributes to a film and is a vital part of it. One can no more separate the shot from structure in actual practice than one can sort out in his library the various molecules of matter that make up a book. But, for purposes of examination and, it is hoped, understanding, it has to be discussed so.

Structure hews to its laws of action and climax, and shot arrangement hews to cinematic laws, but there is no conflict. Cinematic laws must be invoked so that the shots are not merely flat and illustrative, but have a cumulative, emotional effect supporting (never detracting from) the over-all structure, whether it be from literature or other sources. The order and handling of shots can alter the story structure or can shape the same structure into a number of different emphases. For instance, a film about a city can be approached in many ways. One might follow a time sequence through the film, showing first the morning's activity, then incidents that take place at midday, followed by the transformation that takes place at night. On the other hand, the film might be geographical. The city could be revealed in its relation to the countryside, so that its size and position could be noted. Its layout might be revealed in terms of main streets, side streets, and residential districts. Moreover, historic places, parks, civic buildings, and other places of interest could be pictured. Then again, one might handle the subject by contrasts—business areas with residential areas, slums with well-to-do housing, old architecture against the modern, centers of culture and the honky-tonk, or quiet parks with busy markets. The film might also be developed by showing the people who inhabit the city, in any one or combination of their various aspects. Within each of the four broad approaches mentioned here are possibilities for many, many variations. What the film-maker sees, what he photographs, are the shots. The characteristics, arrangement, and tempo of these shots can not only decide where the emphasis will lie, but can change the original structure of the story. The working of shots according to values inherent in and among them, in turn, shapes the structure so that it becomes uniquely its own—filmic.

The city film based on time sequences might include opening shots of people in various parts of town. Morning activity might thus be built in any number of scenes leading to a minor climax (a sequence), and the same with afternoon and night shots. A film contrasting slum areas with well-to-do homes might be arranged in counterpoint, either by juxtaposing individual shots from both areas, or by presenting the cumulative effect of a scene in one area followed by a scene in the other. The time sequence film could be developed in three distinct opening scenes: scenes of breakfast, scenes of people going to work, scenes of people busily engaged in their daily activities. Depending on the nature of the shots selected to portray this activity, the climax for the sequence can come at the close of the second scene or at the close of the third. In other words, if the scene dealing with people going to work includes shots that mount in tension, show increased activity, and are followed by shots in the third scene in which people settle down to work and carry on their chores, then the third scene acts as a transition for the second sequence. The scene arrangement might be as in Arrangement No. 1.

Arrangement No. 1

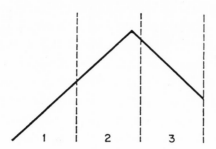

If shots in scene three are selected to build in intensity and interest with the activity being fuller and richer, Arrangement No. 2 might result.

Arrangement No. 2

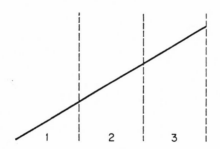

A counterpoint arrangement (No. 3) in a film on contrasts might develop in terms of a main scene interlaced with pieces from related but contrasting scenes, the whole serving at the same time as a sequence.

Arrangement No. 3

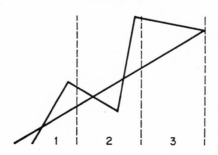

Thus the arrangement is similar to No. 2, except for a further varied internal complexity. It may be made of two scenes leading to parallel editing, or many more than two scenes, leading to multiple arrangements in parallel. This would depend entirely on the arrangements of the counterpointed shots within the scenes, as well as on the nature of the shots themselves.

By using only two units and separating them—developing the scene dealing with the slums fully, and then following it by the scene of the well-to-do areas fully portrayed[3]—the arrangement might be diagrammed as in Arrangement No. 4.

Arrangement No. 4

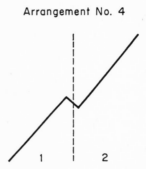

Shots cannot be discussed without mentioning specific content. Whatever might be said about the angle of a shot, or about the distance between camera and subject, ad infinitum, the shot does not assume a specific function until its content is clearly established. Beyond this, it is clear that the content of each shot and its successor, and their relationship, take on a definitive shape. This shape is the structure. This does not imply that the

---

[3] Such a structure may be likened to the whole of the Willard Van Dyke-Ralph Steiner film *The City* (1939), although there is question whether in that film the second rise surpasses the first. However, it should be noted that scene arrangements lead to total film structures that may or may not be organized similarly. In short, what is true of a small piece of film is equally true of the whole. This does not mean that they are structured in exactly the same manner. They may or may not be; but the essence of the artistic work is just this kind of dovetailing within a framework, permitting exploration and thus giving rise to richness and insight of subject matter.

shots necessarily come first. They may or may not. In some cases, a very loose structure might first be realized by the film-maker, who then firms it up with shots that more or less fulfill the original plan. No matter what the film-maker's starting point, the shots he chooses and his final structure are invariably wedded and are expressed in terms of one another.

By reviewing the various sample diagrams, however, one sees that scenes and sequences fall into patterns comparable to those found in literary pieces. One might structure a highly abstract film, but still on analysis will find a recognizable pattern based on artistic principles. At least, it is so hoped. So no matter what is done with the individual shots—whether they are assembled in a pedestrian way or dynamically in montages—they give rise to age-old patterns based on long traditions.

INTERNAL STRUCTURE

The inner structure of the story film is in most cases similar to that of the play. This is the case even in the more recent films, where there is a seeming break with known methods of structure. The difference lies not in the structure, but in the way in which subject matter is handled in terms of that structure, giving rise to a high degree of believability and resulting truth. Diagram No. 1 refers to the slow, steady build of the material

Diagram No. 1

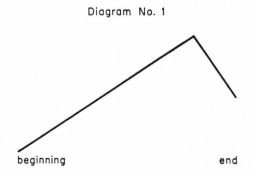

beginning   end

leading to a climax and conclusion. Diagram No. 2 represents a climactic opening followed by a drop and subsequent build

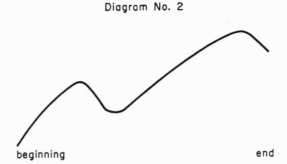

Diagram No. 2

beginning   end

that must surpass the opening. Diagram No. 3 refers to a play within a play, or even possibly a flashback, where the separate units rise to their own climaxes, but are related to the main story in between and lead to a final climax.

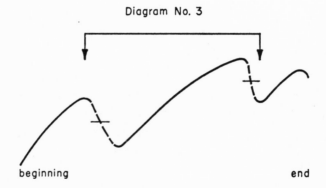

Diagram No. 3

beginning   end

To understand these internal structures in terms of film, any one of these diagrams would have to be realized in terms of the outer structure diagram. The complexity of film structure, therefore, is represented in Diagram No. 4.

Each small square in each box under the scene headings in diagram No. 4 represents a single shot, of which there can be any number, edited, of course, at the discretion of the film-maker. When developing a film story, the film-maker invariably

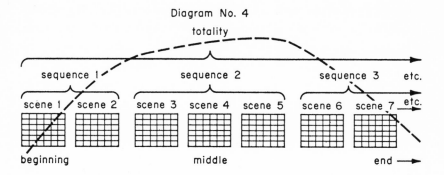

Diagram No. 4

approaches his material in these terms. To be sure, he thinks in the specifics of his story and his shots, but the shape and form he gives it can be abstracted as the diagrams indicate.

Bearing this in mind, it is profitable to look to the playscript, not only because it is the oldest of script forms and still provides the basis for modern films, but because the elements contained in it are still uniquely sound. They deal with exposition, point of attack, complication, discovery, reversal, conflict, rising action, crisis, climax, falling action, and resolution. Added values are the elements of probability and surprise; these are not placed in the initial group because they deal with ideas permeating the whole structure, while the initial group contains a steady and mounting progression. It conveys the classic idea of a beginning, a middle, and an end, and contains a satisfying unity and completeness.

To define these terms briefly: *exposition* presents introductory material in the nature of time, place, atmosphere, characters involved, and background information pertaining to them; *point of attack* deals with the meeting of opposing forces (the conflict) and the stating of the problem; *complication* has to do with the involvements of story—those interesting facets of character and action that reveal the successes and failures in the fortunes of the opposing forces; *discovery* introduces new information about the characters as the story unfolds, having to do with other people, new events, or the central character in

4 3

terms of himself; *reversal* refers to the changes of fortune that come about, often for the worse (and it is here that further complications are elaborated); *conflict* is the clash of forces and may be external, as when characters are opposed, or internal, as when the attitudes, ideas, or feelings of a single character are opposed; the *rising action* is that section of the story that deals with the major plot development and leads from the point of attack to the climax; *crisis* arises when complications and reversals have reached a point calling for a major decision from the characters involved, thus foreshadowing a turning point. *Climax*, of course, is the high point of intensity and interest, often occurring simultaneously with crisis, where the characters must take a major action; it often suggests two or more possible outcomes and engages the audience most keenly. *Falling action* is the dropping off of the climax leading to the *resolution*, in which all major and minor questions are resolved and the structure is brought into balance. All loose ends are tied off, and there is, hopefully, a catharsis in a tragedy, a happy ending in a comedy.

Probability is constantly present to assure understandable development of cause and effect. What eventually occurs must be motivated by what precedes. In the old classics, when events became so hopelessly entangled that a natural working out was impossible, the authors resorted to the *deus ex machina*, in which the gods descended by machinery and straightened everything out. Many of today's weaker scripts use the same technique in a more "subtle" way, much to the dismay of audience and critic. Closely linked with probability is *surprise;* the unexpected may take place, but it too must be motivated. This motivation is often the difference between a satisfactory resolution and a *deus ex machina*. When the cavalry arrives in the nick of time, some time earlier a message must have been sent for help, or the coincidence of their arrival is strictly from above.

It is by no means accidental that these elements are strung together to suggest progression. They specifically provide for clear organization; unify and complete the story, and are absolutely necessary for involving an audience. But these elements can also produce stilted and trivial scripts, obvious in their unfolding, saccharine, and maudlin.

The renascence undergone by the modern theater since Henrik Ibsen (1828–1906) attracted international attention with his plays, circa 1870, has been experienced by the motion picture during the last forty years. Ibsen, called the father of modern realistic drama, became concerned with social issues and problems that were considered taboo by the society of his time. His plays started a movement that was further advanced by George Bernard Shaw, and found its culmination in the realistic plays of Eugene O'Neill. This rebellion, however, was against the substance, not the external structure, of the traditional plays of their times.

Filled with treacle and sugar-coated with boudoir nonsense, the so-called "well-made" play at that time observed the structural rules slavishly. The exposition, climax, and resolution were easily identified, being artificially contrived and obvious. Usually the opening scene introduced a maid and butler who, while engaged in housecleaning chores, discussed the events of the previous evening—these events naturally dealt with the glamorous lady of the house. Result: exposition. In short order, the upstage doors would be thrown open and the lady would appear, beautifully gowned, her hair flowing freely, stars in her eyes. But the exposition hinted at trouble, and so it was. The lady would be deeply embroiled with the difficulties of amour. Result: complication. The doorbell would ring and the wrong lover would be announced. Embarrassment. Excuses. White lies. On and on it would go, in precise order.

Throwing out the treacle, Ibsen, Shaw, and the realistic playwrights who followed gave freer rein to inner structure, while still observing, generally, the orthodox external structure. Ultimately, this led to substance gradually taking precedence over

45

external structure as well. The revolt had to do with a dying Victorian Age and the emergence of twentieth-century realism, but it altered the writer's attitude toward structure. Structural elements became servants, not masters.

The movement developed slowly over a considerable period of time. During the 1920's, while O'Neill was carrying on the realistic approach of Ibsen and Shaw, Clyde Fitch's plays, *Beau Brummel* and *Captain Jinks of the Horse Marines*, were still attracting the public. In the latter play, a New York City pier replaced the French living room, a host of stage-door Johnnies replaced the butler and the maid, a gangplank leading to an ocean liner replaced the symmetrically placed upstage door, and the leading lady was a diva returning from a successful European tour. All proceeded as before in the perfectly conceived structure.

As entertaining and successful as the film plays of the 1930's were—*The Big House* (1930), *The Front Page* (1931), *It Happened One Night* (1934), *Mr. Deeds Goes to Town* (1936), *Mr. Smith Goes to Washington* (1939)—they were all linked to the well-made pattern. A look at the development of film fare from the 1930's to the 1960's (with Luchino Visconti, perhaps, as the foremost post-World War II exponent) reveals a significant change over to the realistic tradition, and with this change a break from the well-made structure that had become common to film. More notable recent examples are *Room at the Top* (1958), *Saturday Night and Sunday Morning* (1960), *La Dolce Vita* (1960), *L'Avventura* (1960), and *The Easy Life* (1963), among many others.

Changes in taste, revolts against staid traditions, the probing into life's meaning or donning rose-colored glasses for an idealized view of life will constantly occur. No special brief is held here for one or the other. But out of these trends come additional craft attitudes that are important to the film-maker. Traditional structure is closely observed and adhered to, or is recognized and violated, according to the way in which the storyteller approaches his material. In both instances there are examples of marked successes. In the successful "well-made" films of the 1930's, freshness, ingenuity, and cleverness of incident and characterization masked the creakiness of structure. Audiences curled up their noses only at those films that were vapid and obvious. In other films, where the actors' personalities were carefully chosen to fit single-dimension characters in firecracker situations, structure drew no complaints. The rigid structure, in fact, was a necessity.

In today's realistic Italian and English films, the rigidity of structure has disappeared. But this is not to say that the films are unstructured. *Saturday Night and Sunday Morning* (1960), for example, is closely related in many ways to the slice-of-life naturalistic plays of Elmer Rice and Sidney Kingsley. The film unfolds as if life itself were being witnessed, with the usual type of exposition, climax and resolution lacking, nevertheless present in the film's own terms.

In summary, the classic elements—exposition, point of attack, complication, discovery, reversal, conflict, rising action, crisis, climax, falling action, and resolution—that form the basis of play structure also form the basis of the film story. These elements are utilized and developed in varying degrees in order to organize the story. The degree to which they are exploited depends primarily on the film-maker's attitude toward his material. The film-maker must know exactly what he wants to say and all of the ways that it can be said, so that he can pick the best way for his purposes and thus bring form and substance together in a happy marriage. Ironically, however, the effort is seldom, if ever, a conscious one. If anything, conscious or studied effort would hinder rather than help the artistic process involved. Rather, the character of structure emerges naturally from two sources: the way the film-maker perceives his material, and his knowledge of the storytelling craft.

STRUCTURE AND SUBSTANCE

The point is often made that the only way to learn how to write is by reading and writing. By reading constantly the would-be writer subjects himself to theory. By examining the writings of others he becomes aware of structure, style, method, and manner. The would-be writer must move a step beyond the simple enjoyment of a story or the gleaning of information from a nonfiction piece into an analysis of the writer's technique. Thus, through his critical faculties, he sets up in his own mind a series of frames of reference.

Successful writers often tell how, in their beginning years, they conscientiously read hundreds of novels or saw hundreds of plays. But they never stopped with the reading or seeing. Invariably they became critics by making notes of their reactions, their evaluations, and their reasons for believing a piece to be a success or a failure. Alexandre Dumas, *fils*, interested in playwriting, related how he would visit the theater and see only the first two acts. He would then rush home and write the third act, return to the theater at a later date, and compare the actual end with the one he had written. Out of the comparison would come a conclusion as to which of the endings was better, and why. George Bernard Shaw tells of his days as a critic, how his observations and written criticisms sharpened his insight into the play form. To give a contemporary example, there is the story of a young man interested in television drama who locked himself in a hotel room for a week with a television set and typewriter. He observed and wrote throughout that time. There is no saying how good his results were, but it is certain that he developed some familiarity with the form of television drama.

The next step in learning to write, of course, is application.

In this step, the writer moves from an observing role to a creative one. However, the idea that the writer simply repeats what he has observed could not be further from the truth. The reading, seeing, and learning must be converted into an integral part of the writer's being. They must provide him with depth and background but, seen through his own personality and point of view, be transmuted into a creation of his own.

Similarly, the film-maker must approach his material with a point of view that is singularly his own, a product of the integration of his experience and his personality. In the heyday of motion pictures, the 1930's, one could not criticize a film quite the same way as a play. This was so, not because of the difference in media, but because of the creative differences in approach to substance by the artists involved in each; it is even so to a great extent today. Plays can be criticized for plot weaknesses, failure of character motivation, or lack of logical development. A play may succeed despite structural weaknesses or other defects because the playwright's convictions, theme, or insight into character causes the play to transcend its flaws.

The bulk of films, however, cannot be criticized in this way. They are structurally perfect, or nearly so. Characters and events are motivated (at least conventionally), all loose ends are tied up, and everything is very logical. But in most cases there are no convictions, no insights, and very little theme. In the early days of film, as many as seven different writers would be called in to work on one script. In such instances the greatest concentration would be on the mechanics of development. To get seven men, with seven different personalities and seven different points of view, to agree on, develop, and communicate one given theme is manifestly impossible. Therefore, they concentrated on the nonthematic aspects of the script—its mechanics, its external structure. This resulted in "perfect" films, with no heart or guts.

Structure cannot exist for its own sake, or come to life

without meaningful substance; its weakness or strength, effectiveness or ineffectiveness, is related directly to the way the film-maker assesses his subject, for this assessment determines the film's internal structure. In other words, his knowledge of technique (external structure) must be so thorough and so much a part of him that it almost unconsciously guides him in the presentation of his subject; while his sensitivity and awareness of the world about him, his feeling for people, and his passion to communicate all provide the structure with freshness and vitality. Depending on the film-maker's maturity and experience, the two develop concurrently. Thus, although the film-maker is primarily engaged in creative work, his critical senses, sharpened and refined by training and learning, shape his work almost automatically. The importance of studying structure, therefore, does not lie in one's ability to set up a neat, or correct, shot-scene-sequence progression, but rather to present specific material in the most effective shot-scene-sequence. The more the film-maker explores his material, and the more familiar he is with his craft, the more able he becomes to combine the two in filmic terms.

This supports the previously stated idea that films, like plays and novels, have both external and internal structures. External structure can easily be recognized and understood, but internal structure has no sure-fire formula, no pat method, no slick and polished mold. Where the two types of structure pull in separate directions or fight against each other, the work suffers as art. The internal structure, having honest substance and an individual point of view, is the more important of the two, but it has to be understood—and structure is its vehicle, for it is the individual way the substance is organized. Either type of structure can be conventional or experimental. Internal structure, however, must grow out of the material; and the substance of the material must be rich and meaningful, or the final result will at the very best be slick, pat formula.

OUTLINE TO SHOOTING SCRIPT

A film script goes through four distinct planning phases: out-line, treatment, scenario, and shooting script. Although these terms are often loosely used, they do define specific stages of development.

The *outline* covers the most elementary planning. Its objective is to state the point of the film—what it is about. It also includes a rough grouping of the major and minor points that lead to this objective. The outline has no specific form; its order is usually based on the thinking method of the film-maker. In some instances it may be no more than a series of single sentences having some element of progression. The film-maker looks it over and, either consciously or unconsciously, checks the logic of this progression. At this point, the order may be changed, or some ideas may be eliminated in favor of others. The outline itself does not necessarily follow the specific path the film is to take. In other words, the logical order of the outline does not necessarily proceed according to the logic that will control the scene-sequence arrangement of the film in its final form.

Specifically, the outline is the starting point that deals with the thought in the film, as it stands abstractly, and is simply a presentation of ideas or events. When concerned with the documentary, the film-maker will deal with ideas; when work-ing with narrative, he will consider the things happening, the events. Yet, this is not meant as a hard and fast rule, for, in fact, the conditions might very well be reversed. The deciding factor is the thinking pattern most expedient to the particular film-maker. Each film-maker finds his own way of arriving at ideas and grouping them according to his personal needs. The film-maker in this case is no different from the novelist, play-wright, short-story writer, or magazine article writer. What might be called an outline in some cases is nothing more than a compilation of notes, meaningful to no one but the author. Such notes have been gathered on the backs of old letters, bits of newspapers, or pieces of torn paper. (This practice, however, is not recommended, particularly if there are compulsive house cleaners at home!) In such a case, the outline is actually carried in the head of the writer, and the notes are simple guideposts for recalling the arrangement and organization of facts in his head. Other writers may formulate and organize all their material on standard-size paper in a lucid and intelligible system. And, of course, there are innumerable variations between the two. No one can say that one method is better than the other. Whatever the method, if results are good, it is valid. But very few, if any, writers or film-makers approach writing or making a film without some sort of written outline for a start. One cannot put too much faith in the creative flashes that pass through one's mind without putting them on paper in order to examine them objectively in the helpful light of later reason.

The *treatment* is a somewhat developed outline. It not only includes all the minor details that support the story, but generally starts from the very beginning of the story and proceeds continuously from that point to the end. Structure, as it may finally shape the film, is hardly apparent in the outline and perhaps only slightly better defined in the treatment.

Treatment has a twofold purpose: it provides all story background, so that the cause-and-effect progression of the story can be clearly understood and checked, and it develops the frame of reference in which the story is being told. Many details, as well as many premises that might be in the treatment, never live through the weeding-out process that goes on in the further refinement of the film. In some cases, some of these premises are eventually handled through expository devices or dialogue, or are dropped completely.

Story treatment, then, is a detailed account of the plot, mostly written out in paragraph form. A well-handled treatment should include the quality and style of the production. Too often, treatments deal exclusively with plot in a bare-bones presentation. One gets a pretty good idea of the story, but of little else. The point of view of the film, as well as the color surrounding it—the kinds of characters, the degree of realism of the locales, the style of the costuming, the flavor permeating the story—should be worked into the treatment as it unfolds.

The *scenario* takes the treatment one step further and reveals exactly how the story will unfold in the film. A clearer understanding of the transformation that takes place between treatment and scenario might be gleaned by briefly looking at the working methods of some writers of mystery stories, including mystery-film writers. Mysteries are cleverly plotted and a number of threads woven together as the story develops and the culprit is discovered. But in the treatment of such a story, no mystery need be present. Events are set forth straightforwardly, each detail in its order of occurrence, and all the relationships, all the happenings, in a simple straight line. In the scenario, many of the events that occur first are revealed last. The mystery unfolds roughly in the order of the final story or film. Suspense and intrigue are created by the manner in which the information is doled out, and the scenario states what that manner will be.

A story, therefore, in which a journalist picks up a wealthy young nymph and goes riding with her in her dazzling American car might not have such a scene opening the film. More complications of the story might have to do with the journalist's mistress taking poison because of her lover's infidelity. The journalist, on returning to his flat, might find her, crumpled in pain and whimpering incoherent phrases. He then races her to a hospital. Scenes like this might be interlaced with others. In fixing the focus of the story, placing all its elements in proper perspective with thematic values coming through, the opening might show a gilded statue of Christ, swung under a helicopter and being borne aloft over the rooftops of Rome. A second helicopter in pursuit of the first has in it a journalist and a photographer. The sunbathing girls in bikinis, the attempts of the men at conversation and dating, and the figure of Christ all recall Fellini's *La Dolce Vita* (1960). What is happening to whom, and who is thinking and feeling what, will emerge from this as the meaning becomes known according to the way in which the story has been structured. The scenario gives this information.

The scenario is written out in paragraph form and is often broken down according to sequences. In other words, Sequence No. 1 may be described in four, five, or any number of paragraphs. Sequence No. 2 (and Nos. 3 and 4 etc.) will also be summed up in a number of paragraphs. The paragraphs themselves, though not necessarily comparable to individual scenes, will give a general indication of the number of scenes in each sequence. Like the treatment, the scenario should contain the color and point of view of the film.

The *shooting script* is a breakdown of the scenario into shots. Although it might seem desirable to list each specific shot in every scene, more often the shots are listed in a general way. Specifics are left to the director, who approaches his shooting, either by improvising each shot while actually filming, or by making his own detailed breakdown of the shots as he sees them, according to his interpretation of the scene. A first shooting script, therefore, might list only key shots, which establish the setting, characters, time, and atmosphere, and leave further refinements until the time of shooting.

No hard and fast rule governs specific steps to follow when making a film. But prior planning and preparation are mandatory. A film has to be structured. Outlines and shooting scripts provide the film-maker with control. He is at a distinct disadvantage when compared with theater directors, because his external frame of reference is not a proscenium arch, but a screen that is never actually in front of him until the film has been completed.

Because a film is not all of a piece, but made of pieces, the good film-maker must be as aware of editing as of the writing and directing. By editing the film he can make further structural changes for greater effectiveness. Outlines, treatments, scenarios, and shooting scripts are extremely valuable planning phases; when done early they provide the film-maker with a close check on his progress as well as opportunities to heighten the impact or correct mistakes. But whether he believes in them or not, in one way or another, sooner or later, he has no choice but to go through the steps—even if he begins shooting with nothing but an idea and waits until he reaches the editing table. Then, of course, he has cut down his opportunities by one third.

STRUCTURE AND THE DOCUMENTARY

Because the documentary film is generally shorter than the narrative feature, documentary film-makers often do not plan through the specific phases of outline, treatment, scenario, and shooting script. A feature-length narrative can comprise from seven to twelve reels or more, running on the screen from seventy minutes to two hours or longer. Documentary films are handled in units of reels that run ten minutes; the entire film usually comprises one or two reels, although there have been a good number running much longer. Still, with the average ten- or twenty-minute documentary, many film-makers do start with the thematic idea, move to an outline to set up a structure supporting the theme, and develop a shooting script from the structured outline. In such cases, moreover, the shooting script is highly detailed, especially when it comes to the various shots to be taken.

Documentary structures are ingeniously wrought, because in many instances the subject matter does not lend itself readily to film. In order to overcome this obstacle, the film-maker must depend on a strong point of view to provide the backbone of his film. In the selection of his material, a unified point of view sharpens, clarifies, and defines the objective of the film. Knowing what to look for he will recognize it when he sees it, adapting his subject matter to a visual presentation at the very time of its development, thus sharpening and controlling both his material and theme. Lest this seem to belabor the obvious, note how many unsatisfying films show no sign of their maker's —or any particular—point of view.

The simplest and most obvious way of approaching the material is to dramatize it. This method is only as good as the film-maker using it, for he runs the risk of having the dramatic element overpower the content, as well as of having the drama mean something different from what he is after. Careful attention to proportion and balance will avoid this. There are various means of dramatization. A film, for example, might be based on a simple interview that, although dull, contains significant thematic points. To avoid dullness, the scene might open with the interviewee in a dramatic situation dealing with a special problem. Such a scene would motivate the interview to follow. Once the interview gets underway, the camera would depart from time to time to dramatize the points raised by the interviewer. This might be followed by a final scene dealing once again with the interviewee, showing what action he took on the problem.

On the other hand, in place of this last dramatic scene might be a number of scenes, objectively approached, that deal with the basic problem on a universal, rather than a personal, basis. In this case the object would be to engage the audience intellectually, rather than through dramatic empathy, and so to move them to a conclusive action or decision.

The structural arrangements in such instances are exemplified by structures nos. 1 and 2.

In both instances, the structural problem is to have the final scene build in intensity and to top what has come before, so that the last sequence is climactic. The constant danger of such structures, as already stated, is that the dramatic scenes may overshadow the basic communication. The sensitive film-maker avoids this by making certain that he is not carried away by drama for its own sake, but uses drama to reveal truth. It is not

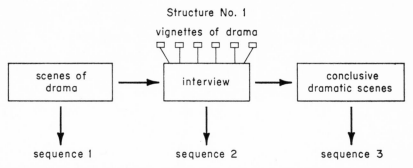

so much a matter of avoiding pyrotechnics and melodrama as of presenting real people dealing with real problems in a real way. Keen observation, honesty, and understanding of the people, the situation, and its meaningful visual aspects are the necessary ingredients that enable drama to support the film rather than to be in conflict with it.

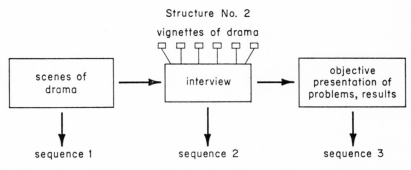

Another structural device is one in which general material is presented entirely in terms of one individual's actions and reactions. Although this one individual states the issues in personal terms, he is so presented that he is always recognizable in terms of the larger issue. This method minimizes the element of drama, but still takes advantage of the audience's tendency to empathize. (See Structure No. 3.)

Simplest of all structural arrangements, of course, is the direct idea presentation. The film capitalizes on the subject's importance to carry the film through. Such films are visual editorials, of course, and their success or failure depends primarily on the clarity and impact of the material in terms of its

5 7

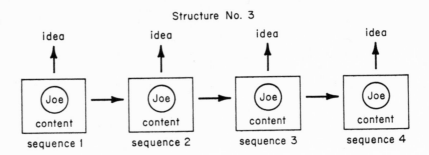

Structure No. 3

organization. This assumes that the shots themselves adequately convey happenings of social, civil, economic, or political consequence. Arrangement then is the key, because through it the plus or minus value of propaganda emerges.

Although the diagram of such a structure looks relatively simple, there must be an element of subtlety in handling the units, ideas, and shots that defies pinning down. Some of the Nazi propaganda films of World War II excellently illustrate this point, for one is led to thinking he is seeing nothing more than actuality, which he is; but the cumulative effect most subtly supports a contention that can be understood only after clear analysis.

When this type of structure is used with less compelling subject matter, an emphasis on mood and atmospheric qualities may raise the interest and effect level of the film. The right music and sound help to do the job. In such cases, sound and music are not relegated to the background, but are brought forward by being given specific functions, very much like a character in a play. A ballad, for example, can not only tie scenes together, thus unifying them into a sequence, but can go a step further in clarifying the thematic intent of the scenes through both lyrics and melody. An interruption of stark sound effects can introduce a reality that further explores theme through contrast. The possibilities are infinite.

The three examples of documentary structure cited here show that although there are endless varieties, there must be a clear and concise path for the viewer to traverse. Any type of organization is valid, as long as it serves to make the film comprehensible. The examples also show that structure can be built on any single element that is in the content. This one element, determined by the film-maker's point of view, becomes the structure's central control point. Structures, therefore, may evolve around idea, emotional progression, mood, atmosphere, and locale. Geographical arrangements, arrangements in time or space, physical groupings, or combinations thereof are useful points on which to build a structure.

The documentary film-maker is also faced, of course, with the problem of intensifying his scenes, building and reaching a climax. Without resorting to the devices inherent in plot structure, he must emphasize his material and achieve his intensification, not by falsifying life, "souping up" the ingredients to create dramatic incidents, superimposing preconceived notions of actuality, or introducing extraneous happenings to liven things up, but by seeing the truth in people, in the things they do and in the lives they lead, and by reacting strongly to this, feeling vividly about it, and portraying it honestly.

On this score there is no difference between the story film-maker and the documentary film-maker—they must both seek truth, the one through imagination, the other through recognition. In both cases, their skill depends on observation and understanding.

STRUCTURE AND THE FILM CONCEPT

When a film-maker shapes up a structure, the abstract is soon forgotten as specific story units are considered. This is a very natural tendency because story units are tangibles, relatively easy to handle and understand, and tangibles are the very things that make the film. All too often, therefore, stories are developed in terms of older, more familiar literary forms—the play, for example. To proceed along these lines leads the film-maker into a series of blind alleys and traps. Despite the film's seeming similarity to other literary forms, there is a basic split, for the film is not a play or a novel or a short story. As previously pointed out, structure is basic to all the forms; but it must be influenced both by the external demands of its particular form and by the internal developments of the specific incidents and actions that have been selected. The best playwright, play director, novelist, or short-story writer cannot successfully move into films without a solid understanding of the film concept. To be sure, he knows structure and is familiar with all the devices, means, and methods peculiar to it as it applies to his medium; but he will only think and proceed in familiar terms, not necessarily filmic.

What then is the filmic concept? It is simply that the story is told through the use of pictures, and it requires just so many pictures of definite content and value to project a specific idea. Simple to say, but difficult to achieve!

Some beginners, aware of flow and arrangement, attempt to secure continuity in their films by resorting to simple and obvious shots of physical action, with little or no thought to other content. Often such a film demonstrates good craftsmanship, but is also a cliché. Many present-day films made for television are good examples of this. The camera work is professionally done, but the development of the material that goes into each shot is in the best comic book tradition. Other beginners avoid the cliché and seek to interpret or explore the world about them, primarily through verbalization. Some extremely fine individual shots may be taken, but no pictorial relationship is developed among them. The final result is a stultifying presentation in which shots are reduced to an almost unnecessary accompaniment to an overloaded sound track.

Film concept takes in both the visual flow and the verbalization, but in harmonious counterpoint. Although basic continuity is important for the audience to understand what is going on, it must be remembered that continuity can be obtained in ways other than by straightforward physical action. It can result from mood, emotion, thematic idea, and character, and even from composition. The level of communication expressed by the continuity will depend a great deal on the selection and arrangement of shots. This is the crux of the matter: the selection and arrangement of shots in a film should be more important than the dialogue or narration. The shots should be chosen for visual connotation and relationships, supported where necessary with an added dimension of words. So chosen they pack a far more vital wallop than when they merely illustrate words that not only can stand alone, but conceivably might stimulate the imagination more if unillustrated. This does not mean that pictures are better than words. The trick is to see a film subject in its own terms, in pictures; or to see those aspects of a subject that lend themselves to the filmic concept, and to write about the others. To see a story in filmic terms calls for experience. To ask how one develops this ability is like asking what makes a good director. The answer is a generalization: by familiarity with craft, sensitivity to the medium and to the subject, interest in people and the world they live in, a keen sense of what is meaningful to an audience, and a personal point of view.

In terms of craft, at least the following three concepts can be made clear to the beginning film-maker. One: The basic story usually follows the recognized literary form. It has a beginning, a middle, and an end, and includes some kind of climax. Two: The film rearranges, telescopes, or draws out this structure to suit its own purposes, through the choice and juxtaposition of shots. Three: The excitement and intensity of the film ultimately depend on the individual shot, not only in terms of its angle, distance, and composition, but on the significance of its content.

THE TRANSITION

A story is usually imagined in terms of its high points, its big scenes, and its climaxes, that is, its major premises. These guideposts, which lead the viewer through a story, have an abruptness and baldness about them because of their climactic nature. In the early stages of story development, therefore, these major premises might be likened to a series of isolated mountains, with no visible valleys. Hence for the viewer the connection is blurred, relationships are incomplete, and the total picture may not only be difficult to understand, but may cause some shock. To have the story unfold naturally and smoothly and to connect the isolated major premises, transition scenes are indispensable. As intrinsic parts of the story, they deal with beginning events and background information, introduce detail, add refinement, and, most important, provide credibility.

A block arrangement (see Arrangement No. 1) might be used to designate a story structure in terms of major premises.

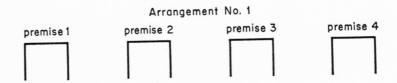

The addition of scenes to make the story more interesting and complete might be outlined in Arrangement No. 2.

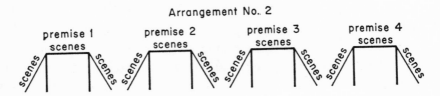

Notice how the elaboration of each of these premises into scenes (which can be any number as needed) develops an individual sequence. To link the story into a fully connected piece, still more scenes are added as transitions (see Arrangement No. 3).

These transitions can be immensely effective or deadly dull, depending on the storyteller's ability. Often the beginning film-maker accepts too literally—or too limitingly—the scene's

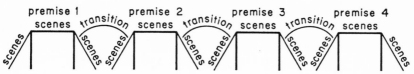

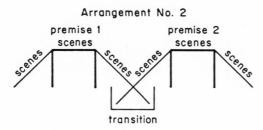

transitional function. Hence he has a tendency to introduce material that is not only superfluous but in another sense inadequate. Transitions are always necessary, but again they need not be confined to simple physical action, or to a specially inserted scene. Often transition can be provided far more effectively by blending the closing scene of one sequence with the opening of the next (see Arrangement No. 4).

In cases where a transition is deliberately eliminated in order to shock or startle the viewer, its very absence must be a contribution to the finished film.

These points are particularly significant in film-making, because pictures lend such emphasis and concentration that in as little as one-twenty-fourth of a second—the time to change from one shot to the next—an acceptable and understandable transition can take place.

In his editing, the film-maker should see that transition shots do not parade across the screen in an endless continuity of boredom and dullness. Often a simple dissolve or a direct cut will carry more weight than a well-knit series of shots included merely to provide a physical transition. Through the editing process, scenes can be eliminated, sequences tightened, and meaningful footage rearranged for greater significance. However, in spite of the tremendous flexibility of the editing process, no amount of rearranging will save a really meaningless shot. True, a kind of cumulative connotation may make a well-arranged series of shots more effective than would seem possible from the simple sum of the parts. Nevertheless, even this effect is heightened when the individual shots are controlled by a specific idea. At the editing table, in spite of the film's flexibility, the film-maker is always face to face with the power or the limitations of his original concept.

CRISIS AND CLIMAX

The action line of any story is the beginning, middle, and end of the main character's striving to meet and deal with an impending crisis, in a set of circumstances involving opposition; the individualizing details are what make the story original and different. The opposition may be internal or external; and the action may be physical, between persons or within one person; but it is not necessarily, nor even desirably, confined to violent physical action. A crisis and a climax are necessary, and are usually the most intense and emotionally charged scenes; but all too often they have come to mean only an intensification of physical action. Two thousand years of drama have contributed to this idea, and a cursory examination of present-day fare will reveal that this interpretation is as popular as ever. Although one might deplore such a conclusion, it is hardly unreasonable.

Crisis and climax, being essential parts of the structural development, bring the developing elements of the story together in an explosive mixture. But the film-maker absorbed with the explosion itself can forget that the viewer must be able to see the conclusions through the settling ashes and dust. Taking the path of least resistance, the film-maker concentrates on the physical action and leaves the viewer with no sense of meaning in the story. It is relatively simple to entrance the audience by overpowering them with action, but not so simple to achieve intensification and impact through revelation (the audience's own, not necessarily the character's). But revelation, a sense of meaning, not physical action alone, is the key. This is the basic difference between the classics and the pulps.

A climactic scene, then, more than any other, should be sharply outlined so that the reason for the action is apparent. The film-maker need not worry unduly about this if he undertook his film with something to say and if all of his scenes were planned with that in mind. A climax becomes obligatory in terms of the scenes that precede it, and in the same manner the meaning of the climax is "obligatory" according to the meaning inherent in the earlier scenes. By the same token, when crisis and climax are accepted as revealing scenes, rather than as merely violent ones, the film-maker has a guide for his camera work. A camera in the hands of a neophyte is like a pencil in the hand of a kindergarten child. Unable to write, the child is entranced by the squiggles he makes on paper. The neophyte is enchanted by shots. One has no more meaning than the other. Once aware that climax can take the viewer a step further into the dimensions of character and story and throw illumination on our lives, the film-maker will no longer take shots for their own sake. Neither will he arbitrarily and artificially devise shots, but will seek to find the visual truth in his subject, thus providing himself with varied shots from which he can select. The meaning and intent of the climax will suggest which elements are important to the story and what all the shots should help to reveal.

It might seem that the same points cannot be raised about the documentary. But, although the documentary does not use a theatrical structure or have a climax in the accepted sense, it does reach a point of intensity, sometimes at the very end of the film. More than anything else, the climax here rests on revelation. Again, if the film-maker has something to say, each of his shots will be motivated, as he seeks and finds the part of life that he wants his audience to experience.

The cumulative effect of such shots, with their revealing insights, is a climax. Sometimes this point is reached a minute or two after the last fade-out, as the audience sits in momentary silence, digesting what it has seen. The picture is not actually over until the audience catches its breath, and the rustle of papers and hushed whispers are heard once more.

STRUCTURE AND SOUND

So much emphasis is placed on shots and their arrangement that planning of the sound is sometimes neglected until the filming has been completed. Even where dialogue is an integral part of the film and the actual spoken lines are worked and reworked for extra polish, the total sound is often overlooked. The beginning film-maker, although fairly well aware of the problems of handling shots, may make the mistake of including sound simply to extend a dimension of reality. Such reasoning is a distinct limitation. The idea of a shot is conveyed not only by compositional arrangement, lighting, and camera angle, but by sound as well. In some instances, sound may be blended and balanced with other shot values; in others it may function more or less importantly.

Sound is an integral part of the film, and as such calls for as much attention as the shots themselves. Sound does not have a structure uniquely its own, but is a contributing part of the shot. It is vitally important in giving more information about the characters, the places seen, the mood, and the style of the film, and in supporting its basic ideas. Sound may be divided into four classifications: dialogue, music, sound effects, and

66

silence. Sound is often used to repeat the idea already communicated through picture, but in such cases, unless it serves a specific purpose, it is repetitive and pointless. Nothing is more wasteful and meaningless than to have the cowboys storm into town accompanied by the sharp clatter of their horses' hoofs. A well-selected piece of mood music can usually do more for effect than the adding of sound cliché to picture cliché.

Once the film-maker understands that sound is not a conventional tag-along, but a basic contribution to the film, he begins to use it with great care, constantly bringing artistic judgment into his decisions. Through the proper use of sound— dialogue, music, effects or their lack—he is often able to communicate with more richness either serious, comic, or symbolic values. The optimum use of sound is not governed by laws, but by insight. For example, the point is made that repetitive sounds are of no value. Still, the harsh, noisy sound of pub activity in *Saturday Night and Sunday Morning* (1960), punctuated by understandable shouts from time to time, produces a characteristic reality that is extremely important to this type of film. But note also that at other points noises are eliminated, and music is used for punctuation.

A different instance is Satyajit Ray's *The World of Apu* (1958), when the uniformed band plays an English marching song over and over in preparation for the wedding that is to take place. Nothing could be more humorously incongruous than the band playing this song over and over again—a little off-key, it seems—as one feels the tender and apprehensive sentiments of the young couple. How perfectly the sound projects this wonderfully crazy world of mixed Hindu and English cultures, and the bridegroom's mixed feelings as he is torn between staying and fleeing. There are innumerable other instances where sound is used to project theme, character, and mood. Such success is not accidental, but has been carefully planned.

Sound takes its structural pattern from that of the film, and is shaped by the arrangement of the shots. In planning, therefore, one must be able to follow the pattern of shots and sound as they are creatively integrated. One method for keeping track is to set up seven columns on a piece of paper. In the first column the sequences are listed; in column two, the scenes, opposite the sequence into which they fit; and in column three, a detailed description is given of the specific shots in each scene. The last four columns respectively are headed dialogue, music, sound effects, and silence. In each of these columns, exact notes are made of the sound desired for each shot, scene, and sequence. The simple description "dialogue" or "music" is not sufficient; one must spell out the exact words, the specific music (including type of instrumentation), and the particular effect, so that one can come as close as possible to evoking the actual end product. By running his eye down the columns, the film-maker will be better able to imagine what the results of his choices will be. He will see the picture and hear the sound, juxtaposed on the paper, but blended in his imagination.

PREPRODUCTION AND POSTPRODUCTION STRUCTURING

The mechanics of film-making provide a unique advantage. Because the finished film is made up of pieces, photographed at different times and in different places, and always susceptible to rearranging, the film-maker can always make changes. Even after going through the process of structuring, scripting, and shooting, he can restructure his film in the editing process. At this point he can check each shot, tell whether his predetermined ideas are present or whether new ideas have replaced them, change the order, or, if necessary, go so far as to come up with a story pattern different from his original plan (presumably better!). This possibility provides the film-maker with three opportunities for concentrating on structure: when the script is being shaped up prior to shooting; during the shooting; and during the editing. Each approach has advantages and drawbacks.

In dialogue feature films and in story films made for television, cost is a major consideration. Hence every shot has to be planned in detail. Experimentation of any kind or trial-and-error shooting are prohibitive. The simplest deviation from a scheduled structural arrangement can cause astronomical expenditures. Stories thus tend to be tight, pat, and often limited. Although fine films have been made in this manner, most often the emphasis is on dramatic storytelling, rather than exploitation of true cinematic techniques, and the camera work tends to be competent, rather than creative. Shooting ratios in such instances range from seven-to-one to ten-to-one or higher. This means that the cameraman shoots seven to ten times the amount of raw stock that will be used in the finished film. The extra footage is shot, not to provide for any deviations from the planned shooting schedule, but to make possible a choice of takes of any given scene, in case of fluffs. A feature film running one and one-half hours would be nine reels long, or approximately nine thousand feet of 35mm film. At the above ratio, the original amount of exposed film would be from sixty thousand to ninety thousand feet.

By contrast, *Louisiana Story* (1948), Robert Flaherty's feature-length film of a wild Cajun boy, running eight thousand feet in its final length, was shot on two hundred thousand feet, a ratio of about twenty-five to one.[4] It must be understood that production methods in both cases were markedly different. Flaherty worked by himself and with a select few, and accomplished the bulk of his structuring in the editing process. One of his biggest expenses, at least in the early days, probably was the cost of the raw stock. In the pre-set story film, raw stock costs are probably among the lowest of the expenses.

---

[4] Karel Reisz, *The Technique of Film Editing* (New York: Hastings House, 1963), p. 136.

The cost factor per se is not the point, however. Rather, it is the effect cost may have on the style and approaches to film-making. Generally, some restructuring must be done in all cases, but in the commercial story film with a large overhead it must be held to a minimum. To be able to produce a film under these limitations, and yet develop it in cinematic terms, using an interpretive and exploratory camera, calls for a film-maker with excellent experience, insight into the relationships of images, and a fresh point of view.

The documentarian, on the other hand, can (and usually does) hold off detailed structuring until after he has secured his shots. However, he should study his material thoroughly, to alert himself to possible and probable variations, and to plan a tentative structure. To capture the essence of his material on film, he must know what he is looking for. Living with the people whose story he is to tell, visiting the locations to study the terrain and to absorb the mood, atmosphere, and nature of the ecology, the film-maker provides himself with an honest guide for his story and his shooting. Shooting on a wide ratio, alert at all times for the telling image, he can then firm up his structure during the editing with artistry and coherence.

Generally, it is wise for the novice to forego dialogue in his first film and to be conscious of structure both before shooting and during editing. Man relies heavily on the written and spoken word—often wastefully—so much so that he often uses language to cover inadequacy. The film-maker is already accustomed to dialogue as a means of story communication. To communicate through the image is a method that has to be learned and developed. Thus, dependency on language is a natural pitfall for the beginner and restricts the growth of his visual sense. Hence the beginner should concentrate first on mastery of picture arrangement. When he has learned to explore his content pictorially, he will be better able to use dialogue—when he comes to it—sparingly and effectively.

In summary, to leave structure to the editing process is extremely hazardous. To adhere to a rigid structure from the outset is limiting. As film is fluid, so should its structure be. In one sense, in the making of a film, structure is at one extreme, while the shot is at the other. The film-maker thinks constantly of one in terms of the other, because his task is to work at both ends to develop a telling pattern, and one that is never fixed. In the expanding film art—commercial or independent, individual or epic—the methods of the documentarian and the narrative film-maker are coming closer and closer together.

3

THE FILM CRAFT

The separation of craft from art is purely academic. Like form and substance, the two have to be inextricably woven into perfect harmony to be effective. But the very fact that art cannot exist except in terms of the other, as good or bad as art might be, provides the key to the limitless ways in which craft must serve the film-maker.

In simple terms, if substance is what the film-maker has to say, craft is the way in which he says it (and the result, one fervently hopes, is art). Craft, therefore, is technique governed by the many rules that guide the ways in which shots can be photographed and arranged to project a story. As important as it is to recognize and understand these rules, it is equally important to be aware that they were introduced by men in the light of what they had to say. Other men then introduced variations, alterations, and, in some cases, outright disavowals of their predecessor's basic assumptions. Through this method film technique has been developed, but its history also points out that technique can never really be an end in itself. To be sure, certain basic principles governing matched cuts, cutaways, and reverse angles are fundamentally sound; but rules are made to do the job, not vice versa. As ideas change, technique must adapt to new needs.

This does not mean that accepted craft practices should be ignored across the board. The good film-maker only breaks the rules for some specific purpose. Nothing can be so devastatingly sophomoric as the startling shot combinations and unusual arrangements, garnished with optical effects, of the beginner, prompted by youthful zeal and anarchism, who ignores the basic rules. In his attempt to say something genuine and honest, he confuses originality of thought with innovations in craft, thus falling into the artsy-craftsy trap (a term with universal connotation among film-makers). Nothing much more complimentary can be said of the old-timer with a finely trained eye whose only aim seems to be a perfect succession of finely matched cuts, proceeding staidly to first-class banality.

Slavish devotion to conventional rules of film technique not only prevents the technique from expanding, but even worse, severs the threads that connect technique to genuine expression. Of the two film-makers described above, one possesses passion and the other know-how. It is from a combination of these two elements that outstanding films are made. A certain amount of know-how comes simply through experience, but the process is speeded up and quality is improved through study. The Museum of Modern Art points out in its *Film Notes* that

the film [D. W. Griffith's *Intolerance*] toured throughout the USSR, where it ran almost continuously for ten years . . . was not merely seen there; it was used as study material for the post revolutionary school of cinematography, and exercised a profound influence on men like Eisenstein and Pudovkin. It is true that Griffith is often disorganized and always instinctive in his methods, where the Russian directors are deliberate and organized: but it was nevertheless in large measure from his example that they derived their characteristic staccato shots, their measured and accelerating rhythms and their skill in joining pictorial images together with a view to the emotional overtones of each, so that two images in conjunction convey more than the sum of their visible content.[1]

As the study of relatively simple techniques led to the development of complicated and varied shot linkages by the Russians, so today the movement toward mature thematic statements in film is not only evoking new filmic structures, but is changing and extending craft practices.

Craft techniques today may be fluid, free, and more given to change than ever before, but it is essentially changes (or violations) born of experience that open the avenues for new and exciting filmic communication. It, therefore, behooves the beginning film-maker to familiarize himself thoroughly with established methods before he attempts to depart from them.

CRAFT TO ART

The basic purpose of arranging shots in an order is to secure depth and meaning through selection, a fundamental process common to all the arts; the nature, kind, and quality of the selection give the measure of the artist. As simple as this idea may sound, it challenges the film-maker constantly and quite often eludes him. The shots not only vary in length, perspectives, points of view, values, mood, closeness, or distance, but also, when placed in the context of the films, they form varied patterns of movement in continuity. Dependent upon their arrangement, such patterns emerge: mood, feelings, continuity, ideas, and artistry are expressed. Thus there exist limitless degrees of expression: pedestrian or artistic, banal or revealing, moving or boring.

A brief study of the rapid strides made in motion picture

[1] The Museum of Modern Art, "Part I: The Silent Film," *Film Notes* (New York: The Museum of Modern Art, 1949), XVI, 17.

craft, from its beginnings around 1895, through the silents of the 1920's and the renascence with sound in the 1930's, up to the present, points up not only the intricacies of the medium, but the expansion of both theory and procedure at such a rapid rate that experimental efforts have become accepted standards almost overnight. The expansion has been, however, more or less orderly and logical, almost in a step-by-step progression. Each step has involved the film-maker deeper in content, so that highly individualized and personal, as well as universal, themes have been conveyed to audiences.

The first step—and this with a loose regard for historical accuracy—was to reveal to the audience what was happening, where, and to whom; and the shots were arranged to make this clear. A story can occur in the span of the hour or two that it takes the viewer to see the film, or it can encompass a lifetime or centuries. Because shots are only pieces that create the illusion of a whole, they have to be arranged so that the who, what, when, where, how, and why of the story are clearly projected. No matter how well a piece of action may be staged, or how simple it may be to follow as one watches it being enacted, the central action may easily be lost if the various shots are taken without some kind of thought organization behind them; or, once they are photographed, if they are arranged arbitrarily.

When a viewer watches action taking place on the screen, he immediately adjusts himself to the basic scene, its given area, and its relationship even to the implied world off the screen. In his mind he notes what is at the left of the picture, at the right, in the foreground, and in the background. He judges distances and sees vast or limited spaces. When he watches a subsequent shot flash across the screen, he never for a moment loses his interpretation of the initial view presented to him. No matter how close up or far away a subsequent shot may be, therefore, he nevertheless relates it to the one that came before it. Should one of these later shots violate the initial interpretation, not only will the viewer be disturbed, but he will also not be able to follow the action. A pile-up of such instances would finally destroy any relationship between the film and the viewer.

To avoid this and to secure continuity, a number of ways to handle the shots were developed and have become a basic part of the craft. Some of the terms used to identify such arrangements are: master shots, matched cuts, insert shots, cutaways, reverse angles, continuity cuts, and screen direction.[2] A series of established rules and procedures exists for using these arrangements to maintain direct physical continuity.

The second step was to develop a way to establish interest, emphasis, excitement, and suspense while physical continuity was maintained. Obviously, to show everything that is happening at a given time would be dull and monotonous. Selection must be exercised, and only those shots included that propel the story forward without losing the continuity. At the same time, shots must be selected that stress the most important aspects of the scene being enacted. Although a long shot might quite naturally be followed by a medium shot, and this in turn by a close-up, a direct cut from the long shot to the close-up might still make the continuity clear, while adding more emphasis to some needed value of that scene. In addition, the film-maker's decision as to which part of the scene will be a long shot and which part a close-up adds to the complexity. On these decisions often hangs the difference between craft and art.

Adding to the complexity of shot arrangement is cross-cutting; the expansion of this idea to take in scenes occurring in different locales set in counterpoint—the "meanwhile-back-at-the-ranch" set-up so popular in the Western—is referred to as parallel editing. The villain is seen carrying out a nefarious act followed by the hero in hot pursuit: pieces of both actions are set against each other, thus introducing suspense and excitement unknown to the older storytelling forms.

---

[2] Excellent diagrams and descriptions of these basic film-joining procedures may be found in special texts as listed in the Annotated Selected Bibliography.

Step three deals with the handling of time. A film contains both actual time and expanded or diminished time. When any given number of shots, arranged in matched continuity, describe action within one setting, the time is actual. A medium shot of a man crossing a room and sitting in a chair, followed by a medium close shot of him sitting, and then a close-up of his face re-create real time in terms of the action shown. To show still another man in another room watching a TV set, and to intercut shots of him with those of the first man would indicate diminished time, because both units in this type of arrangement suggest simultaneous occurrence. To go back to the first man and intercut a series of shots of feet mounting stairs would indicate expanded time, because although the simultaneity of occurrence exists, the nature of the content may be given greater suspense value either by holding the shots longer, repeating them more often, or combining both. Through this method time is actually expanded.

The expansion or contraction of space is equally affected by the same construction methods. In the last example, the second man might be climbing a single staircase of ten steps. Through the intercutting and repetition, those ten steps can be made to appear twenty. Space expansion and contraction are not limited to intercutting, but can be accomplished in a series of shots arranged in straight physical continuity. For example, a subject climbing a set of stairs can be seen through close-ups of feet, face, or hands on the balustrade, so that the stairs appear actually longer than they are. Reversing the procedure by bringing together a shot of the subject at the bottom of the stairs and another of him arriving at the top would bring about a contraction of the actual space.

Obviously, therefore, although shots are arranged by basic rules to communicate action, the knowledgeable film-maker accepts them as starting points, rather than as limitations. In this way, craft elements are controlled completely through the film-maker's approach to his content and his sense of visualization. Thus he determines when and how to alter the basic rules, in order to realize the content fully through a projection of action that is clear to the viewer, and at the same time conveys powerful and compelling insights.

Step four leads to the full exploitation of craft in terms of filmic structures, based not on plays, novels, or short stories, but on the film's own peculiar resources. Only recently have film-makers from all over the world begun to break away from traditional methods. Fresh points of view and personalized outlooks have introduced story structures that have affected the basic craft as never before.

The Russian import, *A Summer to Remember* (1961), for example, deals with an extremely simple story of the relationship between a small boy and his stepfather. It repeatedly demonstrates by economical shot arrangements that continuity is not secured through the boy's actual movements, but through his attitude and mood. The entire film utilizes the technique of continuity through feeling and mood with a minimum of physical shot continuity; it shows that many old rules are ideas of the past.

Traditional craft elements are also ignored in the extremely complicated structure of Akira Kurosawa's *Rashomon* (1950). This Japanese film allows for a flow of shots that blend scenes occurring in three different locales (forest, police station and temple) and at different times (the past, immediate past, and present) without confusion or effort, and with the effect of weighing the relativity of truth. Here too, the dynamic development of shots comes through idea, rather than through physical continuity.

This is not to imply that breaking rules necessarily leads to success. It is not anarchy that is desirable, but a strong frame of reference, a well-developed filmic sense, and a firm grip on the who, what, where, when, and how of a scene. The new techniques do not spring forth without a past, but grow out of the film's history and reach up to today's needs: not stories that provide the barebones of action, but stories that illuminate, each in its own way, a world that demands more of man because he wants more.

Continuity refers to the smooth progression of one shot into the next, or one scene into the next, creating for the viewer the feeling that he is witnessing a whole action, rather than a series of interrupted actions cleverly dovetailed. Common practice refers to such assemblages as pictorial or mechanical continuity. Pictorial physical continuity would be a more accurate term, because the connection of shots is made through physical movement by the subject being photographed; through physically moving the camera closer to the subject or farther away from him (it); and through a combination of these, in which both the subject and the camera move. As explained earlier, such continuity sets up the frame of reference through which the viewer is reached.

An integral part of planning such continuity is "blocking," a theatrical term that refers to the movement given by the director to the actors as they sit, rise, walk, and move about a setting, acting and reacting to one another. Blocking is the stage director's means of interpreting the values of his play physically. The screen director's task is far more complex, for not only must he block the actors' movements, but must also visualize how he is to set up the camera and what shots he is to take. Often, ground plans of the setting, indicating the actors' positions and the pattern of their movements, help to contain the scene for planning purposes.

In the simple plan noted in Diagram No. 1, the husband (h) is seated at his desk, working (position A). He rises and crosses to the door where he meets his wife (w), who is carrying a tray

Diagram No. 1

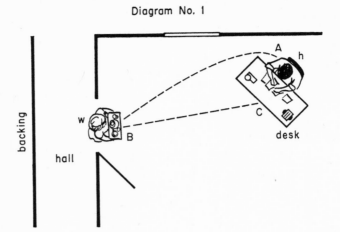

of food (position B). He takes the tray from her and crosses to front of desk (position C), placing the tray on it. His wife has crossed with him, and as she reaches the desk she faces her husband, who by this time has turned to her.

The question is what series of shots is to be taken to depict this action. The scene might open with a medium close shot of the husband working. He reacts to a noise at the door and begins to rise. The camera moves back for a second shot of the husband in full figure, as he rises and crosses to the door. In order to see the husband assist his wife with the tray, the camera moves closer to the couple as the tray changes hands. Within this same shot, the husband moves out of frame, his wife directly behind him. For the next shot, the camera reverses its angle and photographs the couple as they arrive at the desk. Finally, the camera would move in for a medium shot of the two as they faced each other. In the outline this would be as follows:

1. Medium close-up of husband working at desk and reacting to noise at door.

2. Medium shot of husband rising and crossing to door. Camera PANS him as he crosses.

3. Medium close-up two-shot, husband and wife, in which husband takes tray and crosses out of frame. Wife follows him.

4. Medium shot of husband and wife crossing to desk.

5. Medium close-up of husband and wife standing at desk facing each other.

The ground plan (see Diagram No. 2) is of assistance in planning such shots, as not only the action can be indicated, but the camera positions as well.

Diagram No. 2

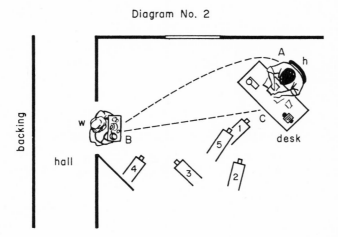

Each camera position bears a number that corresponds to the particular shot outlined. The ground plan helps to visualize each shot as it would look on the screen.

When diagramed further into a rectangular drawing measuring 3 × 4 inches—the proper aspect ratio of the standard motion picture screen—this picture of each shot is called a storyboard (see Diagram No. 3).

The storyboard is essential, because not only does it provide a basis for planning physical continuity, but also enables the film-maker to get his first rough visualization of the scenes and check out their effectiveness. The storyboard is to the film-maker what the outline is to the writer and the rough sketch is to the artist.

In the scene containing the five shots just outlined, the camera is used primarily to record the action. It bears repeating that although recording action is a valid function of the camera and

Diagram No. 3

shot 1 shot 2 shot 3

shot 4 shot 5

is essential to informing the viewer about what is happening, it is still only a preliminary step. Were the camera used for nothing else, the film would be reduced to a moving photograph of a stage play. Hence, by innumerable craft devices, physical continuity is blended with story values explored in depth. Yet, on the level of physical continuity alone, there are multiple choices to be made in the selection of shots dealing with motivation and story elements.

In the scene just outlined, for example, little if any story background was given and specific assumptions were arbitrarily accepted. The design of the shots would indicate that the husband is at home working in his den; the wife is concerned for her husband and brings him a tray of food. The husband is thoughtful of his wife, so he gets up to help her with the tray; she is interested in his work and follows him to the desk, possibly to discuss his progress. So, with no real change in meaning, it would be possible to arrange the shots as indicated in Diagram No. 4, with the storyboard appearing as in Diagram No. 5.

Although the action in this unit is identical to that of Diagram No. 1, the shots, as seen in this outline, are different.

Diagram No. 4

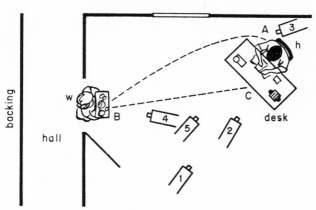

1. Medium long shot of husband working at desk.

2. Medium close-up of husband as he reacts to noise at the door. Turns and rises.

3. Medium long shot from behind husband as he crosses to wife, who is seen at the door at far side of room.

4. Medium two-shot of husband and wife as husband takes tray and crosses, leaving frame right.

Diagram No. 5

5. Medium close-up, husband and wife at desk, as he puts tray on desk and turns to wife.

This second series of shots is presented to point out that many combinations of shots are workable. But physical continuity, though it projects action, is at best pedestrian if the sole purpose of the camera is to record the action. In such cases one series of shots is as workable as another, and the arrangements can be based on mechanical principles. However, where the angles, distances, and order of the shots are dictated by the content of the scene, and are meant to convey more than the simple physical action, arbitrary principles must give way to the artistic choice of the film-maker.

On a basic level, physical continuity contains the elements of motivation and emphasis. The first shot in Diagram No. 3 is a medium close-up of the man, followed by a medium long shot as he rises and crosses to his wife. This first shot, because of its proximity to the husband, places the emphasis on him and his work, while the fuller surroundings are overlooked. Compare this with the opening shot in Diagram No. 5, where the shot takes in a good part of the room as well as the man. He and his work are thus de-emphasized, comparatively speaking, in that the man is shown more in relation to his environment than to his work. The second shot in Diagram No. 5 builds interest and increases the intensity of the scene, whereas in Diagram No. 3 the reverse is true. It should be noted, however, that the second shot in Diagram No. 3 is motivated by the man's movement. The camera pulls back so that he can be seen rising and beginning his cross. In Diagram No. 5, the cross is covered by the third shot, which has the husband rising in the foreground with the wife seen in the background.

Neither of the examples is necessarily better than the other. They merely illustrate that values in terms of emphasis exist, and that in such terms both what is included in the frame and what is excluded are important. Differences in perspective also change the emphasis. Therefore, although physical movement itself is a valid reason for introducing a new shot, other values are also served.

To sum up, physical continuity should be developed along three lines: 1) each shot should picture the action; 2) each shot should emphasize the important actions; 3) a thorough exploration of the content should be made, to determine the one-and-only combination of shots that will carry the story forward most effectively.

The planned progression as outlined in the diagrams is not necessarily a fixed procedure used by the film-maker. Concerned mainly with the flow of images as they appear on the screen, he needs tangible anchor points to shape up his thinking, and may devise variations of the outlined diagrams to suit himself and his needs. Slavish devotion to the diagram can easily lead to theatrical-type staging that would greatly limit the free, flowing quality so basic to the film. Experience takes the film-maker's thinking directly to the screen; the rest are the ABC's of getting there. Shot arrangements cannot surmount the quality of the idea that motivated them; a shot is a result, not a cause.

THE MASTER SCENE

The master scene—one long basic shot used as a kind of framework within which to arrange continuity groupings of other shots —was a method familiar to early film-makers. It works like this: A given scene is blocked out in a specific area. One master shot is made of all the action taking place and called the master scene. Then the particular close-up and medium close-up shots as previously planned are taken separately and cut into the scene as inserts.

This technique did not become widespread until television began making wholesale demands on the film industry. Half-hour and hour dramas had to be turned out on film at an unheard-of pace. Where Hollywood film-makers previously took many weeks or months to shoot a film, television films had to be ready on a week-to-week basis. The adoption of television techniques in some cases, the entrance of television personnel into the film field, and the pressure that television itself brought led to the production of these dramas on shooting schedules as short as three days. Further refinements and added experience cut the schedules down even more. Competition added further impetus to this scramble for time, and, ultimately, films of a half-hour or an hour in length were often made in one day or a day and a half.

The master scene method produced the spectacular quantity, if nothing else, of films; and today it seems as if the master scene method is a credo. The method is ingenious: For example, the camera taking the master scene has an accompanying sound recorder synchronized with it to register the spoken dialogue. Additional cameras located strategically for the insert shots are also in synchronization. All of the shooting is done simultaneously, the main scene as well as the pieces. Editing then is primarily mechanical—merely a matter of cutting the inserts into the master scene as planned.

The master scene is possible even without the advantage of multiple cameras. The action is merely repeated in units for the insert shots. This takes extra time, of course, and puts the actors through the action several times; separate sound takes are made for each insert of dialogue. In such cases, editing is still a routine matter of cutting in the preplanned inserts, but with the additional chore of cutting in the sound too.

Variations on the basic method depend to a large extent on circumstances, special problems, or requirements of the scene. Having to photograph a large church choir, for example, a film-maker might pre-record the voices under extremely favorable conditions, then photograph the choir in a master scene at the actual location, with additional cameras shooting the inserts. To ensure synchronization, the pre-recorded track is played back, amplified for all to hear, and the choir sings along with the recording they previously made. Variations of this kind are not only necessary in cases of impossible sound conditions, but also prove to be the simplest and best way to get the scene.

The purpose here is not to explore the technical intricacies, but to evaluate the contribution of the master scene when used as a basis for production. True, it saves considerable time and cost, but artistically it has singular weaknesses. First, for the master scene to be functional, the staging must be within a given framework and according to a prescribed routine. No matter how cleverly a director may stage his scene, the camera primarily records the action, rather than assists in interpreting it. Once the arrangement veers away from the standard series of medium long shots, medium shots, and close-ups, the master scene technique is useless. The master scene technique fixes the film as a kind of play contained within a number of basic action pictures threaded together by transitional shots—which it is not.

Second, to make use of the master scene, such detailed and thorough technical preplanning must be done that the editing must perforce follow suit. All fluidity is lost, and creative editing is reduced to an almost mechanical process.

Third, the very idea of a master scene is in a way a myth. No such scene ever exists on the screen as a unit. When put together with the various inserts, it is actually just different individual pieces. These pieces, supposed to convey the full impression of the scene and to provide a lucid physical continuity, lack the selectivity available to the film-maker who has approached his shots, not with physical continuity alone in mind, but with the camera eye as an integral part of the developing drama. This also points up the tendency of the master scene toward redundancy. It can easily lead to an extremely literal presentation of the action. Although a clever editor would spot ways and means of tightening and intensifying the sequences, he must still adhere to the master scene with all of its limitations.

A fourth point is that the use of the master scene, truly a

television technique, forces the director to lean toward theatrical staging methods—witness some of the good live dramatic presentations on television—but the art here is primarily that of theater, not of cinema. Theater and television playwrights work their drama through the dialogue and use their shots to portray the story action. Film-makers use their shots to tell the full story, with dialogue as an enrichment and refinement. The difference is far greater than it appears on the surface.

Knowledgeable film-makers base their work on the over-all concept of each scene, and then plan individual shots that will serve to explore, develop, and project that concept. Shots so selected are rich in value and, when correctly handled, eliminate the need for a master scene. In fact, the frame of reference that the master scene is intended to achieve is better done in this way, because it is not confined to purely physical boundaries. References are constantly set up on the basis of emotional and intellectual values, in addition to the physical. The argument that the master scene technique is valuable because of the time and money it saves does not apply when film-making is viewed as an art. Time and money can be saved, but by efficient planning, rather than at the much greater cost of throttling limitations on the artist.

MATCHED SHOTS

Matched shots are any given number of shots linked together in a series to picture one continuous movement. In the scene discussed earlier of the man crossing to his wife with the tray, etc., each shot in that arrangement would have to match the action of the next one, so that there would be a smooth, continuous flow of the action. Therefore, long shots, medium shots, and close-ups, arranged in a variety of combinations to project continuity of movement without interruption by cutting away from that prescribed action, are termed matched shots. When, for example, a master scene has had inserts cut into it in which parts of one shot are revealed in the successive one, the resultant series are matched shots (or cuts). Not just in master scenes, but in any arrangement matched cuts provide a smooth, continuous physical progression with definite points of separation which, nevertheless, the viewer is generally unaware of.

Rules governing the arrangement of such shots deal either with methods for matching the shots, or with justifying the shots to be matched so that they will be acceptable on screen. Although these rules are fairly clear and do work, they should be examined for their relative merits.

The master scene technique will provide matched shots, but so will having the actor "freeze" at the conclusion of one shot until the camera is reset for the second shots at which time he moves on with his action. The obvious disadvantage of this method is that there is no telling how long it will take for camera setups. The actor may also lose all spontaneity through continual "freezes" and restarts.

Another possibility is to have the actor repeat his action, so that the beginning of one shot overlaps the tail of the preceding one. The amount of footage to be shot in duplication depends on the film-maker's estimation of his editing needs. In this instance, the actor has the advantage of repeating enough of each section to maintain his sense of acting continuity. Even more important, the overlap allows for a much broader choice in editing, since there are a number of places that can be selected for the cut. Still another method is to use more than one camera. Here, overlap of scenes is certain, and the actor has the advantage of greater acting continuity.

In the light of all this, it would appear that the master scene is the easiest, but it should be remembered that truly creative cinematic techniques do not result from simple theatrical stag-

89

ing methods; though matched shots are an integral part of film-making, their values are far from terminal so far as whole scenes are concerned.

For justifying shots to be matched, it has been pointed out that the camera axis should vary from shot to shot. The camera axis is an imaginary line directly from the lens of the camera to the subject. Successive shots should not be taken directly along this line, but rather to the right or left of it. The rationale is that shots on the same line tend to become redundant, whereas variation from the line shows the subject each time from a new point of view. Hence interest is increased and motivation for the change is supplied. Such justification is questionable, however, because its essence is mechanical and artificial. For want of anything else such variation may provide intensification, but a good film-maker would not be so indifferent to his subject matter that he would have to take successive shots for purely arbitrary reasons. Slavish devotion to such practices may indicate a polished craft, but will certainly fail to produce a work of art. The rule should be understood, but not applied purely for its own sake.

Still another rule is that successive shots have to be sufficiently different from one another so that the change is acceptable (that is, so that it looks as if it had been done on purpose and not by accident). A cut from one medium shot to another, for example, lacks visual motivation, has a disturbing effect on the viewer, and sets up a "jump" cut—one that does not match and cannot be joined.

Just because successive shots of marked contrast can go together is not sufficient reason for planning and taking the shots that way. Once again, although the rule is true, it tends to instill the idea that shot progression must be long shot, medium shot, close-up, or the reverse. Such progression, when based on the artificial motivation of a rule, leads to monotony and redundancy. The knowledgeable film-maker works with an open mind and an eye alert to story values. Rather than planning his shots on the basis of acceptability or time for a change, he considers the total effect and the amount of insight the shot will project to his viewer.

An important aspect of matched shots is that the particular shots selected—long, medium, close—have highly specialized contributions to make in terms of rhythm. A first requisite is that the rate of the subject's advancement (or the camera's, should the subject be static) at the joining point of two shots should be the same, or else the shots really will not match. Rhythm is induced by the variation of beats in terms of the length of the shots, and the kind of stress given to the joining points. For example, a medium shot flowing smoothly into a close-up of a

Diagram No. 1

soft-beat joining

given subject in a set area, with no subject change through movement, has a soft stress at the cut (see Diagram No. 1). Conversely, a more radical change between the camera angles of the matching shots tends to stress the join more strongly and introduces a more pronounced beat (see Diagram No. 2).

Diagram No. 2

hard-beat joining

These beats might be likened to those of a drummer using brushes (soft) or sticks (hard). Just as the drummer can soften or harden the beats by using his brushes or sticks either force-fully or lightly, the film-maker can control the rhythmic effect of his matched cuts by the severity of the change in camera angle.

Jump cuts—those that do not match at all—are said to be completely disturbing and unacceptable because they disrupt flow of movement and introduce a beat where none is required, or where none can be endured. Yet dissonance can often prove more important than harmony. Jump cuts, when motivated by genuine story values, can add immeasurably. In Tony Richard-son's *Tom Jones* (1963), for example, comic effects are created through just such liberties; and in Jean-Luc Godard's *My Life to Live* (1962) simple scenes project an underlying agitation through disrupted bits of physical action.

Once the film-maker settles in a general way on the cuts he plans, he can sense their rhythmic characteristics by viewing them on the screen. Then he decides more definitively on the par-ticular shots needed with the respective rhythmic qualities that complement or counterpoint the scene's content. Such planning, of course, must grow out of material rich with meaning, highly particular in quality, and not given to generalization.

The movement of the camera, the kind of shot it is taking, and the movement of the subject are all related to the beats. Taking into consideration all these factors, it is possible to vary the beats or stresses in such a complex yet rhythmical way that their arrangement will attract the viewer so that he finds it impossible to ignore the screen, very much as a listener cannot resist the rhythm of a good musical score. Diagrams nos. 1–4 illustrate a few simple rhythmic shot associations and assume that the action involved would be appropriate.

Matched shots incorporating a moving camera (that is, pan shots) could set up rhythms as part of units (see diagrams nos. 3 and 4).

92

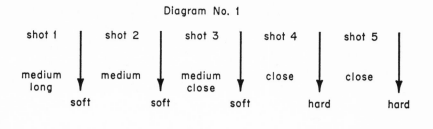

Diagram No. 1

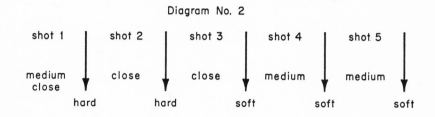

Diagram No. 2

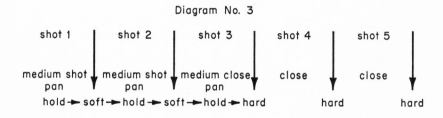

Diagram No. 3

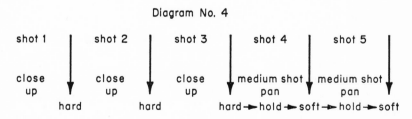

Diagram No. 4

Notice how the stress structure suggests an over-all rhythm and how, with small effort, scenes can be visualized that would work with or against the variety of stresses—how musical in nature the structures are. By the same token, the film-maker intuitively reacts to rhythmic arrangements as he views his film on the screen during the editing process. The question of rhythm enters all aspects of editing and depends on the selection of all the shots. It is mentioned here because too often one is inclined to apply rhythmic principles only to markedly dissimilar shots and to overlook their value in matching. Equally, one is inclined to be aware of rhythm when working with objects, but in the story film to allow the bulk of the film's rhythm to be carried by the acting—representational film-making, so to speak—whereas the film needs not only content organization, but also a rhythmical arrangement that can only be realized in the editing.

In summary, the mechanical principles of matched cuts have to do with changes of camera axis, shots of marked contrast, and mixtures of various types of shots with sufficient difference to suggest motivation; but more vital than these is the natural desire of the film-maker to enlarge on his viewer's vision of life as it is explored through the camera's eye. Bearing these principles in mind, he also considers the hard and soft beats of the individual shots and their cuts, whether they be slow-moving pans, abrupt close-ups, or a series of staccato close-ups. When shots are planned and taken with these points in mind, the film-maker arms himself with material flexible enough to develop into a scene with a wallop.

THE REVERSE ANGLE

A popular method for developing scenes, building interest, and keeping them moving forward is through the reverse angle as when the camera cuts from one character to the other, always with one in the foreground, back to camera, and the other in the background, facing the camera. To pave the way for reverse angles, a fairly standard practice is usually followed. A character is introduced through a few matched cuts; a second character is also shown in a few matched cuts. Most likely the second character is moving through a set, or entering the set, in the direction of the first. The moment both characters are in proximity, a medium shot of both characters is taken as a kind of "pint-sized" master shot. This technique is often used when there is dialogue, and usually shows the speaker's face. Such setups are repeatedly used to get across exposition, character attitudes, or plot elements.

From time to time, as the dialogue progresses, the medium shot of both characters is brought in again, in order to re-establish the physical relationship for the viewer, then a shift is made back to the reverse angles. More commonly, during the medium two-shot, the characters move to another area or change their position (for variety's sake). This may also be followed by a repeat of the reverse angles.

Although reverse angles cut back and forth from opposite points, a matching problem still exists. An extreme, rather than slight, change in camera angle could so reverse the positions of the characters in relation to the master two-shot that the reverse angles would be unacceptable. Where Character A is on the right side of the screen, and the shot is taken over his left shoulder, a severe angle change taken from the far side over his right shoulder would place him on the left side of the screen. The guiding principle in matching reverse angles is not in terms of direct physical continuity but in terms of the positions of the characters on the screen in the "pint-sized" master shot.

The technique of reverse angles has been popular with film-makers, because cross-cuts in which fairly close shots are taken is an expedient staging method. Once characters are in a reverse angle setup, there is tremendous conservation of shots as the camera concentrates first on one and then on the other. But to conserve shots does not appear to be the objective so much as to maneuver the characters into set positions so that they can talk, talk, talk. Reverse angles have been used so often in the manner described that they have become a visual cliché. It is often overlooked that staging and dialogue are not half so important as the action and reaction on which the reverse angles should be based.

The opening scene of Fellini's *La Dolce Vita* (1960) is developed entirely in terms of reverse angles. Shots of the statue of Christ being towed by a helicopter are counterpointed against the sunbathing women on the rooftops of Rome. A reporter and his cameraman in a second helicopter call to the women, attempting to get their phone numbers and make dates. The ensuing dialogue is drowned by the roar of the plane's blades, so that much of what is said is lost, and rightly so. The impact is carried by the reference points—sunbathing belles; men "on the make"; a technological society, as represented by the helicopter, contrasted against the Holy City spires in the background; and the Christ statue, arms outstretched, hovering over all, yet being only a piece of painted stone to be hung on one of those spires.

The film is not only a medium for action, but for reaction as well, and action and reaction are the cause and effect of the reverse angle. Good films resort to this motivation with high flexibility, and from it draw much of their power.

The reverse angle also is useful in conserving shots, as mentioned above, and allows for increased selectivity. As the camera moves from place to place, reversing its point of view, it can concentrate primarily on specific story values, on action and reaction. In this manner much wasted movement and unnecessary action can be eliminated. Pieces that do not specifically help propel the story forward, but which might have been included merely to solve the matching problem in direct continuity, are no longer needed.

A profound grasp of his story enables the film-maker to stage his scene, move his camera, and, with the use of reverse angles, project only those qualities he selects—without disorienting his viewer or having to include a great many matched cuts. This economy also provides a high degree of fluidity. The use of reverse angles thus provides a continuity several notches above that of storytelling on a purely physical basis, by providing a tighter continuity of emotional action and reaction and of thematic development, and at the same time maintaining all the visual relationships for the viewer. Because of the concentration it achieves, this technique steers the audience into understanding and going along with story intensification. The cumulative shots so set up become automatically climactic and provide a penetration into meaning beyond that of any one shot.

THE CUTAWAY

The cutaway, named because of the way it cuts away from the action at one place to action occurring simultaneously at another place, contributes vitally to the free and fluid effect that makes film distinctive. Like the reverse angle, it can be used as part of direct continuity to emphasize and condense the action, or go beyond this to broaden the physical limitations of the scene, at the same time increasing and heightening suspense. Applied on an even larger scale it introduces two scenes at one time, showing the relationship between the two.

This latter use of the cutaway armed the early-day film-makers with new and exciting ways for creating tension and excitement. In film after film, the heroine was trapped by the villain, her honor and virtue at stake, while the hero, mounted on a noble steed, gallantly raced to her rescue. The cutaway and the return to the original scene (the cutback) moved the audience toward the climactic scene with mounting and relentless power, and finally relief as the day was won. In later years, the Seventh Cavalry assumed the role of the hero; the wagon train of settlers, that of the heroine; and the Indians took over as the villain. Still later, the innocent but rich damsel became the heroine, asleep in her boudoir as the mad killer prowled through her home. The heroic young gum-shoe, meanwhile, had to fit the pieces of the puzzle together and realize the killer's whereabouts in the nick of time.

With successive years, refinements and subtleties established the cutaway technique firmly enough to earn it a more dignified name: parallel editing. Today, this technique, too, appears to have undergone the pressures of time and settled down to the stereotype. Actually, the stereotype lies not in the technique, but in the story being told. True, the cutaway intensifies scenes so rapidly and creates suspense so spontaneously, that one is easily inclined to develop the scenes solely in terms of the melodramatic. But this clouds the more meaningful functions of the cutaway.

The cutaway can enable the audience to observe anything from any point of view in any place; but this only begins to touch on its concentrated power. More important, it opens the way for staging whole scenes or counterpointing scenes in multiple arrangements that provide the film with free and fluid staging methods, thus making a clean break from the traditional techniques of the theater.

This idea might best be analyzed by examining the cutaway first in its simpler uses, as in the scene of the man at work in his study with his wife bringing him a tray of food. Diagram No. 1 illustrates the camera position for three shots in a scene, with shot no. 2 being the cutaway.

In outline this would be as follows: (1) Medium close-up of

Diagram No. 1

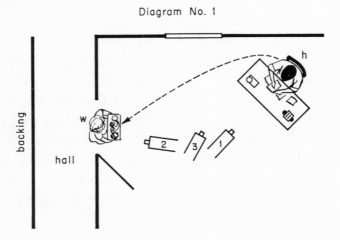

man at work—reacts to sound at door. (2) Medium shot cutaway of woman at door, holding tray of food. (3) Cutback to medium shot of man at desk as he rises and PAN him as he crosses to help wife with tray.

Shot no. 3 can be altered slightly, so that the man can be picked up half-way between the desk and his wife at the door, thus shortening the actual distance and compressing the scene. All this, of course, can be done without altering the flow of physical continuity so far as the viewer is concerned (Arrangement No. 1).

Arrangement No. 1

shot 1   shot 2   shot 3

More likely, the film-maker moves many steps beyond such an arrangement, because shot no. 2 can serve as a pivot for varied storytelling arrangements. Shot no. 2, in the instance described, supports the physical arrangements of the scene and, even though a piece of shot no. 3 is eliminated, provides a connection for all the shots based on content. But examine the different values given to shot no. 1 if in shot no. 2 the wife is seen busily at work in her kitchen (see Arrangement No. 2).

Next replace shot no. 2 with one of a small child bouncing a

Arrangement No. 2

shot 1   shot 2   shot 3

ball on the steps outside the house, and question the effect and the reaction that would seem suitable then for shots nos. 1 and 3 (see Arrangement No. 3).

Arrangement No. 3

shot 1   shot 2   shot 3

Or again, replace shot no. 2 with one of a car pulling up to a curb, the driver hurriedly leaving the car and rushing up to a house (see Arrangement No. 4). Again question the effect and reaction that would then seem suitable for shots nos. 1 and 3.

Arrangement No. 4

shot 1   shot 2   shot 3

Even in these simplified examples it is immediately apparent that although the shots are connected by the direction in which the characters may move (as in Arrangement No. 1), there is a connection that goes beyond the simple action. In Arrangement No. 2, one might assume that the man is going to the kitchen to assist his wife, whereas in Arrangement No. 3 he could be going outside the house to scold the child for bouncing the ball and disturbing him.

In all these cases, the moment the cutaway is presented, the viewer has not only related it to the first shot in which the man was seen working, but also has looked forward to what is going to happen—when the man meets his wife, when he reaches the child with the ball, or when the man and the driver of the car meet. In all, the viewer anticipates news of some kind, and depending on facial expressions, either favorable or unfavorable news. But in all cases the viewer's information and anticipation far exceed the actor's movements. Communication occurs instantly, because the connection between the shots is made through inference in the mind of the viewer, that is, by thought.

The cutaway thus serves in three ways to add complexity and richness to film arrangements. First, although the film re-creates reality through the camera, the cutaway expands or contracts this reality; in so doing it alters the physical relationships, thus emphasizing their connotative relationships and adding emotional depth. Second, the cutaway provides a method for connecting shots through attitudes of character, emotional states, and thematic ideas. For example, examine the subtle use of the cutaway in René Clément's *Forbidden Games* (1952), where the little girl is seen observing her equally little friend being severely spanked for not divulging information. The cutaway holds on the little girl for an inordinately long time, capitalizing on her reaction and thereby projecting an intensity about children's feelings that adults normally overlook. Another example is found in the opening shots of Alain Resnais' *Hiroshima Mon Amour* (1959), in which the embracing lovers in the grip of life are counterpointed with the Hiroshima victims, frozen in death. Although there might be arguments that these shots are not cutaways, they defy standard definitions and can be considered extensions of common cutaway techniques.

Third, the cutaway introduces a freedom of movement in which the camera's only limitation is the film-maker's ability to perceive and to feel. Because the cutaway can take the viewer from point to point, the film becomes truly fluid, not only breaking away from fixed, theatrical staging, but also emphasizing the great wealth in pictorial relationships that probe reality for its meaning.

101

Often the cutaway is referred to as a "protection" shot, meaning that in a scene of direct continuity its use can protect the film-maker from mismatching errors. Some film-makers will go so far as to shoot a series of extra close-ups in a scene, so that they may be inserted into those places where continuity is faulty. In the light of all that has been pointed out, such use of cutaways is false, inartistic, and completely wasteful.

As in all aspects of film, effective use of the cutaway must depend on the film-maker's understanding of and approach to his material. Once he has honestly explored and analyzed his story, the cutaway will help him to project it; but the cutaway follows the idea, not vice versa.

SCREEN DIRECTION

Although the screen can create the illusion of depth, it remains a flat surface on which images are projected. When a series of shots in which the subject moves progressively are to be matched, the film-maker considers these movements primarily in terms of moving right or left, simplifying them from the viewer's point of view. Hence, a subject moving from left to right in one shot is seen moving in the same direction in subsequent shots. If the subject changes his direction, the change is shown. The reason for this is that screen direction is a basic part of physical continuity to which the audience relates in an over-all impression of the "lay of the land" and the subject's relationship to it. When a shot is not in correct relationship to this pattern, the viewer may be so disoriented that he is not able to follow the story.

In the typical Western, as the traditional villain was pursued by the traditional posse, the cross-cut device was completely dependent on proper screen direction for understandability. Awareness of both the relationship between pursuer and pursued in terms of the direction being traveled, and of spatial and temporal differences, was maintained by having the subjects pass readily recognizable landmarks. For instance, the villain would be seen leaving town as the posse is alerted, men running to their "hosses." Next, the villain would be seen on the outskirts of town, going by a low, overhanging tree branch (from right to left). Then the posse is seen, fully mounted and reaching the town's outskirts. Again the villain appears, this time passing a mountainous area. The next shot of the posse reveals them reaching the overhanging tree branch (and still going from right to left). By this time the direction of travel, as well as the distances between the conflicting units, has been firmly implied. In addition, sufficient information has been provided to indicate how long it would take for the posse to catch up, based on the relationship between the shots of the town's outskirts, the branch, and the mountainous area. Once the villain has begun to scramble among the boulders and the shooting has started, screen direction is reinforced by nods of the head, hand gestures, and dialogue such as "Keep him pinned down here, Sheriff, and I'll git 'round him."

Thus, as the movements become more complicated, the viewer is provided with ample reference points and knows at each moment who is facing whom, who is stealing around the boulders, and who is being caught in what trap. Although such scenes today are boring or laughable, or both, similar craft techniques in the so-called "adult" Westerns are still holding the attention of countless viewers on television.

Nevertheless, the principles governing screen direction, with its correlating values of information provided and suspense created, are fundamental. The technique is vital and indestructible, and its worth is directly related to the content of the film-maker's story. In the example given, as well as in more "up-to-date" stories—where, for instance, the villain and posse combination is replaced by the weary, emotionally sick gunslinger who wants to settle down, and a gun-crazy, ignorant kid who wants to shoot him as a villain—the story is dependent on obvious physical continuity. The shots themselves have little value beyond maintaining this progressive action in terms of simple, straightforward melodrama.

Screen direction, however, can go further than this. The artistic use of screen direction not only widens a given scene, breaks out of the boundaries of any prosceniumlike restriction, and shows time and space relationships between moving figures, but can transmit thematic points, character values, or emotional states. In such instances, screen direction is not necessarily concerned only with the movement of the actors, but of the camera and of both actors and camera in relation to the setting and to each other.

Screen direction for thematic impact, for example, is well demonstrated again by Fellini in one of his early scenes in *La Dolce Vita* (1960). Marcello, the reporter, is in a white Cadillac with Maddalena, a bored, blasé, nymphomaniacal heiress. A pick-up prostitute, Adriana, is offered a ride home. Throughout the entire trip, Fellini ignores the conventional methods of connecting the shots through the action, relying on the setting and its value to the story. The lights of Rome are seen in the background, receding in the distance, lessening in intensity with each passing moment. Finally, the camera swings to a reverse angle full shot, as the car is seen pulling up to a drab apartment dwelling stuck up on a barren piece of ground (the drab and barren quality is that of a site still under construction). Once the car occupants alight, the force of the direction continues as Adriana leads them to a flooded basement apartment and into a newly made mess of a room, as if they were descending into a modern Hell and being swallowed up by it. At this point, Marcello turns to Maddalena and asks, "You want to make love here?"

Throughout the entire sequence the sense of continuity is never lost, and significant linkages are achieved through the receding garish lights of Rome, to the gloomy, deserted area of the city, and down into the prostitute's "cave." These shots provide a movement that physically projects thematic content. The usual pattern of actors moving left or right through shots is not the guiding principle.

Screen direction for psychological value is well demonstrated by Akira Kurosawa in *Rashomon* (1950). He more or less adheres to the rules, but expands them considerably through composition, camera movement, and rhythm. As the bandit in the forest discovers the wealthy lord and his lady, the camera begins an encircling movement to follow the bandit's dash through the forest. Compositionally, the camera is placed to shoot through the foliage and is moved along with the bandit, so that the feeling of rushing is increased considerably. As the camera trucks along at breakneck speed, it supports and projects the inner excitement of the bandit. The intercutting of still shots with moving shots introduces a directorial pattern that explains both the cunning and the wild abandon of the bandit. Screen direction in this case delineates character.

Still another use of screen direction is demonstrated by Sergei Eisenstein in *Potemkin* (1925). The townspeople come to the wharf to pay tribute to a sailor who was killed by his officers. Various shots show crowds of people on the streets, bridges, and steps—all taken at various angles, all set up in deliberate patterns. The crisscrossed lines formed by the moving people in each shot create a cumulative pattern that almost reaches a nonobjective state. The viewer becomes anxious and anticipates trouble to come. A feeling of strength is transmitted by the straight, moving lines formed by the people; tension is secured by presenting these lines in a crisscross pattern, and further heightened by the disjointed quality introduced by each successive shot. Screen direction in this case is deliberately disorganized, with a framework of carefully organized composition. The actors are used primarily to create these patterns; they have no personal identity except as "the people."

A minor use of this technique is made by René Clément in

the opening shots of *Forbidden Games* (1952). People are seen on a bridge hurriedly leaving Paris, some in autos, some in horse-drawn carts, others on foot. Overhead, German bombers are attacking. One shot is taken from the right side of the bridge, showing the pedestrians moving from left to right. A follow-up shot is from the left side, and although the pedestrians are still moving in the same direction, on the screen they are moving from right to left. This kind of dynamic opposition helps support the feeling of the chaos and confusion of the helpless Parisians fleeing the Nazi bombs, and is an intentional and justified violation of the rule. Movement that has taken full advantage of thoroughly planned screen direction will bare to the viewer character attitudes, states of mind, or concepts; or will subject him to compositional designs and flowing arrangements that convey the story's emotional and psychological qualities. Similarly, a man's eyes, watching a skyrocket, are led up into the sky to see a glorious burst of stars in multicolors, patterns within patterns revealed through multiple explosions.

To achieve these ends, basic rules must not be ignored or flouted—connecting shots in terms of the actors' movements must still mind their lefts and rights—but the psychological, rhythmical, and other values of movement must be taken into account, and those values that are important then brought out by the imaginative use of screen direction.

THE ESTABLISHING SHOT

The term "establishing shot" is a hybrid, in that it grows out of the master scene principle, but its function is only partially related to that of the master shot. It is used by some film-makers, ignored completely by others, and indiscriminately tossed around by many. Essentially, the establishing shot is only the first full long shot, the shot that establishes the environment of what would be the master scene. Where the master scene has in it all of the action that is to be taking place in a scene, with subsequent medium, medium close, and close-up shots cut into it, the establishing shot is only the first full long shot of what would be the master scene. The term is not applied, however, when the first long shot is part of an actual master scene. Theoretically, use of the establishing shot instead of a whole master scene gives a somewhat freer approach to staging and shot continuity; subsequent shots do not have to follow as tight a prestaged pattern as in the master. The point is moot, however.

The establishing shot, like the master scene, is a definite part of shots in physical continuity. It is meant to establish mood, atmosphere, time, place, and characters. The rationale is that once these elements have been introduced the film-maker follows with shots that project the action. Since it is assumed that the viewer's orientation might weaken after a number of medium close and close-up shots, the re-establishing shot is introduced. This system can go on and on, and what actually occurs is that every long shot serves to re-establish the scene. The technique, being a variation of the master scene, has just as many weaknesses. Such elements as mood, atmosphere, time, and place are necessary story values; and as a result it is thought necessary to indicate them separately. But this separate or establishing shot is wasted, like the long-winded introduction with which a poor storyteller prepares his audience for the real story to come.

The artistic film-maker becomes as conscious of the value of each shot as the effective playwright is of words. Shots, like words, have to be selected and carefully brought together for specific meaning, so arranged that layers of information are in a subordinated order. An effective presentation introduces the core of the story and immediately sets out to explore it. The background elements have to be carried as well. This does not mean that matters of time, place, etc., take care of themselves.

They are subordinate values used by the film-maker to enrich the storytelling shots, rather than subjects of equal emphasis in an expository shot.

In the area of playwriting, for example, Henrik Ibsen proved the master of what might be called the concentrated technique. In his plays, all his scenes, including opening ones, deal primarily with conflict. Expository material is worked in as part of the natural development of this conflict. It is difficult, if not impossible, to find a purely expository scene in an Ibsen play. The viewer's attention is secured and immediately led into problems and difficulties of character, while he unconsciously absorbs the background information. One can take an Ibsen opening scene and examine it for emotional values as well as expository ones. In *The Master Builder*, written in 1892, the opening scene is set in a draughtsman's office, which is a workroom in the house of Halvard Solness.

Knut Brovik: (Rises suddenly, as if in distress, from the table, breathes heavily and laboriously as he comes forward into the doorway) No, I can't bear it much longer!

Kaia: (Going up to him) You are feeling ill this evening, are you not, uncle?

Brovik: Oh, I seem to get worse every day.

Ragnar: (Has risen and advances) You ought to go home, father. Try to get a little sleep.

Brovik: (Impatiently) Go to bed, I suppose? Would you have me stifled outright?

Kaia: Then take a little walk.

Ragnar: Yes, do. I will come with you.

Brovik: I will not go till he comes! I am determined to have it out this evening with (in a tone of suppressed bitterness) —with him—with the chief.

Kaia: (Anxiously) Oh, no, uncle, do wait awhile before doing that.

Ragnar: Yes, better wait, father!

Brovik: (Draws his breath laboriously) Ha-ha! I haven't much time for waiting.

Kaia: (Listening) Hush! I hear him on the stairs.

108

One's appetite is whetted in short order. The scene has tension and builds anticipation, yet son, uncle, and niece relationships have been quickly established. The setting, which in the text is fully described, provides the mood, time, place, all as secondary values. Ibsen, of course, uses dialogue plus visual setting to open his play. This is mentioned, not to argue over visual versus verbal elements, but to point out how much Ibsen establishes in twelve short speeches while at the same time pushing along the conflict. How drawn out and weakened the scene would be if these two aims had been developed one at a time!

The same weakness is apparent in the establishing shot that conveys background information only, or attempts to prepare the viewer for the story by establishing the scene and the relationship of the people in it. Once this premise of moving directly to shots with layers of meaning has been accepted, it can be appreciated that every shot can be an "establishing" shot, and that the film-maker's concern should always be how much of what he is establishing.

Another weakness of the master scene—that points of reference have to be introduced for the viewer in physical terms—is also true of the establishing shot. Using the establishing shot to fix time and space relationships is as wasteful as using it solely for exposition. All three of these points—background information, time and space relationships, exposition—can be incorporated subtly into a shot that basically carries more weight.

Examine a scene containing the following shots:

1. LS car on highway
2. MS driver as he hears motor sputter
3. MLS car slowing down
4. CU tail pipe—puffing gusts of smoke
5. MS car coming to a halt
6. MCU of motor hood with smoke seeping out
7. MS driver coming to hood and lifting it
8. CU smoke pouring from engine

In this series, shot no. 1 might be referred to as the establishing shot, while nos. 3 and 5, still part of the continuity, maintain and re-establish the scene. But what would happen to the scene if it were altered as follows?

1. CU tail pipe of car puffing gusts of smoke
2. MS driver as he hears motor sputter
3. CU hood with smoke seeping out
4. MS as car halts, driver comes to hood and lifts it
5. CU smoke pouring from engine

In dropping two shots and combining two others, does the second scene tell the viewer as much as the first? It does, while at the same time providing a build-up of tension and concentration. This example points out that long shots are not absolutely essential, and that often the same quality, or better, can be achieved through close-ups and medium close-ups. This does not deny the value of the long shot itself, but of its use as an establishing shot in the hackneyed sense. If a film-maker wishes to use the technique of the establishing shot, that is his prerogative, but he should ask himself what it is that he is establishing and whether it is really telling his story.

The opening shots of Serge Bourguignon's *Sundays and Cybele* (1962) show a flier on a bombing run in a series of angular and tight close-ups. As the plane screams through these shots the face of a young girl in the path of the attack comes clearly into view. This establishes the motivation for the entire story that follows, and the psychological effect of this experience on the flyer. Further, the viewer, because of the nature of the shots, experiences the horror and terror of the scene. All other story values are subordinated to this one.

In Roman Polansky's *Knife in the Water* (1963), a man and his wife are seen in a car, medium close from in front, while the reflections of trees are caught by the windshield as the car barrels along the road. This establishes as a prime value the boredom and lack of rapport between the two: a somewhat pompous male, and an attractive woman who puts up with the situation for want of anything else.

In Elia Kazan's *America, America* (1964), seemingly traditional long shots establish a beautiful mountainous countryside with fertile valleys; in short order the menace of the Turk is injected into it, thus setting up the thematic point around which the story develops.

THE USE OF OPTICALS

The term "opticals" refers to various special effects achieved primarily through an optical printing machine and used between shots in place of cuts. These transitional effects are fade-ins, fade-outs, dissolves, wipe-offs, push-offs, flips, turns, dissolves that zoom or diffuse, and spins and wipes, to name only a few (Note: see definitions in the Glossary). Of the wipes there are innumerable patterns: up and down, diagonal, across, as well as patterns that swing, split, expand, and contract. The development of the optical printer has provided the film-maker with the possibility of creating just about any kind of transitional effect that he is able to imagine.

Of the hundreds of types of effects available, the most frequently used are the fades and dissolves. The remaining effects, which often run rampant in television film commercials, are used sparingly by knowledgeable film-makers. This might best be explained by likening them to punctuation. Where fades might generally be equated with periods and dissolves with commas or semicolons, the wipes, flips, and other effects might be more closely related to dashes and exclamation marks.

Just as the experienced writer is highly selective, and never employs dashes or exclamation marks as a substitute for the right words, so the seasoned film-maker phrases his shots with equal care and resorts to the sensational effects only when they make a basic contribution to the story—which is extremely rare. Wipes, flips, and spins are somewhat self-conscious and often call attention to themselves. Their use might impress the viewer, but in so doing they dissipate his interest in the true value of the subject matter.

The dissolve, where one shot slowly blends through another, and the fade, where a shot goes to black or from black to picture, although frequently used, also cannot be inserted into a film without discretion. Dissolving shots in television is extremely easy and great fun. Buttons are pushed to activate shots, and a lever is pulled or pushed to effect the dissolve. Because of its simplicity, the dissolve was repeated again and again in television's early days, and is still often overdone. But such haphazard, impulsive transitions contribute nothing to the total unit. Such simplicity attests to the marvels of science, but hardly to good video presentation.

The uses of effects have to be considered in terms of the following purposes: 1) as a guide to the viewer to help him follow story continuity; 2) to bridge gaps in physical continuity so that the story can be both tightened and propelled forward; 3) to assist the viewer to react emotionally to the structural pattern of the story; and 4) to fortify and illuminate the rhythm of the film.

These considerations at best, however, are vague, and if too broadly interpreted serve as an excuse to drag in effects for effects' sake. It does not always follow, for example, that a dissolve from a man entering an apartment building to a shot in which he is at his apartment door, inserting the key in the lock, will necessarily serve as a good bridge. The straight cut should be examined for its value to the story as compared to the slower, ponderous dissolve.

The dissolve frequently separates scenes that differ in time, place, or atmosphere. But when relied on religiously for this purpose, the dissolve tends to set up an extremely formal pattern of picture arrangement, often depriving the film-maker of a natural flow of images, possibly causing the structure to show, or slowing the rhythm when not called for, or both.

Again, it is a question of content. In Satyajit Ray's *The World of Apu* (1958), for instance, the young would-be writer, Apu, in one shot is seen observing factory workers pasting labels on bottles (he needs money and is in search of work), and then in successive shots on a streetcar, crossing railroad tracks, walking around some children at play, and finally in his room; but not one dissolve is used. Although it would have been quite plausible to dissolve between these shots in order to smooth out the abruptness of the cuts, actually the dissolves would have destroyed the continuity of feeling of the young man, which is used to connect the shots; the straight cuts emphasize this emotional continuity. The young man is desolate, without money, with only a room to go to where the rent is due. In addition to the consistency of mood maintained through the shots, further connection is made through the backgrounds: the preoccupied attitude of Apu as the conductor's hand comes into the frame asking for the fare, the endless railroad tracks going off into nothing but emptiness, and, finally, the walk through the carefree, innocent children at play, which adds an ironic note.

At the time of viewing, one is not conscious of these details, but reacts emotionally. Dissolves in such a series of shots would lessen the impact because they would blur the cumulative effect of the shots, each of which enriches the meaning of Apu's mood, not only in its own right, but by the relationship to the shots before and after it.

Still another point to be raised deals with rhythm, an extremely subtle value in film. It is often pointed out that the key to good film-making lies in editing. One of the big reasons for this is that through editing the film is given rhythm, which in turn supplies the film with definition. A natural rhythmic stress results from the direct cut. The dissolve gives a soft stress. Used indiscreetly, it can raise havoc with the material. To dissolve from a person playing a piano, for example, to a shot of his hands fingering the keys is not only confusing, but destructive. The dissolve would prolong the stress, provide an unnatural hold, and contradict the content. In a combination like this, each shot should be held long enough for the rhythm of the movement to be established, with the cut coming in between the shots for a stress.

The value of dissolves, fast pans (called blur pans or flip pans), and similar effects is well demonstrated in Orson Welles's *Citizen Kane* (1941), in which changes in character relationship are introduced almost instantaneously by selecting high points of scenes made up of only two or three shots and connecting them through an effect. In essence, a single scene is developed by taking the climaxes only of a number of scenes and linking them together through effects. Effects in this instance contribute psychologically to the scene, for agitation and disharmony are created as the man and wife reach the point of no return in their marriage. Yet, even here the film has been criticized for effects that draw attention to themselves. Today there are film-makers who possibly would make similar linkages through straight cuts.

All in all, no generalization can be made about the use of effects. In each instance, they can serve to support or destroy a scene, depending on the sensitivity of the film-maker toward his material. The questions that should constantly be asked are: What purpose do they serve, and is the film better without them?

ANGLE AND PERSPECTIVE

Once the film-maker has fully digested the limitations of direct physical shot associations and moves to linkages through thought and feeling, he can appreciate the use of camera angle and perspective to provide more telling arrangements. Specific emotional values are achieved through various placements of the camera. This is true should the subject matter have a neutral value to begin with; and if the subject matter has strong values of its own, camera placement can then either complement or counterpoint such values. In this way, the film-maker can heighten and intensify an existing emotion, subtly underplay it by presenting it softly, or, through vivid contrasts between subject value and camera placement, introduce the comic.

To be specific, camera angle refers to the distance between the camera and the subject (near or far) and the perspective in which the subject is viewed (high, low, or oblique). When the camera looks down on a subject, for example, the point of view can increase the viewer's feeling of pity; and the subject generally appears overpowered, downtrodden, beaten, pitiful, abject, or lost. This assumes, of course, that the subject has induced a feeling of pity to begin with. Notice that the adjectives used to describe the effect on the subject of such an angle are not only varied, but markedly different in meaning. The angle generalizes the value, whereas the subject deals with it specifically. The combination results in an intensification through use of the camera.

Consider the same situation with the distance between subject and camera increased until the subject is reduced on the screen to one-tenth or one-twentieth of its actual size. If the subject was lost initially, such intensification stresses the hopelessness of his position. A striking example of the use of such an angle is to be found in Fred Zinnemann's *High Noon* (1952), in which the sheriff is alone on a street, abandoned by the people of the town, who know full well that he is to be killed by the returning gunmen. The camera pulls back to a full long shot, catching the weakness of the man's position by reducing him in size in relation to the fairly large town, now underscored in its emptiness. If you imagine the same subject, still in a lost situation, but seen from a low angle, with the camera looking up, his plight loses its edge. But if the camera is pulled a great distance away, to look up at the subject it would be necessary to give him elevation. The subject's predicament would be unchanged; but to get the desired camera angle, he would have to be placed on a cliff or other high place. The up angle not only would eliminate the feeling of hopelessness, but would actually introduce strength and a strong implication that the subject would maneuver himself out of his predicament. One further change would provide the shot with a value diametrically opposed to the first one introduced: a change in the subject's body position, so that instead of standing with slumped shoulders and bowed head, he stands erect and tall, sure of himself and his surroundings. He would then take on strength, even to the point of assuming a godlike quality.

The camera with a low angle, looking up, can introduce strength, security, and stature. Yet, depending on the emotional qualities of the subject, the same angle can serve to intensify horror, fear, or the feeling of being overpowered. A standard procedure for monster films is the use of this angle. Nothing can be so frightening and bloodcurdling as a horned, smoke-bellowing, scaly creature, towering above on the screen at an extremely close perspective. The camera may pull away for a distant shot, but as the low angle is maintained, the respite is brief—only long enough for the viewer to catch his breath before the monster is seen again, belching fire and smoke and appearing very close. This is an obvious example, but subtle variations involving more serious themes are used again and again by outstanding film-makers.

An examination of Ingmar Bergman's *The Seventh Seal* (1956) reveals the repeated use of angle and perspective for intensification: when he introduces Death as an omnipotent force, the accused girl as an object of pitiful suffering, the flagellants as earth-bound creatures of misery, the accused girl as an innocent sacrificed to ignorance, and the eternity of life reflected in a silhouetted death-dance on the horizon. His constant use of high and low angles blended with perspective conveys particular conceptual patterns modulated with emotional tones.

The close-up itself, coming closest to flat perspective, has a unique value: its emotional characteristics come purely from the subject being photographed. The close-up converts the viewer from nonparticipant to participant; it introduces so many specific details and stresses the subject in such a personal way that an intimacy is established. The kissing scene, almost always done in extreme close-up, is one of the most powerful means yet devised for establishing empathy. No commercial director in his right mind would dream of doing a kissing scene in a long shot. However, although such a shot might arouse considerable frustration, the actual value of such frustration in a particular context might be worth attempting.

The close-up is as effective as the angle, but in a different way. A great many of the feelings experienced by man can be conveyed through the close-up for others to experience in a highly personal way. The close-up reveals a confidence, and in a sense the film-maker steps aside to permit the secret to be shared between the subject and the viewer. The close-up does not simply make a statement about the subject; it is the subject.

Moving shots, pans, tilts, and trucks have values closely allied to those gained through angle and perspective, and add the sensory dimension gained through the movement itself. To return momentarily to arrangements in physical continuity, motivation for moving shots is secured purely through the movement of the subject. An airplane taxiing and taking off would give sufficient motivation to pan the camera through the movement of the airplane. A car, parked at curbside, then starting up and leaving, would justify a pan shot. A character walking across a room would justify keeping the camera trained on him, thus resorting again to a pan. The motivation in all of these examples is provided by the physical movement of the subject. A more sophisticated justification rests on psychological motivation stemming from the concept in the shot and the emotional

117

characteristics accompanying it. The camera tilting down, for example, tends to convey a feeling of sinking, of being earthbound, restrained, held in. It is linked to the high angle, looking down; except that in addition the movement provides a precipitous, rushing feeling, like that experienced when a fast-moving elevator stops suddenly. The downward movement is like being catapulted into an abyss, if the movement is rapid, or being dragged into a bed of quicksand, if the movement is slow.

Reversing the movement by tilting up relates to the low angle looking up for loftiness; grandeur and stateliness are the values introduced. The added movement gives a feeling of release, discovery, or enlightenment. It is the feeling one gets after a dismal day of rain, when the sun breaks through the clouds and warms the earth; or when a man who has suffered immeasurably stops fighting and calmly accepts whatever else is to come, knowing that nothing more can hurt him; and when a child plucks a flower from the earth to examine it closely and then turns to his mother to share the discovery. Depending on the concept, the movement up can contribute to catharsis.

Should the camera move forward, the viewer begins to anticipate, seek, hunt, and expect. A forward movement is a preparatory one and must be followed by a shot that is climactic in nature. Leading a viewer to a point of expectation, but then having nothing there, results in disappointment and frustration.

Having the camera retreat de-emphasizes the subject matter and induces isolation, loneliness, and abandonment. Depending on the content, such use of the camera can help to create a shrinking revulsion, a feeling of disgust.

The camera, then, through sheer placement and movement has the power to create human, physical, and emotional values in a nonobjective way. But the moment subject matter is brought before the camera, conceptual values are also introduced. The camera immediately begins to interplay and blend with these concepts, and is thus capable of expanding or diminishing existing emotions.

MONTAGE AND DYNAMICS

The dictionary gives three definitions for the word "montage" as used in motion pictures: (a) the production of a rapid succession of images to illustrate an association of ideas; (b) the process of producing several images that revolve around each other or that rush one after the other to a sharp focus in the foreground, as newspaper headlines; (c) a portion of a motion picture using montage. This briefly sums up the various interpretations given to this often misunderstood picture arrangement.

The theory and the word "montage" were first brought forth by the Russians—Eisenstein and Pudovkin being the foremost exponents—after careful study of the advances in film craft introduced by D. W. Griffith, and innumerable experiments in films of their own. Explained in simple terms by Karel Reisz in *The Technique of Film Editing,* the basic characteristic is that "shot A contrasts with shot B (the juxtaposition giving rise to a new concept), is further illuminated by shot C, etc. . . ."[3] to develop full meaning in depth through an accumulation of linkages.

Although this definition gets at the gist of montage and is most quoted by teachers and film scholars, at best it merely generalizes the point. Further, Eisenstein does not see montage as an aspect of film-making, which many people seem to think, but as the whole of film-making. He describes five distinct and different types of montages, as follows:

1. Metric: In such an instance the lengths of the individual shots are precisely measured and arranged very much like measures in music. The content within each shot is completely subordinated to the exact cuts, and the montage proceeds purely in terms of the rhythms set up by the cuts.

---

[3] Reisz, *op. cit.,* p. 112.

2. Rhythmic: In this instance content is given equal consideration with the lengths. The shot lengths selected are practical according to the structure of the sequence and the rhythm inherent in each shot. Acceleration, for example, is achieved through shortening the pieces according to the action. Often counterpoint stresses are introduced by violating this rhythm.

3. Tonal: The basis for the arrangement here is the tone of the shot. By "tone" is meant a degree of soft focus or hard delineation. Color (in terms of blacks, whites, and tones of gray) is equally considered. Such montage is built up on a rhythmic basis, but the rhythm is found in the mood of each shot, rather than in spatial arrangements.

4. Overtonal: This is a further extension of arrangement of shots through mood, but to a heightened degree, so that specific ideas grow out of the combination. Shots set up to provide mood may in turn touch on thematic values, these having to do with nature, man, or the world in which he lives.

5. Intellectual: This is an order that introduces a thematic statement, usually an interpretation of the true and the ideal in human experience. Here the shots support an idea fixed not necessarily in the outward aspects of life, but in the changing, unique flow of life. Such a montage is thematic and is often coupled with physical and emotional values as well as intellectual.[4]

Raymond Spottiswoode describes six types of montages—primary, secondary, implicational, rhythmical, simultaneous, and ideological—and introduces variations of these, all of which are methods for connecting shots, much like Eisenstein's.[5] The differences between the various kinds of montage come about through the changing relationship in the content of the shot, the nature of the shot (angle, perspective, tone), and the

---

[4] Sergei Eisenstein, *Film Form and the Film Sense*, ed. and trans. by Jay Leyda (New York: Meridian Books, 1949), pp. 72–83.

[5] Raymond Spottiswoode, *A Grammar of the Film* (Berkeley: University of California Press, 1950), pp. 206–38.

manner in which it is cut—all done with a purpose. In other words, one of the basic characteristics of montage is that it is motivated by the artistic intentions of the film-maker. Spottiswoode stresses a most significant point about montage: not only does control over the small pieces of a film lead to a specific whole, but, much beyond this, obliquely supports a "community of experience." It would appear that Spottiswoode's "community of experience" is the same as Eisenstein's intellectual montage in that meaning can be derived through shot arrangement. This is referred to as a "great commonplace," found in all art, with "a condition of the artist's experience of the truth as he is attempting to communicate."[6]

Montage, therefore, cannot be regarded simply as a way of cutting or, much less, a way of cutting a few shots to be inserted into a film. Rather, all of film-making is a montage, conditioned by two factors: 1) a revelation of truth as experienced by the film-maker, and 2) secured by him through shot linkages. All that has been said here about film craft has been for the purpose of achieving montage. Montage is the film's dynamic.

---

[6] *Ibid.*, p. 205.

4

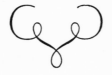

PLANNING THE FILM

Methods for planning a film are as varied as the wide range of material that goes into the making of it, from industrial and social issues at one extreme to highly personal artistic expressions set in narrative form at the other. Film-makers take various approaches, therefore, from a completely pre-scripted beginning or a partially scripted one, to one in which no plan is evident and film is exposed and shots collected. Content is not the only determining factor in planning approaches; economics is a vital consideration, and if ignored can very easily destroy a film production unit.

It is quite evident that a script is a necessary prerequisite; but what constitutes a motion picture script, as distinct from a play script, is another matter altogether. In the usual dramatic narrative script, where pre-scripting is law and where planning smacks of orthodoxy unknown in religious circles, a paralyzing rigidity is introduced based on dramatic concepts. In other words, dramatic film scripts most often are not written as film scripts but as film plays, drawing their conceptual patterns from the theater, rather than from the motion picture. The film-maker or director is confined by the script, and there is a tendency in such instances for the film to follow conventional lines: the camera records action only, and communication is effected through dialogue. This is generally the case when the script is written by a neophyte writer, or by one who comes to film already steeped in other disciplines, having been writing plays, novels, or short stories. A writer knowledgeable in filmic techniques, however, appreciates the camera "eye" and understands its relationship to movement and dialogue.

A most interesting and meaningful development in motion pictures since World War II has been the appearance of a new kind of film man: the writer-director. He is interesting because he is introducing changes in the motion picture form as we know it, and meaningful because, in addition to his artistic influence, he is strikingly successful at the box office.

Most of the films of recent decades that have caught the public's imagination have been either written and directed by one man, or directed by a man who collaborated with his writer to the point of co-authorship. The following men wrote and/or adapted their film stories in addition to directing them: John Huston with *The Maltese Falcon* (1941), *Treasure of the Sierra Madre* (1948), and *The Red Badge of Courage* (1951); Joseph L. Mankiewicz with *Letter to Three Wives* (1948), and *All About Eve* (1950); and Billy Wilder with *Some Like It Hot* (1958), *The Apartment* (1960), and *One, Two, Three* (1961).

Murray Schumach, reporting the Hollywood scene in *The New York Times*, pointed out that "movie companies may soon be engaged in cut-throat competition for the rarest of talents—the top writer-director. The tip-off was a deal Columbia Pictures made with Richard Brooks, one of the most eminent writer-directors."[1]

---

[1] Murray Schumach, "Hollywood Joust," *The New York Times*, January 28, 1962, Sec. 2, p. 7.

Almost a year later, Bosley Crowther wrote in *The New York Times* that

this seems a good time to take full notice of something that has been happening of late in a quiet, persistent fashion and that cries for candor and concern. That is the widening divergence in the nature and quality of the best American films and the nature and quality of the best films coming to us from abroad. . . . It is evident that American motion pictures have been lagging in quality this year while British, Italian and French films have been conspicuously forging ahead.[2]

Mr. Schumach's assessment of the value of writer-directors has proved correct, but not so much in America as in Europe. Mr. Crowther goes on to point out that the outstanding foreign films

have displayed advanced and mature dramatic content and strong cinematic qualities. They have in most cases been in touch with the modern world, in tune with the interests, the problems and the realities of our time.

The American films, for the most part, have been big, gaudy, full-of-air displays—what we, in search of a quick tag, have characterized as supermarket films. . . . When you take such Hollywood pictures as *My Geisha*, Hemingway's *Adventures of a Young Man*, *Mutiny on the Bounty* and *Gypsy* or, to expand the range to take in all "American" films, such other ones as *The Miracle Worker*, *The Longest Day* and *Long Day's Journey into Night* and put them alongside such sensitive and contemporary foreign films as *Whistle Down the Wind*, *A Taste of Honey*, *Through a Glass Darkly*, *Sundays and Cybele*, *Last Year at Marienbad*, *The Long Absence* and *Divorce—Italian Style* the difference in contours should be evident. . . .[3]

Almost all of these foreign films Mr. Crowther mentions were made by writer-directors. Notable among them is Federico Fellini, who started as a screen writer for *Open City* (1945) and *Paisan* (1946), then became director-writer for *La Strada* (1954), *Nights of Cabiria* (1957), and *La Dolce Vita* (1960).

[2] Bosley Crowther, "Theirs and Ours," *The New York Times*, December 9, 1962, Sec. a, p. 5.
[3] *Loc. cit.*

Another is Ingmar Bergman, writer-director who took prizes at Cannes three years in succession and broke all records. Even the following partial list of the best-known writer-directors attests not only to their foreign origin, but to the recognition that as film-makers they bring to their writing a camera point of view: Jacques Tati, François Truffaut, and Jean Cocteau (France); Michael Cacoyannis (Greece); Luis Buñuel (Mexico); Akira Kurosawa (Japan); Satyajit Ray (India).

In the writer-director of today is found the most natural evolution of further film craft development: cinematic storytelling. Successful film-making from a planned script—an economic necessity—demands experience beyond both writing or direction alone, in that newly found combination of directing, writing, and film-making.

Cinematic storytelling can best be learned by getting behind a camera, exposing film, and then cutting and editing it oneself. Although feature-length films made by such a method are almost impossible because of cost, the benefits derived make smaller films—especially one reelers—well worth it.

However, even in this approach the film-maker does not work without a plan. Simply to expose film is anarchistic. The film-maker must have an object in mind: what the film is about, what he wants to say, and how he plans to say it. Because progression is necessary, he structures his story in general, knowing in advance how he hopes to begin, how he hopes to develop, and how he hopes to end. With those targets in mind, and keeping to a small scale, he can proceed.

In summary: to make a film without a planned script can be artistically as well as financially disastrous. A successfully scripted feature-length film requires more of the writer than a knowledge of dramatic structure. Even when no script is written, the film-maker should work from a structured outline; making films from such outlines enables the beginner to understand cinematic characteristics. A film must be approached as a vehicle for visual communication; this means that the film-maker must be absolutely clear as to what he wants to say before he proceeds, and then he must transmute his verbalizations into visualizations.

FRAME OF REFERENCE

Good film-making is good story-telling, catching the audience completely. The audience sees itself as one or another of the central figures, and reacts emotionally to the success or failure shown, the fulfillment or disappointment. More than this, the audience expects to derive meaning from the experience, even if the story characters are not able to do so. The audience expects this whether approaching the story through laughter or sorrow. They seek to empathize, and for their pains they want the satisfaction of the experience—perhaps to know a little more, to have seen a point of view, to make a judgment or come to a conclusion, or perhaps merely to heave a sigh of relief for the excitement they have endured.

Successful storytelling, then, communicates with an audience on an emotional level. Outstanding storytelling, with artistic merit, also does this, but goes further by introducing meaning as well. The difference between an ordinary story and one that is outstanding is a difference in degree and depth, but the factor basic to both is emotional appeal.

The film-maker must avoid a number of pitfalls and traps in the planning of his film. He must make sure that his story is consistently presented in emotional terms that will reach his audience. However, too much zeal in this direction may make the story so maudlin or saccharine that it quickly taxes the audience's willingness to believe. Too much zeal in the opposite direction, seeking depth and meaning, often leads to an intellectualization that sacrifices the emotional qualities of the scenes. A balance must be found and maintained, but this is particularly difficult because film-making, unlike other arts, has no working frame of reference. The frame of reference not only provides a kind of physical unity, but also enables the artist to judge the probable emotional impact of his work as he goes along, because he can see it taking shape more or less as a whole.

In a painting, for example, the painter works within the framework of his canvas. He may proceed from outline to sketch to paint, with his work constantly before him. He sees it grow, making changes and improvements as he proceeds, checking each step against his initial creative aim, and maintaining his creative attitude all the while. In brief, nothing gets between him and his work. Much the same is true of the sculptor or the musician. The sculptor works from his own sketches and applies his own chisel to the marble; the musician writes down his composition or works it out on his musical instrument. The theater director has his stage and shapes his play over a given period of rehearsal time, while he watches the action and works out its development.

In the film, not only do the large number of people involved depersonalize the work, but the only available frame of reference is the viewfinder, which is proportioned to the actual screen size in a ratio of three to four. As he views through this device, the film-maker does not see an entire film, or even a complete scene; he sees one small piece, which eventually is to fit into a broader pattern. To appreciate the challenge fully, imagine a painter doing one piece of work on twenty-six different canvases, painting a different piece of the same scene on each one, moving back and forth to do so, and finally pasting it all together with the hope that there will be a complete artistic coordination of all the elements.

The film-maker has a difficult time being genuinely creative during the actual filming. His working reference point is within himself, buried deep in the recesses of his own thoughts and feelings. To achieve any degree of success as a storyteller, and to develop scenes of emotional content that will work correctly for him, he must find a way of fixing in his own mind the very first emotional surge that overtook him as he read the story initially or reacted to the incident, person, or idea that led him to tell the story. At that time, without any intellectualization or analysis, the film-maker gives himself to his subject matter very much the way an audience gives itself to the screen when the film is shown. The audience understands and participates without raising such questions as why is that happening, why was that done, what does this mean, or what is the significance. The audience does not fall away and begin challenging unless what is on the screen does not reach them. Once the story starts working, nothing is so beautiful as the way in which an audience wants to be led along, wants to take part, and wants to react emotionally. The film, like any other artistic work, is only half of the artistic experience. The remaining half is contributed by the audience.

Because this emotional interplay between story and audience is a key characteristic, the film-maker attempts to pin down its nature as he first experienced it and to set it up as an over-all objective and frame of reference as he works his way through each shot and scene. This quality is the emotional tonality encompassing the degree, kind, and depth of feeling engendered by the over-all work. The mark of talent is that the film-maker, during his long work period, evokes this living emotion through his film, rather than commenting on it editorially or even pictorially. This, then, is the film-maker's fire and flame, the feeling that will excite him, provide him with enthusiasm, give him the strength to wade through endless obstacles, and serve as the guide against which he measures each part of the film.

Nevertheless, once the film-maker has found this key, he does not for a moment trust it. Complete faith in the emotional view will lull him into too subjective and uncritical an attitude. The audience is entitled to have its emotional "fun," and the film-maker must sense it and set it up; but he must also understand how to bring it about. This necessity in turn calls for a breakdown of the content in fine detail, and in a cold, calculated way, leading to an analysis of each individual part. Although emotion and analysis usually neutralize each other, the film-maker must use both, and in such a way that they do not cancel one another out. In this process there can never be too many checks and counterchecks. The subject matter of the story and the emotional tone that it engenders, although eventually coming together in a whole film, must first be picked apart, understood, and carefully fixed. The film-maker's working reference lies within the measure of his own feelings.

UNDERSTANDING THE FILM

It has been repeatedly stressed that a film's effectiveness is directly related to the ways in which the film-maker explores his content. Camera setups, shots, lighting, sound, acting, and the innumerable other components that go into the making of a film all go by the board unless they are well motivated. Motivation, of course, springs from the film-maker knowing what he wants to say, but this is not sufficient. He must know better than anyone else all the ramifications of his message, its parts, connecting links, individual pieces, and their meanings. He must probe constantly into his own thoughts and feelings, challenging himself repeatedly as he tries to understand how he is going to relate to his film and how the film in turn will relate itself to the audience.

As we have already noted, the very first axiom of the experienced film-maker is not to trust his emotions. This does not mean that his approach should be colorless or without enthusiasm. Thought and feeling about a projected film must come together and be kept under control.

The second axiom to be followed when starting on a film is

to put the thoughts and feelings on paper in a logical break-down. All too often, the word "breakdown" refers merely to a listing of the order in which the shots are to be taken. This purely mechanical assemblage *is* necessary to save effort, time, and money; but equally important, if not more so, is the break-down that the film-maker must make if he is to know and re-member what his story is about. For the practical-minded this effort will also save time and money.

A simple and direct way to make such a breakdown is to diagram the entire film into its parts, to make general comments on each part, and then to make specific ones (see Diagram No. 1).

This method is flexible and can be applied to a pre-set script or used as a series of notes on structure prior to scripting. Most important, it must not be given lip service, but must be used to constantly question the intent. By describing the nature of each scene unit as a whole and then stating its meaning, the film-maker provides himself with a check on whether the particular event actually builds toward the idea he wishes to convey.

The sequential description shows the logic of development: do the scene units actually provide a link toward a major premise? The description of sequential meaning examines the parts as they relate to the whole. Then, if all the pieces support the central idea, the film-maker has set the groundwork for be-ginning a film.

Constantly re-examining the breakdown not only allows the film-maker to check the effectiveness of each part, but also to become utterly familiar with these parts to the point of mem-orizing them. Such closeness accomplishes two things: one, it starts the film-maker memorizing a lot sooner and prior to shoot-ing; and two, it gives him an advantage under field conditions when he may have to make substitutions or changes either of locale or meaning. As accurate and detailed as the film-maker may be in his breakdown, quite often new ideas suddenly come up while shooting. Decisions have to be made on their appro-

Diagram No. 1

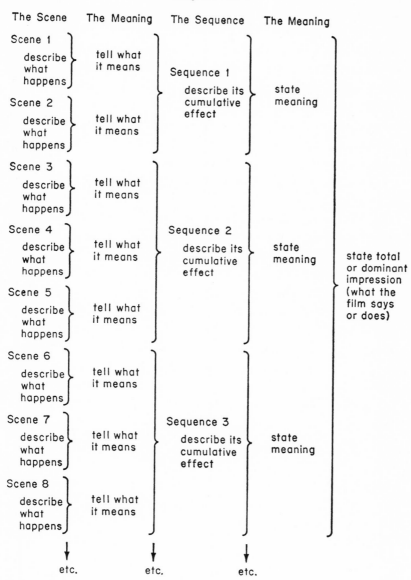

priateness, effectiveness, and significance; and such decisions can only be made when the film-maker is totally familiar with his intent.

Total familiarization, of course, calls for more than a few generalized ideas. Each scene and sequence contains many particulars that are subordinate to the main idea and support it. These have to be worked out in detail, because the nature of the film-maker's approach to a scene and the way in which he interprets it are based on them. A film's success or failure can be determined at this critical point.

A scene, in a sequence or in a total film, is developed to project something that informs the audience about the event taking place and the people involved; beyond this, a philosophical, religious, moral, or social point is made, transcending both the action and the people. To be sure, a well-planned and thought-out scene includes all three values, but never with equal emphasis or weight. One of the three forms the core of the scene, and, in turn, of the sequence and of the entire film. Through this balance of values the kind of film is determined: it may be an action-packed thriller, like Hitchcock's *North By Northwest* (1959); a story of people and passions, like Martin Ritt's *Hud* (1963); or a film of ideas, like Orson Welles's *The Trial* (1962).

The film-maker's background and experience strongly influence his taste, selection, and judgment as he determines the individual values and the relationships between them. These values are seldom, if ever, fixed and separate; more often, they are subtly woven together. Judgment exercised at this point affects the film considerably, because the total effect will depend on how well the shots do the job of communicating these values.

In addition to the dominant values there are details dealing with mood, atmosphere, character, and language, all of which further develop and enhance the scene. The initial diagram of the scene breakdown might be elaborated as in Diagram No. 2.

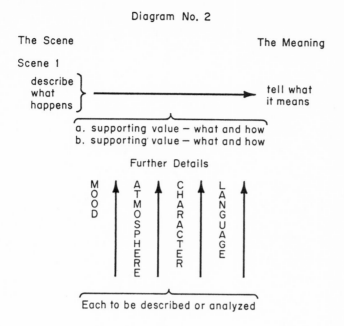

Diagram No. 2

The Scene | The Meaning

Scene 1

describe what happens } ⟶ tell what it means

a. supporting value — what and how
b. supporting value — what and how

Further Details

MOOD   ATMOSPHERE   CHARACTER   LANGUAGE

Each to be described or analyzed

The film-maker may not necessarily follow a breakdown diagram of this type, but he will analyze to this depth and go even further as he raises questions for each and every scene and sequence, and for the whole film.

There is a natural temptation at this point to imagine the scenes as they would be played, with individual shots constantly forcing themselves on the mind's eye of the film-maker. Giving in to this temptation is a sign of his impatience and unwillingness to get to the bottom of his story. He may be eager to get into the relatively simpler work of film mechanics, and be caught up in the process of creation without sufficient gestation of what is being created. Understanding of the scene must be handled initially as an abstraction, whether it is diagrammed, written out, designed, drawn, or prepared as a series of notes. Once satisfactory understanding is arrived at, the film-maker is prepared for the next step: moving from verbal to visual articulation.

VERBAL TO VISUAL COMMUNICATION

Communication comprises not only what is being communicated, but the vehicle through which the message is imparted. Man uses language to express himself; the better versed he is in it, the more selective and careful he is in his choices of words and syntax, and the more fluent he is in conveying his thoughts to others. But language is not the principal element of the film. In the primary visualization of a film, the film-maker has to deal with pictures, not words. Knowledge of film terminology does not automatically insure full understanding of how to assemble a series of shots that are visually expressive.

Because of man's conditioning through the use of language, he is given to constant verbalization; but it is not enough to translate such verbalization into pictures. The pitfall of using the pictures as mere illustrations is too great. Furthermore, all feelings and thoughts suffer some change and limitation when forced into the form of words, just as they do when they are expressed in pictures. But if an emotion is first stated in words and then in pictures, it goes through a kind of double filter that certainly limits and/or distorts its impact. What is necessary is a direct movement from thought or feeling into pictorial presentation. This is certainly easier said than done.

Film language, or picturization, is in some ways a foreign language; and its acquisition as a skill is in some ways like studying a foreign language. The student is bombarded with grammar and rules that he must memorize; but he also needs to be constantly surrounded by the language, so that he can hear it and speak it. The ultimate objective is to reach the point where he no longer gropes for a word, flubs an idiom, or makes a literal translation. He is proficient when thought and language flow as one. In the film, thought and image have to come from the film-maker in much the same way. When the film-maker translates from word to picture, he gets illustrated words; when he gropes for the right picture, he may come up with "arty" effects or hoary clichés; and when he attempts the film idiom he may come up with a film that is understandable only to some specialized minority. By experience and exposure, the film-maker must learn to understand and think about his film in terms of seeing it. As he analyzes his work, pictures, rather than well-turned phrases, should spring to his mind.

It has often been remarked that people listen, but do not hear. Based on this little fact, playwrights have made elaborate plays stressing man's isolation and alienation. What is true of our hearing is equally true of our sight. We see, but we do not perceive. The successful film-maker must see for us. He must open our eyes, provide meaning for what we see, and thereby break through our isolation and alienation, if only temporarily.

The stress in language has always been on care—to eliminate sloppiness, to be precise, to understand and formulate the thought, and to express it directly. Achievement of the same ends through pictorial presentation is even more difficult, particularly when the tendency is to reach for a word.

Before the film-maker can reach the point where he naturally sees the movement of shots unfold, he must develop a deep awareness of what is being photographed. Simply calling for a cut, a reverse angle, or a dolly is not sufficient. If a shot shows a man, bent over a machine in a dim light, scribing a turning piece of metal, or if many men are seen at machines in daylight illumination, what is being related; what are we to see? If one tree is seen against the sky, or many trees, what is being related? If a woman is knitting, a young girl knitting, a child knitting— think of those images—what is being related? Many more questions arise when any one of these situations is visualized. How is the man bent over? How dim is the light? Do we see the man's back or his face? What is his expression?

Each of the images is a vague generalization. In order to get a precise quality, more and more information is sought. To visualize one of these images as fully as possible, the line of the body, the expression of the face, the pace of the action, and the tone of the lighting must be seen in the mind's eye. In this way, a picture clear enough to convey an emotion or a state of mind is arrived at.

By contrast, we should consider a scene developed through the logic of verbalization. In a sleepy Western town, a young man dragging one leg hurries around a corner, looks into this window and that, and rushes into a saloon where men are gathered at the bar, hoisting drinks. The young man sees the person he has been seeking, rushes up to him and says: "That feller's comin' back, the one you threw out of town yestidy. An' he's got them ugly brothers of his'n." Finishing his brew, the sheriff wipes his mouth and says, "Yeah." The Western is an American institution, and the point is not to poke fun at it, but to show that the shots in this action look at life no more perceptively than the average individual. Here essentially is a written playlet, with shots that illustrate verbally realized action and dialogue.

Speaking through shots is as alien to the written story or play form as English is to ancient Greek. Even though the basic thoughts and feelings might be the same, the order and arrangement definitely are not. Seeing is not hearing, and although the two senses supplement and complement one another, in any given situation one must take precedence. Many other media enlarge life by hearing, but the very *raison d'être* of film is to enlarge life by seeing; therefore seeing must take first place, and language and sound second place.

The film-maker cannot show you what he does not see himself. He must first learn really to see, and to develop a total awareness of all the nuances of what is seen. The tilt of a head, or a raised eyebrow may be relatively clear to any reasonably sensitive person, but there are an unending number of clues for the deeply aware person. The film-maker must also temper his sight with objectivity. Pictures record the real world about us, but they also project connotative values, just as words do, and convey thoughts that are uniquely their own. Without objectivity the film-maker may project a value of which he is not aware, while thinking that his pictures relate something else. Depending on our own experience and psychological bent, we constantly read into things significances that may or may not be there. A film-maker must be constantly alert to such possibilities, so that he can use them when they serve his purpose and avoid them when they might mislead. On the other hand, he must avoid assuming that certain meanings will be read into a situation. A shot showing a child looking down at a plate set before it, seeing its reflection in the plate, and banging on it with a spoon, does not signify that the child is hungry; yet there are instances in which the film-maker's subjectivity has misled him into making this kind of assumption, with a resultant failure in communication.

The second step in gaining visual fluency is to move from seeing individual units to seeing relationships. Shots with no connection make about as much sense as a list of unrelated words. The simplest connection between shots is physical action, and there is a strong tendency to take this easy way out. We see a man move from point A to point B, return to point A, and then proceed to point C. The shots are all related, but what have we seen? A kind of pictorial "Look, Dick, look! See Jane run."

Pictorial presentation, however, does have one thing in common with spoken language: although they are both infinitely flexible, they are both dependent on the talent of the user. Although basic talent may be something one is born with, the skill to use it comes from practice, study, experience, and motivation. The film-maker must acquire facility in arranging his shots without stringing them together in verbal terms or through simple physical action. He must learn to think in a free flow of images so that he can secure complex thematic patterns by photographing real people and things. He has no way of achieving these ends save by constant observation and practice. As one becomes fluent in a foreign language by using it steadily, so one learns the language of film by exposing it, cutting it, recutting it, and then recutting it again, always carefully observing what emerges from the cumulative shots and their relationships. After a while the awareness comes that film is as exacting and demanding in its own terms as any other language.

Although pictures have been used to communicate since man's earliest days, more and more of late they are being turned to sophisticated and literate ends. Federico Fellini in *8½* (1962) demonstrates shots that fuse reality, dream, and fantasy to explore a film director's inner torment against an outer world. A sly sense of humor and balance is projected through shots marked by subtlety in both selection and arrangement.

FILM AND STYLE

Style according to the dictionary is "the quality which gives distinctive excellence to artistic expression, consisting especially in the appropriateness and choiceness of relation between subject, medium, and form, and individualized by the temperamental characteristics of the artist." When the word "style" is applied to film, its definition is not nearly so clear. At one extreme, film has suffered from too much so-called "style" (the way-out, avant-garde experiments) and, at the other extreme, from unconcern and lack of any style (the average run-of-the-mill Hollywood release).

Some stylistic distinctions are made, such as "the documentary style," "the Hitchcock manner," and "the theatrical manner." But these phrases do not define film style so much as kinds of film, referring as often to their subject matter as to any artistic connection between subject matter, film, and film-maker. Style in film is complex because it can refer to the way in which a film has been cut, to the way the actors and story have been handled, or to the nature of the story and its treatment. In the broad sense it is all of these combined.

One difficulty in assessing a film's style stems from the dual nature of film; it is an art in itself, but is also compounded of many other arts. In addition, it has been on the scene a comparatively short time, and yet has behind it the heritage of two thousand years of drama and two or three hundred years of journalism. Considering its complexity, it is no wonder style has been one of the least talked about filmic elements and has only recently made itself felt among the film-going public. It is interesting, too, that style in film becomes most strongly felt when the particular piece of work is unusually significant, a truly creative and artistic expression.

In the early days of film, style was practically nonexistent. Film-makers simply recorded everyday scenes of activity. The one outstanding exception was Georges Méliès who, because of his highly inventive and imaginative mind, left his mark on every film he made. And although he used story material essentially his stamp made itself most evident in his settings.

Yet film itself has an authority about it, a realism, an authenticity that in itself suggests a style. Even when film-makers turned to literary sources for story material, the story made the transition to film without whatever style it may have had, its place taken in a way by film reality.

The early stories reflected the dress, manners, and modes of the time. The acting itself was mostly styleless and, if anything, "ham." Theda Bara slinking downstairs, Mae Marsh jumping with joy, or Pola Negri with her big, wide eyes were not exemplifying a style so much as overacting. Nor were the directors, even the best of them, necessarily imposing their own highly individualized marks on their work. This does not lessen the contribution made by the early film-makers, but reverence for their work must be qualified. They made important contributions, but they were also groping for their way and in some cases stumbling through a new mode of expression.

The first important stylists in film were perhaps the Germans who introduced a theatrically stylized series of films, much of it an extension of the expressionistic German theater. In these films, the sets, story, and character interpretations, along with a mobile, fluid camera, all came together with a new-found excitement. In this sense, these films can be considered the first fully developed use of theatrical style in film—Murnau's *The Last Laugh* (1924), Dupont's *Variety* (1925), Lang's *Metropolis* (1926). The Russians, on the other hand, having developed film out of a reportorial point of view, used the documentary approach for their narrative films and placed their stress on arrangement and cutting. This produced a refinement of film theory along with a development of film style, the whole montage theory.

Film never has and probably never will lose its deep authenticity, its sense of reality, its awesome documentation, and its ability to make people believe that what they see is absolute truth. Even in fanciful excursions to unreal worlds, the unreality is broken through by the camera's sense of realness. This penetrating characteristic of the camera introduces not so much a limitation of style genre, compared with the theater, as an extremely subtle refinement of style within the framework of realism. The theater, with its innumerable periods of development, has many styles, among them classicism, romanticism, naturalism, realism, and expressionism. And there are further refinements of these within each classification. For example, romanticism covers a considerable range, from an idealized enactment of a story (feats of derring-do and fair maidens) to a more realistic approach to a period story (a queen caught in the conflict between love and duty). Naturalism, essentially a branch of realism, calls for as authentic a re-creation of life as is possible within the framework of artistic effort. Within realism itself, refinements range from farcical or melodramatic stories at one end to serious character dramas at the other. All played within the realistic style, they are nevertheless subject to subtle variations and stylistic differences, from arbitrary writing, directing, and acting (double takes, abrupt action and reaction, direct movement) to a more rounded and complete writing, directing, and acting (follow through of movement, action and story brought closer to life, low-keyed, natural).

All of these theatrical styles and traditions have been utilized in films, but they have been heavily tempered by the camera's unerring eye for the real. The result is that the styles, though present, are very finely delineated, and highly subtle in presentation. Furthermore, editing can be expressive in its own way, providing another kind of individuality to be considered in the development of style in the film. In addition, there remains the final ingredient—the film-maker's unique point of view—all these elements to be blended into a cohesive whole.

Today, more than ever before, an audience recognizes a film by Bergman, Fellini, Antonioni, Resnais, or Truffaut—stylists all. Most important about the works of these men is that each one assumes a highly personalized attitude toward his work. The last part of the definition of style sums it up: "and individualized by the temperamental characteristics of the artist." So heavily represented thirty years ago by clichéd soap opera and blunderbuss shoot-'em-ups, film has come into its own stylistically through the highly personal and artistic point of view of the individual. Style is the lifeblood of creative effort; and because film takes so freely from so many sources and adds to it an authenticity of its own, successful film-making demands an unparalleled degree of selection.

INTENSIFICATION THROUGH DETAIL

Film has a sense of command uniquely its own. From the moment the auditorium is darkened and the first flickers of light appear on the screen, audiences accept what they see before them as truth. Whether the "willing suspension of disbelief" that takes place in the theater occurs in the same way at the cinema, or occurs at all, is open to question. Film is so close to real life, often depicting life itself, or selected slices of life, that authenticity and documentation are inherent in it.

This point was quickly realized by the Russians, particularly by Lenin, when he issued his well-known decree in 1919, placing the sanction and financial support of the state behind the early film-makers. This brought the entire film industry—production, distribution, and exhibition—under the People's Commissariat of Education. In this way, the inherent authenticity of the film was made to serve the ends of the Communist state.

Because the film draws its strength from re-creation of the real world—either with constructed sets or by location shooting —does not mean that its artistic possibilities are limited. On the contrary its artistic value lies in the selection and intensification of reality. It is a kind of academic snobbery to cling to the notion that artistic interpretation cannot be secured within the realistic framework. To assume that the distinction of the classics or of Shakespeare rests primarily on their being period pieces, or on their removal from reality, is to ignore those very characteristics that give these works their universality, or reality. Furthermore, this universality and reality have nothing to do with the language of the classicists and the Renaissance playwrights, or with the settings they used, or the subjects they dealt with. Rather, they stem from the *way* in which the language and the subjects were used. It is a mistaken notion that poetic overtones and the emotional effect caused by apt expression of feeling and idea can be achieved solely through nonrealistic means.

Two points should be borne in mind: one is that the realistic nature of film, which establishes immediate credibility, is not a flaw or weakness, but its greatest strength; the second is that this reality, if properly explored, opens a wholly new filmic dimension. Such dimensions are achieved through selecting detail that not only can intensify the material, but also can go much beyond that to reveal the artistic statement.

Detail manifests itself in a film in innumerable ways. It might, for example, provide background enrichment through set decoration. In Erich von Stroheim's *Greed* (1924), every stick of furniture, the wall decoration, foreground, middle ground, and background properties are handled with such authenticity that in themselves they make a comment. Detail may also manifest itself in the care given to the individual actions of the players. In Tony Richardson's *A Taste of Honey* (1961), the actions of the mother, daughter, and the young man are so painstakingly drawn that it is difficult to distinguish between acting and actuality, yet the camera moves among these performers capturing detail after detail to point up the greater ironic reality of their lives. Then again, attention to details can appear in the sheer mounting of shots, as in Carl-Theodor Dreyer's *The Passion of Joan of Arc* (1928) where close-up after close-up in succession presents each face, projecting belief and conviction on the one hand against shades of bias, prejudice, and doubt on the other.

Details can be planned for and emphasized in all the elements that go into the making of a film: setting, lighting, acting, movement, and camera work. But although detail by itself will heighten a film's realism, it does not automatically convey real meaning. The handling of detail can be deceptive when one is working within the realistic framework, for it must be chosen, guided, and controlled with the ultimate effect in mind. For greater expressiveness, detail must be motivated. Motivation depends on the story's viewpoint which brings us back again to the film-maker's need to be absolutely clear about what he wants the story to convey. Motivated detail, through camera work in particular, is the film-maker's method of achieving a new language and a new dimension. It is his way of remaining within the framework of reality, yet being able to express the interpretation and significance he sees beyond that framework.

143

A significant amount of detail, both on a grand scale and in character particulars, is handled in David Lean's *Lawrence of Arabia* (1962), yet between the two there is dissipation rather than concentration: grandeur is present, but muddied by a camera that fails to provide sufficient definition in terms of theme, plot, or character development. On the other hand, Jean-Luc Godard uses highly selective detail in the camera work in *My Life to Live* (1962), to show how a woman's quest for identity may combine with self-indulgence and lead to self-destruction. The camera not only controls the scenes, but also narrows the point of view and concentrates on details to provide the insight.

PROPORTION

Proportion as it relates to an artistic effort has a fairly simple and universal meaning: the relationship of one part to another and to the whole are harmonious in accord with their respective degrees of importance. It is a matter, therefore, of harmony and emphasis. A piece of writing that has action as its focal point would be out of proportion if the characters stood around indulging in philosophical talk while the essential action lingered somewhere in the background. Indeed, it would most likely be dull. The same holds true of other arts, of course, but in different ways. In painting, for example, proportion is a principle of design, not only as part of perspective, but also in relation to the emphasis on various colors or the placing of the compositional elements.

The necessity for proportion grows out of the fundamental idea that an artistic piece does not re-create life as such, but a part of life. The artist works to interpret life as he sees it, and interpretation depends on his personal emphasis. If his emphasis is too far from life as others know it, or if there is no emphasis to orient his audience, then communication usually fails.

Writing, having behind it a long, successful history and tradition, has nicely transposed its requirement to the screenplay. Therefore, in the screenplay proportion and its related value, emphasis, are automatically—sometimes, alas, almost mechanically—handled. Yet, in the planning of the shots that are to tell the story, proportion in both harmony and emphasis is now considered by only a few film-makers and ignored completely by too many. Once the idea of the scene is fixed in the film-maker's mind, proportion should be considered on three counts: the number of shots required to project the idea most effectively; the composition within each shot; and the tightness of the flowing arrangement.

Film-making in its fullest sense is not really understood when a scene is blocked in a traditional theatrical method and the camera is used to record this blocking, with some emphasis added by an inserted close-up or two. Such treatment is much like padding in a piece of writing, and reveals the film-maker's inability to appreciate either his story or the relative weights and values of his shots. Scene concepts can be singularly altered, strengthened, or varied by the manipulation of the camera to lend emphasis to a scene's important parts.

In scene after scene in Tony Richardson's *Tom Jones* (1963), traditional techniques go by the board as the camera selects high points and thrusts them dynamically into prominence. Even in such a simple scene as the one in which Tom goes to rescue Sophie's pet bird, let loose by that jealous knave of a nephew, the three dominant points of interest—Tom, Sophie, and the nephew—are the main reference points for the camera eye, all else held as secondary values. Compression is achieved through just this kind of proportionment, not only adding immeasurably to the value of the scene, but rendering it delightfully exhilarating as well.

Knowing on what to focus the camera, and how to emphasize

and subordinate shots so that they clarify scene intent—building the scene, dropping, providing transitions, and rendering climaxes—is like knowing where to apply the blue pencil to a piece of writing. Yet, equally important is the film-maker's awareness that the language of film runs counter to the known and accepted storytelling methods. In the novel the writer may use long descriptive passages to establish a mood, locale, elements of character, or idea, but the film-maker can accomplish this in one or two shots, at the same time relegating some of these elements to the background and keeping his story moving forward in the foreground. As simple and obvious as this sounds, it is the basis for a variety of ways to handle the material.

Proportion in shot planning cannot be spelled out with specific rules, as it is related directly to intent. In the planning stages, the key question is: in what way are the shots serving the story? There is danger here for the beginning film-maker who, after pulling a series of shots together, is disappointed to find that what he thought he was getting is not apparent. The fault may lie in his own subjectivity, confusion in understanding the scene objective, poor choice of angle and framing, muddied compositions, improper selection, redundancy, or any combination of these. If any suggestion can be made, it would be to drop a shot, bring the remaining two on each side together, and see what happens.

François Truffaut and Jean-Luc Godard are perhaps the foremost cinematic proponents of finding the correct relationship between shot selection and story content, as they utilize the camera and editing to project subjective values. They bring their desired values into perspective and proportion by dropping frames, heightening scenes by choking off shots, at times ignoring transitions by bringing together scenes of different locales or moods, by jump-cuts, by inserting cutaways based on abstract ideas, by intentionally cutting counter to staged physical movement to support thematic or character values, by abruptly interspersing subjective and objective camera points of view, and by using "holding" shots as memory devices. Often these techniques are referred to as cinematic tricks, and there have been as many successes as failures. But to see these attempts merely as tricks is to ignore the sense and purpose of why and how they are used. Expansion of film language has but recently gotten underway; and proportion, both in story development and the planning of shots, is impossible to obtain unless the film-maker approaches one in terms of the other.

Modern audiences are inclined to be impatient with traditional methods of film storytelling. Witness the lack of enthusiasm for countless filmed television programs, not really because of the techniques used (of which the audience is probably unaware), but because the sophisticated audience wants more than superficial Pollyanna morality playlets, be they tales of gangsters or cowboys, psychological thrillers, courtroom dramas, or mysteries. Naturally, proportioned shot planning by itself will not make the difference between success and failure; but through shots in proper proportion it is possible to project the more subtle, intangible values that grow out of character relationship and conflict in an exciting way so natural to film. The best of plays, transferred to the screen in the stage idiom, despite exceptional cast handling and acting, will remain curious museum pieces that lose both vitality and pertinence for want of camera selection. An example is Sidney Lumet's *Long Day's Journey into Night* (1962). Even the older film classics, such as those by Thomas Ince or D. W. Griffith, although dramatically heightened, still remain limited by today's standards because both method and concept were earth-bound.

In summation, a film story that strives for artistic interpretation calls for shots so planned that they need not pander to hidebound rules of master shot and inserts. The success of shots is determined by the proportion given to specific story values that have been previously evaluated by the film-maker. On this score, there simply are no "do's" and "don'ts"; experimentation is called for. With film-making in existence only a little over half a century, it seems odd that so many film-makers should accept initial discoveries as final ones. Failure need not be a deterrent; even only a part of genuine intent that comes through often proves more profitable to both the film-maker and the box office than films featuring oversexed "babes" and cliché gags. It is almost axiomatic that correct proportioning of story content with depth and point of view leads to correct proportioning of shots and introduces exciting and imaginative imagery.

THE PRODUCTION DESIGN

The phrase "production design," commonly used by feature-length film-makers, refers to the layout of the shots, the locations, settings, costumes, and generally to the entire visual array that will unfold on the screen. Better yet, it should be a kind of detailed account of all the goings-on of a film's production, including the periods before, during, and after production. This entails both a written and graphic account dealing with everything about interpretation, as well as with shot layouts and scene and costume sketches. Included would be the style of the production, in terms of the kind of acting, nature of shots, methods of cutting, types of scenery, lighting elements, and any or all phases of production.

In all likelihood the term has come to film from the theater, where the production book (a book made to house the whole production plan and design) has long been in use. The thoroughness of planning and control instituted by the theater production book makes it a worth while addition to cinematic production. Containing the script and used as a prompt book, the theater production book holds the director's preparatory notes, changes made in the script during the direction, all of the gestures, movements, and staging assigned to the actors, lighting notes and plot, and, to keep the record complete in every detail, all scene and costume sketches, opening-night comments, reviews, etc. Maintained by an assistant director or stage manager, the production book has the immediate value of organizing and recording all the preplanning, and at the play's termination is a historical record of all that has happened. Most important, it is the control center where the director puts down his ideas, thoughts, feelings, and attitudes toward the script he is to direct.

In the move to film—not that there is any formal connection —the word "book" may have given way to "design." Then again the need for planning, along with its requisite design, may have developed quite naturally, for a great part of film planning is given to the design of the shots. The word "design" is used here in its broadest sense to mean anything pertaining to the composition of each shot, the flow of shots in series, or the over-all pattern of these shots as they project the story values. The production design of a film is built on two foundations: the story, and the way it is told. Both aspects unfold in the flow of shots that is the core or design of the film.

A most useful device in planning and arranging shots is the storyboard, actual drawings of each shot in a ratio of three to four inches in direct proportion to the traditional screen. The storyboard may have originated in the animation studio. The cartoon, being completely a work of the imagination, required a working reality. It is a direct step, of course, from the general flow of storyboard drawings to the highly detailed drawings of the animated cartoon. Advertising agencies and producers of television commercials also depend on the storyboard, as here again something tangible is needed when ordering or approving a filmed commercial.

The storyboard is about as close as the film-maker can get to providing an integrated plan for his film. He can plan his shots and the action within them, check the relationship of shot to shot, and check the shots as they relate to story idea. A story-board can actually be read much as a musician reads a score.

149

STORY BOARD

PRODUCTION:_____ DATE OF SHOOTING:_____

LOCATION SHOT # SCENE # FILM TYPE ROLL.# EDGE NUMBERS

TYPE OF SHOT:_____

ANGLE:_____ LENS:_____

SOUND:_____ SILENT:_____

SPEED:_____

FRAME DIRECTION:_____

EXPOSURE:_____

SHOT LENGTH:_____

TAKES:

1	2	3	4	5	6	7	8

REMARKS:

CODE: F S is "False Start"
      N G is "No Good"
      — is "Fair"
      / is "Good"
      X is "Best"

CHARACTERS	WARDROBE	PROPERTIES

SHOT DESCRIPTION:

As the notes on the sheet indicate melody and arrangement, the drawings on the storyboard indicate the flow and movement of the film.

But the storyboard is only as effective as the film-maker makes it. It can render a film rigid by restraining all imaginative impulses, or it can serve as a general memory jogger from which to plan fluid and moving shots. Many film-makers devise note-taking systems or shot-planning layouts of their own, eschewing the storyboard to avoid any stultifying influence.

At worst the storyboard can lead to contrivance. There is a marked difference between imagining a shot and seeing through the viewfinder the actual shot as it is to unfold. When the film-maker sticks too literally to the record of his imagined shot, artificiality, rather than creativity, dominates the film. If, in addition, the beginner is ignorant of lenses, angles of fields, and lighting, the storyboard is useless anyway, because the planned shots could never be realized.

Nevertheless, working points of reference are sorely needed and can be provided by a storyboard. An experienced film-maker offsets the disadvantages by going over his locations or sets, checking angles and shot possibilities, keeping his story points firmly in mind, and guarding against physical continuity becoming more important than story value. He is inclined to visualize his shots freely and place them on the storyboard purely for purposes of reference and recall. During the actual shooting process, he may deviate considerably from his original plan. The storyboard then can serve the film-maker much as a general outline serves the writer. The idea is to work with an outline, but not to let it be so rigid that one cannot depart from it.

The most important value of the storyboard is that it prepares the film-maker for the very difficult task of shooting. It serves to bring his thinking before him, so that he can examine it objectively and check to see if it will serve him properly. The more he reviews his plans and examines his reasons, the better prepared he becomes to reach his objective.

Subsidiary elements that go toward making up the whole film —sound effects, music, titles, art work—should definitely be considered and related to these initial stages of planning. The over-all production design might well be developed to include the following areas: script, script analysis, camera values, story-board, music, sound effects, costumes, technical lighting, and graphics and art work. Although each of these areas eventually will be developed in full detail as it applies to the specific film, it is best in the early stages to cover each in an analytical rather than in a technical way. Thus, rather than immediately entering into a discussion with the lighting technician, scene designer, costumer, or composer, the film-maker at first works independently to pin down his personal interpretations of the script through each of these areas. No doubt the contributing artists will have valid suggestions and may even make contributions beyond the film-maker's scope; but his is the guiding hand, and it is his preparation and interpretation that later enable him to discuss intelligently and choose well from among the ideas of others. Again, nothing helps this development so much as thoughts clarified by writing. Writing is a mode of expression that forces one to think clearly, as was so aptly expressed by the newspaper columnist who complained when his paper was on strike, "How can I know what I think if I don't read it in my column?"

The way in which the film-maker plans his ideas and feelings about costumes, music, sets, etc., is purely a matter of preference. Sound effects, for example, can be charted or diagramed; graphics or costuming can be sketched. Still, it is wise to leave sketching, diagraming, and designing to those who do them well. Usually there is a tendency in such layouts to become involved with outward trappings. It is best for the film-maker to express himself clearly to co-workers so that they can execute and arrive at the desired values. Carefully organized and arranged notes, written out, help to gain this end.

THE SHOT PLANE

"Plane" refers to the way the shot has been set up in terms of shallowness and depth. Theoretically, the more the subject moves toward or away from the camera (or the camera from it), the more realistic the scene. Conversely, the more the scene is flattened—played from side to side in one plane—the more artificial it seems, giving an illusion of the appearance of reality, rather than of reality itself.

In the early days of television, and perhaps even today when studio space is limited, the rule was to shoot from depth, staging the action in a plane moving away from the camera (deep), rather than horizontal to it (shallow). The shots were set up that way for expediency only, and not because of any regard for their emotional connotation. However, even a simple series of reverse angles, which might seem to be unaffected by their staging, since the camera always cuts from behind one subject to look over the shoulder of the second, can be made to express subtle connotative differences. This is because the camera has no real "front" view. Unlike the playgoer, the filmviewer—because of the camera's mobility—is not confined to seeing from only one vantage point. The camera has unlimited perspectives and the planes shift constantly, deep in a long shot and shallow in a close-up. Second, the generally flattening effect of a close-up can either be increased or decreased both through camera angle and lighting. Therefore, in the traditional reverse angle, despite its seeming "sameness," as the camera takes a two-shot from in front to set up for the reverse, the tendency is to flatten; and as it moves into a reverse, to a point of view of one of the subjects, it deepens. Thus even slight changes in the camera's point of view affect mood values and can heighten the scene's tendency toward the comic, serious, sentimental, or menacing.

Realism in film comedy is not helped by shots in multiplane

staging, but by the basic truth of the comic departure of the subject matter. The story is immediately recognizable as actual life, highly selected in terms of satire, character foibles, or action; and the single-plane staging emphasizes this relationship. The seeming artificiality of the single plane, or flatness of the shot, heightens the ludicrousness and introduces a comic incongruity. For example Chaplin films of the middle and later period immediately point up the extremely human, true quality of the tramp, no matter how incongruous his situation. The desires, hopes, ambitions, and frustrations of the little character with the cane and moustache were universally felt and understood.

It is said that the Mack Sennett comedies faded away because of the advent of a little mouse who was animated, and that animation was more appropriate for comic rendering. The point that does not seem to have been considered is the much greater degree of human attributes possessed by Mickey Mouse than by the characters of Mack Sennett. Certainly, animated drawing made possible the rendering of impossible situations that challenged the wildest imagination, yet these were acceptable and believable because of the realism implied in the mouse's characterization.

The flat and shallow plane shot is as realistic as the shot in depth, but its realism is founded on appearance rather than on actuality. Yet another part of plane shot that affects final values is depth of field. The more the lens aperture is stopped down, the greater the area that will be in focus from foreground to background. The more the lens aperture is opened up, the shallower the depth of field and the narrower the area that will appear sharp. Therefore, staging of the action in whatever plane is also affected by the lens aperture setting, which increases or decreases the depth of field. Therefore, the effect of action staged in a shallow plane and moving from right to left could be cancelled out by being photographed with the lens aperture stopped down too far. The greater the depth of field, the more multiplaned the effect of the shot; and the shallower the field the more single-planed the shot as recorded by the camera.

Again, hard and fast rules cannot be set down as to the degree of depth of field or its relationship to staging of the comic film in terms of depth. Its use must naturally grow out of story content. Not only are there comic stories providing an extremely wide range of situation comedy, character, satire, tragi-comedy, and farce, but the degrees of realism in each may vary as greatly. Although it is true that success relates to believability rooted in reality, the degree of actual realism found in shots may be considerably varied. Backgrounds in some cases may be indistinct blurs, depending on the point of view of the film-maker, and rightly so, because stylistic consistency is achieved by such control.

Although the choice of planes is important in the comic film, it is just as vital in the serious film, where its effects are still more subtle. In a serious realistic story the range can extend from shots so real that they smack of actuality itself to more generally realistic representations as found in the melodramas. These are differences of which the viewer is unaware, but to which he reacts emotionally. Yet the film-maker must decide on staging in terms of plane, as well as on the amount of depth of field. The decision is not so simple as merely superimposing depth or shallowness in the staging, or shortness or depth of field on a series of shots. The total effect of the story must dictate the choices.

Certainly, Tony Richardson's manipulation of shots in *Tom Jones* (1963), or Pierre Etaix's arrangement and staging in *The Suitor* (1963), is not by accident, but by design. The degrees of difference in the use of plane as handled through the camera in those films might well be compared with the use of plane by René Clair, one of the masters of comic inventiveness, in *Le Million* (1931) and *Á Nous La Liberté* (1931). All four of these films are first-rate examples of film comedy; yet René Clair is given to more angularity and formal symmetry in his staging, with the shot plane kept mostly shallow, while Tony Richardson stresses incongruity by jumping from deep to shallow and the reverse, mixed with "frozen" frames and stills—a kind of organized abandon. Pierre Étaix, on the other hand, uses flat, shallow shots as points of emphasis, generally staging in some depth, and then pulling his camera around for a single-planed shot at appropriate moments. In all these films coordination of all the elements has been mastered perfectly, and the proper use of plane has been worked in to coincide with the basic design.

OBJECTIVE AND SUBJECTIVE APPROACHES

The word "theme" among film-makers, at least those in more rarefied circles, is sometimes ambiguous. It is used freely to mean what the story is about, rather than the specific point of view growing out of the story and having to do with philosophical, religious, or ethical attitudes. By this definition every story does indeed have a theme, but the issue lies in whether the theme is a subject for discussion and argument. If what the story is about is not worth discussing, if it is so trite, innocuous, or general (like being against sin) that no one would argue about it, then it really does not have a theme. A cops-and-robbers film, for instance, where the robber gets his "comeuppance" at the end, has a moral but not a theme.

The difference between films with stereotyped values and films that truly affect man's thinking is the difference between the pulp story and those classics of literature that seem ageless and fresh in their richness. Yet somehow these distinctions, long accepted in the literary field, have not been so universally accepted by those interested in film, much less the filmgoing public; still the handwriting on the wall is growing clearer. However, the film, like other creative endeavors, has various levels of attainment. The film-maker, like many an author who sits down to write the Great American Novel, may find that he can only be as successful as his talent will allow. And, like his fellow author, he will find that all successful artistic effort demands heat, passion, inspiration, and a rational foundation.

However, it is just as stuffy and pedantic to insist on themes with philosophical, religious, or ethical overtones as it is vapid to stick to simple, moralistic stories. Whatever philosophy, religion, or ethic shapes the film-maker's point of view will shape his approach to the film and ultimately the film itself, if he resolutely pursues the truth in his story as he sees it. Only with such pursuit can the multiple elements of his film be artistically realized.

The top-notch film, then, is both implicit and fluid, given to all sorts of movement based on craft and intent, and constantly seeking to ignite the viewer. Through the story itself the film-maker can communicate his deeply felt attitudes toward life, utilizing either a subjective or an objective approach.

The objective approach is that of the rationalist. He stands apart from his subject matter, seeing it coldly and clearly. Analyzing and understanding the natures of the people involved in the story, he brings them together to shape up a structure, to have a point of view emerge from the character's actions and reactions. As a film-maker he is at least once removed from his material, not associating himself with it directly. He accurately and carefully works out the refinements of story that take on a universal quality, seemingly devoid of the film-maker's presence.

The subjective approach is that of the emotionalist. He becomes involved with his subject matter, not separating himself from it, but rather becoming a definite part of it. He is deeply affected by mood, tone, and related ideas, feeling strongly the undercurrents of what he has to say, bringing together those elements he finds exciting and excitable, and precipitating causal relationships to arrive at ends that, in all likelihood, are not too clearly defined. Because he sees so much through his own eyes, emotion may give way to passion, and passion to bad judgment.

The objective approach is the disciplined one, and the film-maker is relatively assured of having his audience understand him and his story. The motivation is clear, the effects precise, and the relationships and development of ideas accurate. The typical failings are a lack of heart, the absence of compassion, and a bareness leading to sterility. The subjective approach, conversely, may lack the discipline necessary for understanding and clarity. The heat and the passion may be useless because too much of the film is obscure, with shots coming across as a pretension, appearing to have purpose yet signifying nothing.

The average Hollywood film, for example, is primarily objective and affects no one appreciably. The audience's reaction is often a bland "So?" For an example of the subjective approach one may look to the self-styled new American cinema movement, whose films are thoroughly understood and enjoyed by only one member of the audience, the film-maker himself, because he lacks the necessary discipline to communicate.

Neither method is best as a basic approach, nor is there necessarily any kind of connection between these approaches and kinds of film, say the narrative or the documentary. These differences are purely working methods growing out of the personality of the film-maker. Both types of approach fall short, each in its own way, yet both are valid and essential. The danger lies in that, even in the final stages of the film, the film-maker will never pick up the attributes of the opposite method. This does not mean that through effort and development one approach blends with the other to introduce a new and perfect one. The film-maker whose attitude is objective must achieve the necessary subjectivity, not by assuming the point of view of his counterpart, but by a continuing study of his characters and story in depth. Penetration into the subject supplies a kind of subjectivity without altering his point of view, thus allowing the film to develop power and passion. On the other hand, compensation for a subjective approach does not entail a pullback from keen insight into character and story. Discipline is what is sorely needed. Often, the so-called depth and insight are in reality lots of smoke and little fire, emotionalism without substance. The subjective film-maker must clarify his substance by analysis and structure development, with close scrutiny of the causal relationships. Thus themes worthy of attention and developed through both approaches can convey the emotional and intellectual stand of the film-maker for an impartial audience to participate in and enjoy.

MECHANICS OF PLANNING

In the making of a film, aside from creative effort, much is required of the film-maker in the way of technical knowledge and organizational know-how. Unfortunately, his mastery of these areas can lead to such a sense of accomplishment and satisfaction that he may be trapped into forgetting why he initially set out to make a film. It is not unusual, for example, for him to become so absorbed in the technical aspects of lip synchronization that he overlooks what is being said. Nor is it unusual for him to forget about the meaning of his scenes, after having spent countless hours absorbed in the details of charts, graphs, and layouts that are used to indicate the ways and means for the film to be made. There are levels of creative work, of course, and just about all of them are present in the production of a film in one way or another. Much of seemingly routine work in film is such a challenge that it also has its compensations—the satisfaction of seeing the successful birth of each little unit (artistic or not), as well as the excitement of logistics.

The film-maker, or the director in the case of feature productions, has the job of keeping the basic concept as his constant objective and having everything else satisfy this end. The script itself serves as the control center. Since all the breakdown planning relates to the script, it has to be realized as fully as possible. Tales are only too numerous about actors and sets being held up at exorbitant costs, while writers hastily put the finishing touches to scripts.

Planning naturally reflects the complexity of film production and covers many areas of the operation. Some planning has to do with the expenses involved, with the operation of production, and with postproduction as the film reaches the editing and recording stages. And all this is separate from the creative planning already mentioned.

Budgeting the film calls for a detailed breakdown of costs for the script, producer, director, cast, the producing organization, production expense, film and laboratory costs, editing, studio and facilities, and any indirect expenses from items of travel to miscellaneous props. Generally these are arranged into "above the line" and "below the line" expenses to distinguish the actual cost of making of the film from salaries, fees and/or percentages for the writer, producer, director, and high-priced actors. Experienced production managers are absolutely indispensable when it comes to arranging and handling the innumerable production details.

Production planning, handled by assistant directors and script supervisors, calls for the assemblage of a breakdown sheet, shooting schedule, call sheet (designating cast, crew, equipment, time and place of shooting), cross plot (designating scenes to be filmed, actors involved, extras and crew over a given period of time or for the length of the shooting), actor and costume lists, and prop lists. During the actual shooting, a daily film production report is kept to show the work completed, time involved, cast and crew involved, and the over-all costs. A separate camera report sheet is an exact log of every foot of exposed film. It accompanies the film to the processing laboratory so that only designated shots are printed.

The operation of a major feature is not much different from running a good-sized manufacturing plant. If anything, it is even more difficult, considering the arrangements to be made and the movement involved as the cast and crew go from location to location. Smaller film operations are not much simpler, as the involvements are identical.

On student productions, which are greatly limited in scope, much of the organizational planning can be accomplished on the single sheet storyboard. The shots are laid out in the three-by-four inch square, following the sequence as prescribed by the script. A shooting order can be set up by rearranging these shots in the order in which they are to be taken. Through this arrangement the storyboards are no longer in continuity, but are grouped according to ease for shooting. Groupings may be set up according to silent and sound shots, varying locations, or numbers of actors involved. During actual production, these sheets not only guide the shooting, but also serve to log pertinent information concerning the shot taken. Finally, with the film completely shot, the storyboard serves the editor as a written account of all that has been made available on film and the details pertaining to it. This kind of storyboard is a combination of the breakdown and shooting schedule. It is fairly effective for a single reel of film, but certainly not broad enough in scope to carry the details required for a feature-length picture.

The move from the breakdown plan to the taking of the .irst shot is a giant step and the beginning of a totally new type of activity. An initial inertia brought about by paper work has to be overcome. The first setups may be slow in getting started, the crew not yet up to smooth and coordinated teamwork. The film-maker, feeling his way, perhaps a little insecure and uncertain, must take creative command as the film-making gets underway. It is obvious, however, that in film-making, no matter how lofty and idealistic the intentions of those engaged in the work, success or failure go hand in hand with economic planning, efficient organization, and a functioning integrated unit. The latter is the base on which the artistic effort rests, and it is undertaken, not principally to save time and money, but to use it well. Interestingly, in so many behind-the-scenes accounts, "botches" usually result not only from artistic failure, but from inadequate planning and organization.

On major film productions, of course, there are units and departments specifically set up to handle and arrange the whole organizational pattern. On small productions, some of these tasks may well fall to the film-maker. But the pitfall is the same, whether working on the large scale or the small—that the film-maker will be caught up in the manufacture of a film, rather than the artistic creation of one. Because the film-maker's prime concern is the artistic rendering of his production, the best procedure is to leave the planning breakdown to those who do it well.

LIGHTING, LENSES, AND FILTERS

Because light is the basis on which the feeling, tone, and mood of the shot are developed, it has to be planned as part of the over-all pattern to coordinate and project the scene. It is motivated, of course, by the story line; but all too often the lighting is planned only in terms of the individual shot, rather than of the way the shots will come together. As related shots form a pattern depicting the story, light patterns—evaluated in blacks, whites, and grays—also form a pattern to delineate the story further.

The implementation of these patterns through the physical setup of lighting units often proceeds on a trial-and-error basis, rather than on a pre-set plan that supports the ultimate objective. Light is the essence of visual articulation and has to be constructed as part of the total story design. Light, therefore, has two specific functions: the first and obvious one is that there must be sufficient light to illuminate the scene so that it will register on film; and the second is that the light must characterize the scene. The two are not mutually exclusive.

The general use of the terms "high key" and "low key" to describe kinds of lighting—a predominance of light areas for comic or gay scenes, or of dark areas for mystery or drama—tends to oversimplify light's varied and subtle contributions. To speak in the broad terms of comedy, mystery, or drama is far too vague to provide the technical specialist with sufficient information for him to use his lights with purpose. To determine the nature of the lights to be used, their amount, and kind, a specific and detailed breakdown of the emotional progression of the story is required, to reveal those values emanating from actual setting, characters involved, and the resultant action. This information is then incorporated into a light plot.

Obtaining emotional values that further enhance and interpret scenes is a matter of using light with design in mind. Differences between crisp morning light and the diffuse, soft light of late afternoon are immediately apparent. Yet these are obvious extremes, the nuances of shading and extent of control are as limitless as shot content. Growing out of these uses of light are general feelings that contribute emotionally to the story: feelings of heat or cold, of acceptance or rejection, of confinement or release, of fulfillment or frustration, of life or death. In addition, as light is used from shot to shot it takes on a progressive movement, and thus can be worked into a meaningful pattern. This pattern, like shots, can be worked to expand or diminish the emotional qualities of the scenes. In Alan Resnais's *Last Year at Marienbad* (1961), such planning is carefully worked out and, in addition, specific values are found through shock arrangement as evenly lit scenes are suddenly contrasted with hard-lit overexposed ones. More than this, the frustration of the failure of memory is also achieved, and transitions are instantaneous.

In working out particular patterns and plots, the film-maker sets his lights either from an arbitrary or a justified point of view, depending on the nature of his story. In those instances where the approach is arbitrary, justification for the source of light is not necessary. The scene is illuminated with no apparent central source. The audience accepts illumination as a convention, not questioning the well-lit expanse of scene before it. In a justified situation, the scene contains a specific fixture, a table lamp, an overhead light, lamppost, car headlight, or candlelight and, using this as a central visible source within the scene, the film-maker develops his lighting plot around it. Both of these approaches are general in nature and simply lay the groundwork for the detailed working out of fixture selection and placement.

Further aspects of light as it contributes to pattern are to be found not only in terms of light and dark, but also lightness and heaviness, flatness or depth, shape and form, and hardness or softness. Design values remain nonobjective, yet, when properly coupled with content, assume telling proportions. An extremely good example of this is to be found in Ingmar Bergman's *The Seventh Seal* (1956), from the opening scene foreshadowing doom, in which the morning light has an expectant sharpness, to the murky dimness of the forest, and so on to the final scenes of the dancers silhouetted against the sky. In each and every scene—the confessional, the performance followed by the flagellants, the scene in the inn, the scene outside on the street between the girl to be crucified and the knight—the lighting provokes intensified feelings related to, but separate from, the articulated characteristics of the scene. The light has become a functioning part of the pattern.

The lighting specialist proceeds according to his craft to determine his key light (source light), side light (for depth and dimension), modeling light, back light, background light, fills, kickers, and boosters, in order to achieve the required effect. But for all the technical matériel and know-how involved, successful control of light can be no greater than the film-maker's understanding of his scene's objectives.

Strongly related to light in terms of mood values is the relationship of the central subject in each shot to the area around it within the frame. This is determined by the specific lens used. It is not enough, for instance, to decide on a long shot. In three long shots of the same subject, each taken with a different lens— say, a normal lens, a wide-angle, or a telephoto—the relationship of the subject to the amount of visible background in the frame is totally different and projects a different feeling and mood. Each such relationship also has its own compositional value, which in series with other shots makes a pattern that should contribute its own values to strengthen those of the story. When such values are blended with those of action and movement that grow out of the story, the total effect is one of heightened impact.

In addition, lens selection is based on degrees of distortion. The wider angle lenses, for example, give much greater distortion, whereas the normal lens more closely approximates the human eye and therefore gives the shot a more "normal" sense of reality. Also, desirable as sharpness may be in a film, within the range of acceptable focus there are degrees of sharpness that affect the mood values. The sharply etched characteristics of a Dürer work or the softer miasmic feeling of the French impressionists can be reproduced by use of the appropriate lens.

Filters too have a precise function. They correct the photographic image to get light values as they actually appear when shooting, or alter these values by heightening the contrast, creating haze, or eliminating it. Filters should not be used to "pretty everything up," but only to help clarify the basic values.

Numerous technicians, of all sorts and many talents, are essential to the successful completion of the film. If left alone, they will automatically find a *raison d'être* for their work; they cannot function without it. But if each proceeds on the basis of his own *raison d'être*, the various units of the film will be at odds and in chaotic conflict. All the technical work that is carried on must be motivated and controlled by one source: the film-maker's interpretation of the script. And for this to be possible, the plan must be clear.

MUSIC, SOUND, AND ART WORK

Because the planning and taking of the shot is the hub around which a film develops, the beginning film-maker is apt to delay decisions concerning music, sound effects, title, and art work, areas that can contribute immeasurably to a film's success. The failing is easily understood, as shot planning calls for a host of decisions to be made. The addition of music, effects, and titles simply increases this number. In addition, these extra considerations force the film-maker, at a time when he is least inclined to do so, to see the film as a whole, with all the components interwoven. The task becomes particularly onerous because he finds security in the abstract values of his story and sees its reality on one level, that of the physical setup of the shot. But now the point is pushed almost to the very presentation of the scene as it will appear on the screen, which requires an extremely precise, piece-by-piece development of every unit and all units, at a time when the film-maker may not be in complete control of his material. The shots and their development, although planned in detail, still contain an element of fluidity to account for the variations, changes, and doubts about the effectiveness of some of them. Still, as important as the shots are, they alone do not make up the total film. Their success is based on their relationship to those components with which they blend to yield content. Often the shot itself is quite incomplete without its full definition through the rhythm of music, or through sound effects acting in complement or counterpoint.

Another reason for the beginner's hesitation to move readily into this area is his unwillingness to share his work with those who can seriously contribute to it. With the full knowledge that eventually he wants the services of others, the beginner, either through inertia, laziness, or selfishness, is inclined to regard his work as singularly his; outsiders are to remain outside. This attitude is immature and unprofessional, and is roughly akin to the attitude of the amateur writer who cannot bear to see one word of his masterpiece changed by anyone else. Alas, the result of such an attitude is often that the film at best may end as a compromise.

Film requires the services of many artists proficient in their specialized areas. Furthermore, such artists can assist the film-maker immeasurably, bringing an objectivity to the work; ideas and suggestions they provide may open new avenues for development; the questions they ask and the information they demand act as challenges to the film-maker to check on his own feelings and thoughts about the work at hand. Composers, sound-effects men, and graphic artists contribute to a film as interpretive artists in their own right. The composer, engaged in the actual work of scoring for the film, needs a precisely measured count of every foot of film, and the film itself has to be cued. But decisions he faces as to kind, type, style, and amount of music, instrumentation, and purpose can well be taken up in the initial phases of planning.

A column breakdown, in which the film development is laid out with corresponding columns set aside for notes to be made by the musician and effects man, serves as a working point. Such a list provides all concerned with a clear account of the ways in which the various elements will work together, where one leaves off, where the other takes up, where one backs the other, or where two share the contribution, etc. It brings the basic elements—unity, proportion, emphasis—into a clearer focus, so that the film as a whole may be checked and evaluated.

For all that might be said about the film finding its greatest strength through the personal statement of the film-maker, it remains a combination of arts. This statement is neither untenable nor contradictory to all that has been said before. The impetus of the film and its dominating influence still must come from the film-maker himself.

ARTINESS AS A PITFALL

A word of caution is in order to the young film-maker, who may very easily be carried away by techniques and tricks. All of the topics thus far discussed have belabored one point at the risk of being repetitious: the film's value lies in its substance, and the successful communication of that substance lies first in its exploration. No matter how much may be known about lighting, camera angles, movement, staging, or the innumerable other factors that must be considered in the production of a film, all are nothing more than tools for putting across an idea. Most important is that even the mastery of those crafts can lead to the production of ineffective and pretentious films unless the mastery is at the service of a meaningful story.

All the works of the men cited as examples demonstrate this point. Craft techniques that run counter to traditional methods are not successful simply because they are opposed to the usual way of doing things. They are successful because the ideas to be communicated necessitated their use. Michelangelo Antonioni in the opening scene of *The Eclipse* (1962), for instance, shows a man and a woman breaking up a relationship. To project the agitation and denial of such a scene, to show the actors as entities each in a separate world, the camera and cutting set a pattern through the jump-cut and the severe angle. Yet it is not a sufficient explanation to say that because two people are shown breaking up one may take whatever liberties with camera and technique one wishes. The very nature of the breakup is finely delineated in feelings and attitudes; the mounting pressures within the characters and on each other are carefully analyzed and understood; and the progression of the scene is most carefully calculated to reflect these developing pressures. Thus the camera is aimed.

The externals of film-making—the equipment and the craft technique—can be the film-maker's greatest enemies as well as his working tools. For a film-maker to understand what he is really saying—what his relationship is to his point, and where, how, and why he stands as he does in regard to his subject matter—is tedious, arduous labor. And the labor is most difficult because it is emotional and intellectual in nature. Conversely, setting up cables and lights, making countless thousands of splices, or becoming involved with the logistics of production, as enervating as these may be, provide a release or a defense behind which one can hide.

The film-maker can very easily exhaust himself by undertaking untold amounts of physical labor, feeling the full satisfaction of such effort, but all the while avoiding the real work that must be done. Sometimes he is unaware of his tricky sidestepping until his film is on the screen and his audience begins to cough, talk, and move about in their seats restlessly.

Yet, to say that substance has to be explored in depth, that motivation must be found for what is being said, and that all technique springs from this source is really vague and unsatisfactory. How does the film-maker know when he is in full control of his material? How can he differentiate between a trick and a valid technique? How can he be certain that his feelings are genuine, that certain values are truth, that an insight has been gained? There are no pat answers, because these conditions are directly related to the film-maker's individual talent. Many men have spent their lives seeking the unattainable. There are many levels and degrees of talent, and one of the most significant steps the film-maker can take is to determine the nature of his ability. Even this step is sometimes impossible. Nevertheless, the film-maker can only arrive—if he arrives at all—through trial, error, and experimentation; he develops sensitivity and maturity through his work and through constant analysis of the work of others; he learns to see, think, and feel as does any practitioner of the older arts. To avoid the superficial trappings that might well engulf a picture, he must constantly challenge himself, and yet move on with conviction.

THE FILM
PRODUCTION

The tendency among film-makers engaged in the mass production of film is to pre-set a script down to the last detail, so that the shooting and editing of it are by and large purely mechanical processes, much like the printing of a book. This working method deprives the film of its possibilities, and yet to blame all on economics is to find a convenient scapegoat. For example, a good number of international film-makers have broken from that method, yet do not appear to be on the verge of bankruptcy. The key issue lies in the nature of film-making and, from this, the interpretation and purpose of pre-planning. Much of the film's creative processes are in the shooting and editing, in the execution rather than the planning. The function of the plan is to bring the film-maker as close as possible to an understanding of his objective, rather than to the specific way in which he is going to work it out.

To be sure, he plans with specifics in mind, but he might devise two, three, or four different ways of setting up the shots for one scene, and then spontaneously create something totally new at the time of shooting. Planning with thoroughness prepares him for such spontaneity, and this is the value of the plan —to get to the heart of the material, not to set up limitations and restrictions. Preplanning for film has to be thorough, precise, and detailed, so that the abstract values of story can be brought into clear and sharp definition.

Film production calls for an even greater creative molding throughout all its processes—planning, production, and editing —than the stage play. In the days of the silents, a film was often based primarily on a rough story outline, with many of the shots improvised during the production; and the final development of the story emerged in editing. The advent of sound brought in restrictions, along with precisely set scripts. The precisely set plans followed. Although technical developments brought considerable freedom once again, it is highly questionable whether that freedom has truly released the film from the bonds of dialogue, or whether tradition has set in to such a degree that the minds of some film-makers have already "jelled."

The crux of the matter lies in the distinction between the stage play and the film script. To be able to differentiate among long shots, close-ups, and medium shots in the writing stages of a film script is a far cry from combining the aural with visually intensified shots for storytelling in filmic terms. The film is made up of action and reaction based on movement, with a camera in the midst of it, now looking at it one way, now another, and constantly bringing out relationships. The work done in planning clarifies the objectives within a general framework of abstract story values, but the shooting and final selection remain spontaneous. Such spontaneity goes hand-in-hand with sophistication, and reflects the film's growth. The film today is in a period of just such growth and expansion. The essence of its growth lies more and more in finding this true relationship between dialogue and picture, and returning to those discoveries begun by the film-makers of the silent days, temporarily halted by sound.

THE APPROACH

In the early days of film-making the usual procedure was to rehearse the actors while the crew prepared for the shot. To help the actors get into the correct mood, violinists (playing Hungarian strains mostly) stood just beyond the frame of the shot. The stories being what they were and the thinking of the time being what it was—that the audiences would miss any nuances —hand wringing, eyebrow raising, and "hamming" were the order of the day. Although today the musicians have disappeared and the acting methods are subtle and intense, the technique of actor preparation varies considerably, not only among film-makers in Hollywood, but among film-makers of different countries as well.

These differences are governed by many factors: the nature of the story and its requirements; the personal working methods of the film-maker and what he finds most rewarding as he relates to his actors; local working methods, conditions, and quality of experience of cast and crew; the savings brought about by having a rehearsed cast so that the crew is constantly shooting; and the nature of the shots to be taken (the action can be such that live rehearsals with crew are imperative). In other words, directing actors in film is extremely varied, and depends on personal needs and the working conditions that the film-maker finds most suitable. The end result is all that counts; yet because both art and technology are constantly present, the film-maker arrives at his working methods by examining the needs of one in the light of the other. Actors in some instances might be completely ignored, as all of the attention goes to the work of the camera crew. In other instances, the reverse is true. Unlike the theater director, the film-maker cannot give himself constantly to his actors at all times.

The prerehearsed cast, therefore, introduces important advantages. With actors prerehearsed, the task becomes one of recall and spontaneity, and the time the crew spends waiting is reduced considerably. Also, the film-maker must not only be of assistance to the actor, but must also observe and establish the characteristics of the shot as well. The latter can be so demanding that with mounting pressure little or no time is available to assist the actor to develop his role. Prerehearsal gives the actor the opportunity to understand his role. Because films are shot out of sequence and in bits and pieces, the actor has the problem of securing continuity in his acting while acting out of continuity.

In the theater, plays are generally directed over a six-week period, and the actor has the opportunity to grow and develop in the role. The structure of the play is relatively apparent, so that cause and effect appear as motivating forces and the characterization becomes complete. In any kind of work, the worker usually functions better when he understands the objective of his work and the way in which it contributes to the end result. This is equally true of the film actor, but he has a more difficult time.

A number of steps can be taken prior to shooting to secure and fix the role of the actor. First, much as in theater, stories can be read and discussed, so that basic familiarization is achieved and the actor can come to understand his character and the way it relates to others. At this time, the actor can begin to assimilate his role on an intellectual level, as he learns what the character seeks, why he does what he does and feels as he does, what happens to him, and the nature of his reaction. Because this understanding must link with related emotional reaction, the actor can get further help by becoming familiar with the places in which the story occurs. The second step, therefore, introduces a familiarization with environment. And third, for the actor to develop the role, pieces can be rehearsed in or out of continuity, with the actor sometimes being apprised of the nature of the shots that may be in mind. To fix the entire continuity of staging in the actor's mind may be difficult, for he may attempt to relate physical areas and things to mood and plot progression, as he would in preparing for a stage play. It is advantageous, therefore, to rehearse freely in terms of sequences or scenes in and out of continuity, developing the actor constantly so that his interpretation of the role is seen as a life in constant being, rather than as a succession of organized and steadily mounting disclosures.

Film in the making is a kind of disordered order. The actor must become a part of this kind of fluid life, rather than a prescribed characterization developed within a fixed framework. Working in a Shakespearean play, for example, with its multiple scenes and fluid staging, is good experience for a film actor.

Sufficient prerehearsal, then, is not only invaluable to the actor, but is well worthwhile to the film-maker. The actor, through recall and association—with a minimum of discussion —frees the film-maker to control the shooting from the over-all view: interpretation, interrelationships, harmony of playing and style, composition, mood, tone, movement, angle, distance, and build. The film-maker is not only engaged in a creative and artistic effort, but also in governing and guiding the creative and artistic efforts of others. Prerehearsed periods enable him to establish a rapport with his actors, to make clear his own objectives, his personal involvement, his meaning, and his intentions, thus earning respect and revealing his appreciation for those who would work with him.

Yet, for all that may be said about prior preparation, there are many film-makers who would take issue with the point, and rightly so. Because of the demands of the story and his personal attitude toward it, the film-maker may not want the actor to act at all, but simply to be. Rehearsal in such instances can prove disastrous, as the actor may act when all he need do is be himself, or an absolute blank, or nothing but a figure moving from point to point. Departure from theatrical tradition can be total as the camera takes on the bulk of the work. Then again, the film-maker has his own talent to contend with: does he work actors best under pressure? Can he reinstill spontaneity if his actors are prerehearsed? Can he capture more subtle reactions in a moment than with hours of rehearsal? These are difficult questions and can only be determined by the film-maker through his experience.

By the same token, periods may or may not be set aside for thorough and complete briefings of the technical staff to discuss the story elements in considerable depth. Many film-makers will undertake a film only if they can work with a specific camera-man—the point being that a rapport has been established. The cameraman, through past associations, knows his director and his aims, and can anticipate his needs. Technicians, interestingly enough, not only understand the artistic point of view and can make excellent contributions, but also have a refreshing earthiness about them to jolt the film-maker out of wild and fanciful dreams.

Briefings and discussions may appear time consuming and may arouse an element of impatience, but usually they set up a number of conditions necessary to successful filming. Aside from the values already discussed, this approach provides each working member with a chance to identify with the film, and gives the film-maker the opportunity to check his planning against his crew and cast. They are actually his first audience, partial to be sure, but still sufficiently challenging. Beyond this, he gives himself the opportunity to gain control of the production gradually and with authority. Even at best, film-making is a process of chaos and confusion, and a strong guiding hand is needed. If the film-maker fails to provide it, someone else will, thus wresting control from him.

Squabbles between producers and directors, directors and

actors, or director and technicians occur more often when interpretation is fuzzy, definition unclear, or directions confused. To eliminate these is the better part of field work. True, some difficulties are those of personality, and no amount of briefing or rehearsal can solve them. But briefing and rehearsal periods may bring them to light at a time when something can be done about them, and not just before or while a shot is being taken.

Primarily, the film-maker is in a "hot seat" as he maneuvers his people to get the best from them. The film-maker must look to his own strengths and failings, and from these draw his approach and working methods. Unfortunately, this does not happen until after many pictures have been made.

PREPARING THE ACTOR

It has been said that the documentary film is based on the premise that "there is nothing so interesting to ourselves as ourselves."[1] Today, this premise appears even truer of acting as demonstrated in the work by international film-makers. Such actors as Soumitra Chatterjee, Marcello Mastroianni, Tom Courtenay, Albert Finney, Monica Vitti, and Simone Signoret are but a few of the many who are adding a new dimension to the art. John Crosby, in an interview with Pierre Rissient, the director of the Cercle du MacMahon, a New Wave Film group, reported that "Rissient thinks the most important aspect of it is the insistence that actors live rather than act, that they are not playing, they are being."[2]

Some film directors who are part of the movement might tend to disagree, claiming that cutting and editing have been respon-

---

[1] Paul Rotha, *Documentary Film* (New York: Hastings House, 1963), p. 123.

[2] John Crosby, "The Nouvelle Vague Set," *New York Herald Tribune*, October 1, 1962, Sec. 2, p. 21.

sible for the new film. This point hardly can be questioned, but it is just as apparent that the new approach and development have come through a different handling of all aspects of film-making: approach to script, point of view, methods of shooting, use of camera, and editing. The manner, method, and kind of acting are equally affected. Living or "being" the part appears to be the key. However, a good amount of the "living not acting" school of interpretation might be a reflection of the film-maker's point of view toward the new stories, which demand ultra-realistic treatment because of their slice-of-life orientation. Such stories depend for artistic merit on an extremely sensitive degree of selection combined with utmost faithfulness in representing what has been selected. Thus, the faintest suggestion of acting destroys the impact. One way the film-maker avoids this is by typecasting. Typecasting in this sense is making an actor out of someone who has actually lived the role or been quite close to it. Stathis Giallelis in Elia Kazan's *America, America* (1963) is a case in point.

Such typecasting is not like the age-old Hollywood method of "typing" individuals, as a cigar-chewing, garrulous old soak; or a chuckle-in-the-throat smirking killer; or a don't-know-what-to-do-with-the-hands bird-brained maid. Nor is it the playing of "personality," that kind of acting that is not acting at all, but a case of the actor being completely and utterly his charming self: a long-legged, drawling, handsome individual given to understatement; or a charming, soft-spoken Englishman; or a tough, wiry side-of-the-mouth talker and brawler. Rather the actor is treated as a totality, a human being with dimensions, not as a cliché, a type, nor a one-dimensional personality.

The one or two instances in which types have been found and turned into actors in no way explain the success of Leslie Caron, Alberto Sordi, Vittorio Gassman, and many others who are part of the "being" school. Whether there is a real difference between highly realistic acting as practiced in the theater and this school is a moot point, and the deciding factor may very well be in the ultrarealistic approach. The "being" acting is conditioned by the loose, seemingly disjointed, and flowing quality of the story, in which lines of dialogue are not formulated as in theater, but have a casual, every-day naturalness about them. This "throw-away" conversation secures meaning through accompanying action, with characterization and idea projected through the camera and the way in which it interprets the action.

Acting of this kind, however, is not necessarily easy, nor are the actors less talented than they appear. On the contrary, the acting is singularly good; not only is it in harmony with its material, projecting its own style and dimension, but it also calls for a demanding and penetrating restraint by both the film-maker and the actor.

Although this kind of acting blends perfectly with the "real life" quality of film, it is not really suited to all kinds of stories; therefore, the film-maker must understand the great variety of theatrical acting styles and their adaptation to the film within its essentially realistic framework.

Aside from its various styles—traditional, classic, romantic, realistic, and naturalistic—acting is also arbitrary or motivated. Arbitrary acting, whatever the style, is usually called for in comedy. It depends on abrupt movements, single and double takes, and halting reaction with lack of follow-through, all expressly to point up a line, put over a gag, or secure some specific effect for a laugh. The tremendous range of such acting is apparent when one considers that it takes in not only Elizabethan comedies and drawing-room comedies, but burlesque as well. It can also be applied in the romantic or realistic story.

Motivated acting, on the other hand, is characterized by a greater degree of follow-through; smoother, integrated movements; and more cause and effect. It strives to approximate real life and, with the addition of more and more definition, reaches complete naturalism. However, there is room for variation here too, in that at the other end of the scale from naturalism there are the larger-than-life demands of melodramatic realism or historical romance.

To complicate the picture still further, two types of actor training have developed during the realistic tradition, which has been present in both film and theater during the latter part of the past century and all of the present. In the broader definition these two types are referred to as subjective and objective acting. In objective acting the actor prepares for his role by assuming external traits to develop the character. Its weakness is said to be in the mugging, and grimacing, and lack of depth that result. At present, it is rarely an accepted way for the actor to approach his role. There is a strong relationship between objective and arbitrary acting. Because comedy is developed in breadth, rather than in depth, it calls for ingenious and imaginative bits and byplays, not for introspection; and the objective approach is a definite part of the present-day pattern. Such actors as Zero Mostel, Paul Ford, and Terry Thomas perform in this tradition, as do the closer to burlesque-type comedians, such as Sid Caesar or Phil Silvers.

Subjective acting, on the other hand, has been shaped by the realistic pattern. It found its first clear definition with Constantin Stanislavski of the Moscow Art Theater in 1898. As the post-World War I theatrical fare moved almost completely toward realism, the Stanislavski tradition was revitalized through the efforts of Stella Adler and Harold Clurman of the Group Theater. During the 1930's, this group advanced the concept of the actor building his character from within, through intellectual and emotional understanding of the patterns, stimulation, and environment that lead to the shaping of personality.

Still another movement appeared on the scene after World War II, and is much in evidence today—the Actor's Studio, espousing method acting, under the hand of Lee Strasberg. Some of the techniques of Stanislavski and the refinements and advances of the Group Theater are to be found in the approaches of today's method actor. In this tradition, acting is in depth, and the psyche of the character to be played is given a fine and detailed examination. The performance, when successful, is one of complete conviction, immersion, and belief.

The connection between this development and the "being" acting that burst on the scene in European films during the 1950's and early 1960's is not readily apparent. Method acting is part of the theatrical acting tradition; while the "being" actors are more a part of the over-all film movement and, as already said, may be shaped more by the efforts of the film-maker and the style of his film than by any acting school, coach, or theatrical tradition.

What does all this mean to the film-maker and to his relationship with his actors as production gets underway? Two points are of extreme importance. The first is that the film-maker must develop an awareness of the subtle differences and degrees of acting interpretation, not only so that he can set the level of performance for each actor, but also bring about an acting harmony among all the players. Actors come from different backgrounds, have varying sets of experience and training, and are inclined to use any and all of their previous experience to find a key to their roles unless one is provided. This the film-maker must do, for the actor's interpretation must fit in with the film-maker's complete outlook. The second point is that the film-maker can assist his actor through a discussion of the character's desire, resistance, or conflict; the units of action that occur and the effect of these on the character; the tone and level of the characterization; the proportion of dominant and subordinate traits in the character's make-up; and the way in which these factors intensify the story.

Beyond this, the film-maker must be fully aware that he has intellectualized both his story and his characters for the actor. The best of analysis leads to cold calculation, providing a good understanding, but not necessarily a first-rate performance. He must realize that these means for preparation are fuses that have to be lit so that the actors as well as the production will catch fire. There are no rules, no laws, and no set patterns. Some film-makers are inclined to show their actors what they want, thus having the actor imitate. However, this technique does not provide the actor with true comprehension; it remains purely imitative. Other film-makers work in close confidence with their actors, stimulating, explaining, describing, and using substitute action close to the actor's own experience to re-create the emotion. Still others refrain from entering the actor's domain. They allow him, once he is familiar with the story, to work himself into the part and rise to a certain level of performance; then they comment on its appropriateness.

These methods invariably link up with the personal inclinations of the film-maker and the way he believes he secures the best results. What is paramount, however, is spontaneity, that first-time freshness, the excitement of discovery as people affect one another and as it is seen through a camera eye. In spite of technical encumbrances and details, the film-maker constantly strives toward this end.

USE OF THE NONACTOR

The nonactor has been the mainstay of the documentary film, and Robert J. Flaherty, called its father, has amply demonstrated the superb projection of feeling and thought to be achieved by having people be themselves. Other film-makers have sustained nonactors through feature-length films with excellent results. Penelope Houston in *The Contemporary Cinema* tells of Luchino Visconti, who made *La Terra Trema* (1948) with an "entirely amateur cast, recruited on the spot, and encouraged them to make up their own dialogue and follow their own rhythms of speech." She goes on to say that although the "Sicilian dialect left even an Italian audience at a loss" the film's value lies in its "absolute interlocking of social and human themes."[3]

Similar values were achieved by Georges Rouquier in *Farrebique* (1947), detailing a year's existence of a French farm family, in a film that is a classic of its kind. How much of the natural and real results achieved can be attributed to the raw talent of the persons involved, how much to the film-maker's ability to secure the qualities he desires, and how much to the cutting and editing, through which he selects the convincing pieces that make the performance a success? That success may usually be traced to all three sources simply points up the degree to which a film-maker's ingenuity is taxed when working with the nonactor. For this reason, many documentary film-makers, when asked about their methods for working with non-actors, will heave a deep sigh and say, "anything goes." The implication is that tricks, subterfuges, ruses, dodges, wiles, deceits—just about anything—are allowable procedure for the end result. But this is not actually true. The film-maker most definitely assumes a sense of responsibility for his people and is fully aware that tricking a person into a performance is short-lived and without enduring substance. He is not out to make fools of people, but to present their truth, and he works with them to arrive at it.

His "tricks," therefore, are usually no different from those used when working the professional: creating an understanding of the scene; recalling situations and suggesting associations with other times and other things; actively creating a play or make-believe condition; introducing surprises to foster an emotion or reaction; and, most of all, encouraging the people to be themselves. But simply because people are in their own environment, doing things they normally do, does not necessarily mean that they will perform well. Inhibitions and self-consciousness

---

[3] Penelope Houston, *The Contemporary Cinema* (Baltimore: Penguin Books, 1963), p. 26.

set up barriers almost immediately. Attempts to urge the performers to do well simply induces them to act, and the moment they begin to act the scene is lost. The film-maker must constantly be sensitive and alert to finding those things to which the individual responds.

For example, thinking (not analytic, but within the framework of character) is the basic cornerstone of acting and can be tried with the nonactor. If this results in halting movement or stilted speech, the reverse quality can be tried—doing. Moving through a series of his ordinary routines usually makes the individual feel "at home," relaxes the tension, and actually induces thinking again, but in terms of what is being done. The main problem is not to discover the range of talent of the individual, so much as to learn ways in which he becomes immersed in his own desires and needs. Overshooting, of course, aids immeasurably; for although a performance may be spotty, the effective pieces can be joined so that a consistent quality is maintained.

This introduces the value of editing and, with it, the hazards of dialogue. With no speech involved, more control can be exercised through cutting. With this advantage, many film-makers are inclined to record their people talking in interview sessions, then select speech-takes to use as voice-over to the action. An added advantage is that speech can be counterpointed with the action for further thematic enrichment. But the voice-over method also has serious disadvantages: if the technique is poorly handled the results are grossly amateurish; the technique is limited, in that it might sustain well in a short documentary, but hardly in a feature-length film; audiences are accustomed to actual speech, so that the technique is used in the documentary primarily for special purposes, not to avoid problems; and the rhythmic characteristics of such speeches may be lost for lack of association with doing. Still, tremendous advances have been made recently in portable field-recording equipment, and on-the-spot live sound has taken on greater flexibility with added fidelity. Decisions concerning methods and approaches when using nonactors should not be based on the mechanics of the problem, but on the specific values to be derived from live sound as against voice-over. The mechanics can usually be worked out, but the big problem remains how to draw out a performance.

The key lies in the attitude the film-maker has toward the story being told, regardless of whether it is short or feature length. If he is doing a story about real people in real life, and using nonactors, he refrains from making up situations and characters and derives his meaning by carefully observing and capturing the reality that is there. If he is doing a story that is essentially made-up—and using actors—then he creates his own reality as well as the situations and characters. In the former instance he is not a participant, but an observer; in the latter instance he not only participates, but makes it all up.

When working with the professional actor, the film-maker's approach is to make the life he is portraying smack of truth. He has a script at hand and works together with his actor to interpret that script. The projection of character and theme is synthesized out of assumptions: the script assumes certain conditions because it is make-believe, and the characters are imagined. True, it is made from life and reflects it, but it is seen directly through the film-maker, as if he had placed himself between the subject and the audience. But working with the nonactor and the kind of story that is generally being told through him is the exact opposite. Here reality exists, the truth of the situation is readily apparent, and the film-maker's approach calls for him to stand to one side, so to speak, and guide the audience to see the subject.

In brief, when meaning is already stated in the script and one is working with a professional actor, the task is one of making it all believable and acceptable; when working with the non-actor in his own milieu rather than a script, no meaning is readily available except reality itself, and the task is to get meaning out of it.

The line of demarcation is finely drawn, yet is essentially one of synthesis against analysis: the ultimate objective is the same, although the starting ingredients vary. When working with the nonactor, tricks and ruses are not necessary, as proved by Flaherty; what he saw in *Nanook* or *Man of Aran* was disassociated from Flaherty himself. Yet, once having secured this insight, he most successfully photographed his nonactors for themselves. This does not mean that scenes were not staged and even, occasionally, artificially manufactured. It is said that the scene where *Nanook* fishes through the ice in a tug-of-war with his prey was staged. It is also said that the people of the Aran Isles had not gone out in whale boats in years, but Flaherty staged such a scene also, and it was still within the context of the actual. The important point is that these people were seen, understood, and appreciated for what they were, not photographed on the basis of preconceived ideas. They were not made up, but discovered.

The discovery of a character is the film-maker's job with the nonactor. And when discovery comes, a basis for communication develops between the actor and film-maker that permits natural conditions to prevail. The film-maker's research in such an instance consists of spending weeks, months, and sometimes even years living with his people so that he can appreciate their way of life and come to understand their point of view. George Stoney provides just such a detailed account of his research for the making of *All My Babies* (1954), when he describes making daily rounds with the Negro midwife, understanding her philosophy, seeing the conditions where she worked, and how he formulated his story from this knowledge.[4]

At times a nonactor may be given a lead role in a made-up

---

[4] George Stoney, "All My Babies: Research," *Film: Book I,* ed. by Robert Hughes (New York: Grove Press, 1959), pp. 79–96.

story. Here the film-maker's task is a special one, because on the spot he must make a professional actor of one who is not. This again is a synthesis of a role. It would thus appear that the role of the documentary film-maker is distinct from the maker of story film. Yet, in this very circumstance the documentary and the fiction film are coming closer and closer together. The need for specific approaches for each kind of film and special handling for each kind of actor is being disproved. Today, film-makers ignore boundaries, rules, limitations, and reservations to use the most expedient methods for reaching audiences. The break from traditional theater is causing an amalgamation of those qualities peculiar to the film, with one main purpose: to bring meaning out of reality.

TIMING AND MOVEMENT

The standard operational pattern for shooting by many film-makers is to chalk acting positions on the floor, so that shots can be set up and taken as prescribed by the script. The method is based on highly detailed planning to make possible an extremely efficient production. The shots as outlined by the writer are reworked to some extent and further pinpointed by a breakdown. To turn out a thirty-minute film in a day of shooting—or a sixty- or ninety-minute film in two days—becomes pure routine, and the very word routine is a giveaway of the system's failings.

The method is based on a number of strange suppositions: that the task of the film-maker during the directing process is mainly one of logistics and traffic; that the script is clear as to what is to be said and done, and is the film's control center; and that the great deal of time spent in specific planning is not to be voided—that any creative choices or changes that would enrich, tighten, or strengthen the story should have been made during the planning stages. The fallacy lies in the belief that films are written and not made. It is true that chaotic conditions can develop on a location or set very quickly without a forceful hand to control the operation. But it is equally true that if this control is mainly that of mechanical organization, the shots themselves will follow suit.

The objective at the time of shooting is not a chalk mark that prescribes an actor's movements to "three steps to the right and then a turn away from the camera," but a relatively spontaneous movement, building a series of coordinated rhythms of which the actor is only one part. The actual shooting is a part of performance. If planning is anticipation of the moment, the moment itself calls for passion. Rather than a mechanical process, the taking of the shots should be a high point of creativity in film-making. Editing, although of utmost significance, might be said to be both reflective and selective, whereas shooting is passionate.

During the shooting the film-maker for the first time is creating with his material and can ascertain both the feeling and meaning of his actor's movements. Although his movement is to be secured in units that are out of continuity, the film-maker sustains a flow of these as part of an over-all pattern. Timing and movement must be considered on three levels: the actors as they move in each individual shot; the camera as it moves to take the shot; the over-all rhythm set up both by the actor and the camera, and the way in which they will support the over-all cutting rhythm as the shots are set up to flow one into the other.

Planned and prescribed camera movements force the film more into a theatrical mold, with the bulk of timing and movement carried by the acting personnel. It prohibits fully creative use of the camera, and of the editing to follow, which depend on the film-maker's spontaneous responses to the heat of production participation. Without the planning the film-maker would not recognize the moment, and with too much planning there would be no spontaneity for such a moment to occur. In serendipity there must be an element of preparation, of talent, and of luck;

but the luck really comes from being open to what occurs at the moment.

Of all the units before the film-maker at the time he is taking a shot, and as highly individual as any, are the camera and its operator. The camera is the film-maker's eye and ultimately the audience's eye. The camera, through the technique and sensitivity of its operator, must photograph what the film-maker sees. This depends on two important conditions. First, the film-maker must be able to see what the camera is seeing, or else he is like a man whose optic nerve has been cut. Innumerable film writers and directors have never looked through a camera viewfinder. Second, the cameraman must be creatively involved and working with the film-maker to sense the feeling of movement, mood, and rhythm of each shot. A kind of love affair goes on between the camera and the subject, with the film-maker as matchmaker.

During this time, the film-maker can solidify the rhythmic characteristics of the scene, emphasizing points of stress either by specific movements of the actors, by the actual "feel" of a cut at the end of a static shot, or by securing a release or intensification through a dolly shot or a pan. When the film-maker actually moves the actors and the camera about, he may find a new harmony or disorientation that eluded him at the planning stage, and he may take advantage of the nature of these movements. In all ways, he works constantly toward rhythmic development at this point, freely searching through his camera for the ways in which it can use movement and rhythm to get at content.

Also at this time, the emotional quality of a scene can be expanded or diminished, and the degree to which this can be done depends on its measure at the moment of taking. Despite planning, there are always variables in anything connected with human nature, and only by taking advantage of the living moment can the camera adjust to the nature, the intention, and the hope of the actual activity. Rhythm values can be set (or destroyed) in the editing, but only within the range of what is there. The best seamstress might make a small glove out of a pig's ear, but never a silk purse!

Rhythms are not mysterious, unknown qualities. When playing scenes actors often stop and remark, "That didn't feel right. I'll do it again." Because of a misstep, a poor gesture, or perhaps an awkward turn, they have felt either the loss of a beat or a beat too many. Speech and movement proceed rhythmically in measured stresses that are felt, and the film-maker and his camera have to be a part of this pattern.

Meaning and rhythm go hand in hand. The camera itself, the instrument through which the scene is expressed, can be given still further dimension if handled more as a live force than as a dead instrument. It has already been pointed out how choice of angle, lens, distance from subject, and camera point of view can affect the content of a shot. Yet none of these values will come through to the audience unless the movement of the shot is progressive and given definition through rhythm. Rhythm, therefore, is a correlating factor of film production elements and can strongly support emotion—thoughtful or rash, calm or agitated, sad or happy, angry or delighted.

Yet, all too often, the traditional chalk mark and the fixed action simply reduce the camera's value and force it to be an impartial observer. The clear result of this is that the film-maker is not using the medium to its fullest extent. On the other hand, attempts to use the camera interpretively, without the film-maker getting the feel and intent of movement, sensing and participating in its rhythmic flow, can be just as ineffective. The result is self-conscious camera work, artificial, forced, perhaps even bewildering to the spectator, and often leaving him indifferent. As in all other areas of operation, motivation is the bedrock on which the timing of both the camera and the subject rests. But the success of the effort here depends not only on the film-maker's point of view, but on his creative visual instincts as well.

CONTROL OF THE SHOT

Control of the shot means that the film-maker has taken command of each and every shot and in turn of the production. Lack of control means that the shots have engulfed him, and in turn he is overwhelmed by the production. Command is achieved by considering everything—from the money available to the nature of individual ability—and it calls for a cold and grimly realistic appraisal. The production must be brought within the range of the film-maker's capability so that he can operate freely and without encumbrance.

It may be exaggeration to say that some film-makers are inclined to dream of huge spectacle and gigantic mob scenes when their available budget may not cover the cost of raw film stock. But absurd as this sounds, enthusiasm is often channeled in the wrong direction. Where a more modest and honest outlook could provide the film-maker with free rein to work, his unrealistic ambition could beset him with financial as well as artistic problems far beyond his reach. This is not meant to discourage experimentation, but to distinguish it from foolhardiness.

Films can be made for $500, $5,000, $500,000, and $50,000,000. It is never a question of how much money a film-maker has, but of whether he can make the most of what is available, not only in terms of money, but of his talent. Some men work well with a bull horn and thousands of extras; others in such circumstances cannot fathom one end of a shot from the next. The problem is not one of economics, but of artistic rendering. The film-maker has to take a good measure of himself, his story and its requirements, and how well he can work it and be in command of it.

Once this range is generally established, the immediate point of control is the shot. The handling of the components of a single shot (lighting, composition, framing, etc.) calls for the same amount of judgment and care as the setting down of a good and effective sentence. The film-maker writes with his camera, and his shot components are put to work to communicate abstract or tangible ideas. Yet, all too often the individual shot is taken for granted. The subject is available, the camera is there, the lights are turned on, and the shot is taken. But the result is an assemblage of images on a par with the values of pulp magazines and comic books. A purely mechanical control has led to inadequate use of shot components, which then suffer from a kind of anemia.

As critical as one may be of pulps and comics, their basic ideas are not necessarily bad so much as they are half-baked. The plot of *Hamlet*, or of Dickens' *Tale of Two Cities* or *Great Expectations*, can be rendered in comic book form (it has been done) and the result is just as inadequate as any "purple-eyed monster and maid yarn." The difference between the same story as a classic or as a comic book lies in the choice, arrangement, and use of words, words that reveal perspective and depth. The dignity of aspiration, the telling revelations, the sense of presence and authority—even if present in the author's mind— could not have been secured unless he had control of his words as well as his material.

In the film control is gained in three ways. One has to do with the film-maker and his working group, for the film-maker depends on his cast and crew in the transfer of his artistic vision to film, and purposeful leadership is the prerequisite for their successful cooperation. The second has to do with choice and selection within each shot, and the way in which all the shot components are arranged, set up, and manipulated. This is a shot syntax. No brief is held here for the idea that a shot is fleeting and travels at twenty-four frames per second, hence must be simple, with one idea only. Although it is true that a shot has to make an initial master impression, it should be built on a core of meaning, with all parts related to it in depth. Relationships found in editing begin at this point, and not purely in the cut. Arrangement within a shot, therefore, is a part of shot control. Another part is the way in which the camera is handled at the time of shooting. This is the film-maker's prime opportunity, because control is evidenced in the clean way a close-up comes up on the screen, how a medium shot holds attention in terms of foreground, in background positioning, in the way a pan moves from point to point to show up specific things, and a long shot has purpose beyond the simple establishment of time and place. Each shot gains a distinguished sense of authority as it comes up on the screen, commanding, fresh, sparkling.

All in all, the viewer is taken by the hand through a wonderland of sights to behold. Here again is the clue, for such control is more than mechanical efficiency—a smoothly operating pan, a perfectly timed dolly, a precise tilt. Such mechanical efficiency is important, but must combine with the film-maker knowing where he wants to take his viewer, what he wants him to see, and how he is to see it. The components cannot be arranged or the camera handled efficiently if there is no clear reason behind the shot. The third means of control, then, is purpose, coming out of the story and providing considerable information about the film-maker. It is through such control that style is made possible. Here, the film-maker's personal philosophy comes into play, his attitude toward his material, and his point of view—all coupled with the range of his experience.

There is necessarily an affinity between the film-maker and the kind of shots he takes. Ingmar Bergman does not absorb himself with mystical and religious ideas because that is where the money lies, nor does Federico Fellini ponder the world's morality because he thinks that is a good idea. These men gravitate into these areas and think in these terms because that is the way they are. Their backgrounds and their personalities come together to give them a sense of command over their material.

The challenging requirement, therefore, is for the film-maker to search out and find his milieu—a seemingly hopeless task, but the quest of the artist since time began. As sweeping and general as this may sound, it is through such attempts that individuality makes its presence felt in individual shots. Insights are arrived at in terms of native ability; and the measure of control the film-maker can bring to bear on each shot is directly related to those areas toward which he finds himself moving naturally, where he feels at ease, and works at satisfactory efficiency. Bergman and Fellini may or may not as yet have turned out their greatest films, but every shot in each of their works bears their individual stamp.

The issue really cannot be intellectualized, nor can it be simply explained. Some film-makers spend an entire lifetime and never actually reach a point of full assessment of their strengths and weaknesses, a knowledge of method and genre ideally suited to their individual talent. If anything, perhaps the quest is more valuable than the objective. Certainly the film-maker cannot, in the middle of production, wax philosophical and worry about his id or ego. But after the shooting is over and the film has been edited and released, it should be looked at and studied in retrospect—as painful as that may be—so that working references may be developed for the future.

ACTUALITY SEQUENCES

The chariot race is on, swords clash, arrows cleave the air, hordes of Mongol warriors sack and desecrate the village: thus is the essence of drama fixed in the minds of some film-makers. With such a frame of reference, the shooting of actuality sequences—stories set in a real-life framework, even though with actors, or documentary-type films of people in their own environment—can evoke no more enthusiasm than a pitcher of stale beer. The film-maker so slanted is not only missing the requirements of good film-making, but is even unaware of the essence of good playwriting. He might provide a noisy circus side show, but hardly a meaningful piece of work.

Two points are worth considering: one is that although spectacle is a natural for film, by itself it is like watching a magic act. The audience is tricked, and though delighted at the moment, is more curious about the way the effect was achieved than moved by the actual achievement. Diversion, rather than drama, is the result. The second point is that in spite of the differences between the theatrical story and the one set in actuality, the underlying values that the film-maker seeks are the same: believability, truth, revelation, and meaning. The beginning film-maker, when dealing with actuality, often fails to see the drama in life itself—in spite of the fact that drama is born of life, and obviously not the other way around.

Again, two points are worth considering. One is that all people and things being photographed have physical shape and form that contain a wealth of information. A simple shot of an orange, though readily recognizable, does not always show us whether it is sweet or sour; a shot of a roller coaster may hide from us whether it is terrifying or thrillingly delightful; and a shot of a man can withhold or reveal a wealth of untold secrets. Though his mouth is curved downward in sorrow or upward in joy, thus providing some clue as to his mental state, still the secrets remain. The film-maker must know those secrets so that, through the direction given to his camera and his observation of the action taking place, what is physically represented on the screen projects meaningful story matter.

The second point is that once the film-maker has arrived at the core of his material, knowing and understanding its *raison d'être*, its character's hopes, aims, and ideals, he finds further camera definition by determining his own attitudes, which may be sympathetic, antagonistic, or neutral. In dealing with actuality the film-maker—although he takes his shots with the thought that in the editing stage he will select those that serve him best—does not rely on this technique alone. Simply because he is not a direct participant does not mean that he fails to develop a point of view. His point of view is essential, as it is the motivation for both his camera work and the editing that are to follow. He has to make up his mind about where he wants to go and why he wants to get there.

The same approach is taken whether the subject being photographed is city harbor traffic, automobile jams on busy highways, or fruit peddlers. The point of view has to be determined so that the shooting, though seemingly sporadic and off the cuff, still has direction and aim. The sheer excitement of activity is not enough to produce shots that in the editing will work toward the re-creation of that excitement, if excitement is what is wanted. There are innumerable examples of shots of traffic, traffic signs, policemen, etc., in many films; but of them all, the Willard Van Dyke–Ralph Steiner production *The City* (1939) haunts the viewer, for the simple reason that statement grows out of the humorously presented, frustrating madness of city life.

Aside from understanding his material and developing a personal point of view, the film-maker is faced with still more problems during the actual shooting. Should the camera be hidden, or should it be brought out in the open? Should the action be restaged, or pieces taken as they actually happen? Should sound be recorded at the time of shooting, or should the people involved be brought into a studio and their voices recorded under ideal conditions? Will the action move so fast that it will be beyond the speed and dexterity of the camera crew? Should the camera be hand-held? Should there be one fixed camera and a number of roving cameramen? Asking these questions of experienced film-makers will draw out answers based on specific experiences. This indicates that there are no set rules to follow, and that the film-maker has to rely on his own judgment and ingenuity to secure the results he wants. The solution is usually found through trial and error; success often rests on how well the film-maker can recognize the truth of the moment, and how quickly he can decide the camera angle best suited to capture it. Some film-makers do their own camera work in such instances. In other instances, director-cameraman associations develop where the rapport between the men involved has grown over a long period of time and the two can act as one. In such cases, communication is almost unnecessary, because the director knows that his cameraman's point of view is his own. In yet other instances, the solution is found through saturation coverage: everything is shot from all and any angle, securing lots of footage, so that in the editing the correct pieces will be found and joined. This method has also worked well, and is made possible by the nature of the subject matter. Still, the significant fact is that in all such shooting, as in shooting for any other type of film, craftsmanship by itself is not sufficient. The film-maker has to exercise artistic judgments and bring to bear that most telling of artistic factors: selection. It is through the right choice of seemingly ordinary experiences that, miraculously, a work may become extraordinary and edifying.

In some instances, the nature of the circumstances permits the restaging of actuality, and the film-maker is careful to allow the action to happen. Easy as this sounds, it calls for a genuine imagination that recognizes the real and the true in ordinary everyday living. The ludicrousness of creating the "real" where it should be allowed to develop on its own is well evidenced by those television commercials that present floor-waxing neighbors, sink-scrubbing plumbers, and repairmen who do the laundry. Unless we have been invaded unawares by commercials from Planet X, there is in our midst a sizable group of people who have the most peculiar ideas of what life is like on earth.

Interestingly enough, true understanding calls for objectivity, elimination of self, and an impartial evaluation of things and people. Yet the resulting point of view is by nature subjective. The film-maker achieves this seeming paradox by working in just that way. He makes up his mind after he has collected his facts.

A recognition and appreciation of the truth in life is the key to all of it, as it is the cornerstone for expression in all the arts. In those instances where drama is made up, both in the theater and in the film, success is measured by the accuracy with which the story reflects life and, through careful selection, makes a statement. The wildest theatrical farce, for example, although impossible occurrences take place, must still be deeply rooted in real life lest it become an innocuous, harebrained bit of nonsense, much like the television commercials cited.

Where in the theater a wide range of stylistic representation is achieved through sets, costumes, and manner and method of acting and speech, the film seems most effective when it is explored fully through the actual life (real or re-created) that it can present. Many fanciful sets and trappings have been brought from the theater to film, but generally these have remained more effective as theatrical pieces. The film's power lies in penetrative exploration of the real, with the selection of the image being the film-maker's way of getting at its poetry. In the film all is actuality; the measure of the film-maker is taken by how well he can see into it.

ECONOMY OF ARRANGEMENT

After turning out a successful work, creative people often express the fear that they will not be able to duplicate the feat. The reaction is quite natural, for once having said what he had to say, the creative individual is left temporarily empty and once again must traverse the long, arduous road to another work. For the moment the human well is a void. Fortunately, such moments are generally short-lived, and the problem is not one of getting material so much as having too much. Anxiety brings about a precipitation of story material, but in spite of its abundance there is a tendency to hold back, to keep a reserve so that too much of this material will not be expanded too quickly. The unintentional result is padding. The method for eliminating this is to move into the midst of the story; for that matter, starting with the climax may reap rich dividends.

In a Western, for example, a sheriff may have had a number of encounters with a desperado who wielded considerable power through terror tactics. But the sheriff is persistent and catches the desperado red-handed, thus securing sufficient evidence to insure a long prison term. With the town able to follow its normal pursuits, the sheriff turns his attention to lighter matters, like love and marriage. But on the very day of the sheriff's marriage the desperado, having served his sentence, is to return for revenge. At this climactic point the film *High Noon* (1952) begins.

The film-maker faces the problem of economy or tightness, not only in the construction of his story, but also in the use of his shots to tell that story. The film *High Noon* amply demonstrates economy in both areas. Climaxes are used as beginning points, with the shots moving constantly to explore and elaborate on the individual attitudes of the players, their relationships, and the evolving thematic ideas. The camera constantly ferrets out information and keeps the nature of the conflict before the audience. Such seemingly static and empty shots as the tiny train station and the railroad tracks stretching out to infinity, which are referred to as part of a consistent pattern, serve to provide a recall value, affecting all levels of the story as well as maintaining interest and suspense.

The film-maker should be aware of shot economy during the very act of shooting. Economy or tightness refers to the elimination of shots that simply pad a story, or merely provide a background or an atmosphere. The misinterpretation of tightness, however, can lead to a bald, underdeveloped type of film that is just as ineffective in its own way as one that is redundant. Although the film-maker, both in the preparation of his story and in the shooting, moves fearlessly to the core of it, he should not shoot so as to capture only the key aspects. To take shots of only the most important action occurring in a scene, followed by more, similar shots, would certainly be tight in construction, but far from satisfactory to an audience, as development and en- richment would be lacking. Economy or tightness, therefore, does not mean an emasculated collection of shots, but shots that work constantly toward providing more and more information about the story and the people concerned. It is again a question of selection. The film-maker concentrates on the key aspects of his shots, but achieves economy by having each one carry as many levels of meaning as possible, with a focus to create a central impression and other meanings in perspective based on their importance. Therefore, although it might be more effective to use one shot in place of two, or two shots in place of three, the prime consideration is not the number of shots, but whether the shots are propelling the story forward and neatly dovetailing the plot or incident, character, imagery, sound, speech, and theme. Ideally, as shots unfold they should convey something to everyone in the audience, very much the way the Shake- spearean plays appealed to the educated nobility in the boxes and to the roisterers in the pit.

Economy, then, depends on selection and sensitivity. The task of the film-maker is to be alert to the connection between things and people and to bring his camera to bear on this connection.

Connections of this sort, no matter how well delineated in a written script, can never be so fully realized as at the moment when the camera is trained on the scene. The reason for this is that such connections not only involve the story itself, but the interactions of the players, all the elements that go to make up the shot and the camera and its perspective as well. All of these values have to be fitted one to the other; the resultant developing characteristics not only have to be judged and measured at this time, but, in a sense, created as of the moment.

What has to be clearly understood is that film is not drama as in the theater, nor is it close to live television. The main difference between the motion-picture camera and the television camera in the studio is that one is free to move, whereas the other is tied down by a cable. But in this very difference lies a freedom that provides the film with fluidity. This trivial mechanical detail spells the difference between representational theater at one extreme, and image selection and concentration for intensified communication through the joining of such images at the other. Punching up shots in television, by the same token, is not editing in the filmic sense. Television is said to be at its best with on-the-spot reportage and documentary presentation, with the implication that immediacy alone is the reason for its success in those fields. But it is just as true that in these instances the limitations of the studio have been broken down. Camera freedom in such cases—though still with some limitation—not only puts the viewer in the midst of an actual event, but gives him vantage views that would be unavailable to him if he were there in person. However, for live television drama to be effective—remaining within the studio—it has to be first-rate theater. Its shots picture the action, the story is conveyed mainly through the dialogue, and its orientation remains theatrical. Economy is practiced, but it is one of writing; shots mainly follow the players, and when used properly heighten the drama. In the film, the free-moving camera affects the story, the way it is visualized, and the way it is handled. For example, consider not only the conceptual differences between *Hiroshima Mon Amour* and television's *The Defenders*, but also the manner and mode through which each is realized.

Economy in shooting, therefore, requires a different kind of inspiration that prods the film-maker to see into things and to find the way to comment on them effectively. This ability bridges time and space, outer and inner worlds, the tangible and the abstract, to concentrate on connotative associations. The editing process that then follows demands a creativity far beyond the obvious business of placing shot no. 1 first, shot no. 2 second, and so on.

200

GENUINE VALUES

One of the biggest problems facing the film-maker, as other artists, is making his creation ring true. The phrase "ring true" in this case means more than the dramatic element of believability; also involved are the film-maker's passion, concern, enthusiasm, and excitement for that piece of the world that he has discovered and wishes to portray. Successful film expression, as in other arts, is a constant struggle between the creative artist and the world about him. Such expression, though extremely satisfying when achieved, is perhaps the most challenging of tasks to be undertaken. The reason for this is that in spite of countless explanations, no one can be quite sure about the chemistry that takes place between the film-maker and his craft and content to fuse a film into a dynamic whole.

A genuinely artistic film is usually recognized when it is presented; it is analyzed and interpreted by critics and scholars; sometimes rules and theories are either applied to it or drawn from it to better understanding. Thus attempts are made to explain its make-up and nature. Yet, like life itself, such a work has its own secret, defying the audience with its simplicity and tantalizing with its beauty and scope.

As the audience watches, it is smitten. It thinks about what is unfolding before it, yet there is no time for thought. It reacts emotionally, but before one emotion can be expended, still another rushes in to take its place; there is a constant mounting of emotional surges. The audience refuses to be distracted; it cannot be distracted, for in that very moment something may occur that demands even more concentration. Hence the audience cannot be indifferent to the film. Perhaps the clue is there that in such an instance the film-maker himself was anything but indifferent when he made the film.

For the film-maker not to be indifferent is far more difficult than it sounds. In film-making, as in other arts, a fine line separates the professionally competent work from the inspired. Inspiration is an emotion; and as inspired as the film-maker may be at the outset, the continuing shooting process, along with the mounting technical considerations, renders the emotion increasingly elusive. A film, in general, has three working areas: first, there is the arrangement and organization of the story to be told in terms of the craft; second, there are the people who are part of the story, along with their actions and reactions—the content. These two aspects of the production have to be kneaded and blended together so that one becomes vital and acceptable in terms of the other. No matter what kind of film, effective communication must go hand in hand with effective craft work. This part of the work is so demanding in itself that it is often in the third area—a strong outpouring of feeling for each shot's significance and for the whole film—that the film itself can quite readily fall beyond the film-maker's grasp.

Consideration of a few kinds of films and their effect on us will help to clarify the point. On viewing a well-done murder mystery we feel sympathetic to our hero, through him participate in harrowing and bloodcurdling incidents, and heave a sigh of relief when the culprit is apprehended. On viewing the story of a pioneer moving West with his family, we take his part, courageously fight the Indians, and heave a sigh of relief when the cavalry arrives. On viewing the plight of a little boy who declares his loyalty to his father, although the father has been mistakenly carted off to jail, we shed a tear or two and sniff it away when the boy and father are united. These represent one type of film. But, when we see *La Dolce Vita*, we are appalled by human behavior, shocked, and stunned as we try to deny our instincts and motives, yet see ourselves for what we are. Thus, knowing a little more about ourselves, we may come out the better for it. When we see *Man of Aran*, we sit spellbound at the vast and relentless power of nature, yet we take heart in man's unconquerable spirit and thus know a little more about ourselves. When we see a medieval knight seek the answer to life while in the midst of cruelty, superstition, and ignorance, as in *The Seventh Seal;* or experience truth as something relative, as in *Rashomon;* or become part of a scene in which people meet to determine whether they will help someone in trouble, as in *High Noon;* we are brought face to face with issues that beset us constantly, and we learn more about ourselves and all others who are like us. These, then, exemplify another kind of film.

The first group cited above is well-made and organized story matter, but the latter group has moved several steps beyond that, for it has a core of meaning. Yet, the film-maker cannot willfully manipulate his ingredients to arrive at this end. The situation exists and must be interpreted by the way he sees, thinks, and feels. The task is difficult, for he has the problem of organizing a story to meet the demands of his craft without destroying its reality or obscuring his point of view. Unfortunately, film-makers often produce perfectly constructed films that are well motivated, seem to fall together flawlessly, yet are marked by sterility. This is not meant to criticize such procedure, for many aspiring films that lack motivation and tight construction have been so blurred that audiences are loath to sit through them. But compromise can lead to mediocrity, and often leaves the film with no place to go. In a few short years, from the late 1950's to today, the New Wave, cinema *vérité,* and individual film-makers working independently have contributed to the advancing film art by introducing craft changes and different approaches. In the successful instances these were not arbitrarily superimposed on the film; rather, they grew out of the need for ways and means to project emotion. Because emotion is unpredictable and volatile, it is not always conveyed by normal and routine methods. Hence, in his need for a solution, the film-maker begins to jostle accepted patterns, searching for a method that at the moment may seem to be exclusively his own. And so the craft is expanded, and critics and scholars once again gather to study the new phenomena.

For a film to have genuine value it must include the break-through that occurs when the film-maker sees beyond the tools he is working with, and beyond the vehicle that carries his story. He gives a good piece of himself to his work and reveals himself for a thinking, feeling human being. Thus the work takes on a dimension beyond that immediately apparent on the screen.

The beginning film-maker has the most trouble in this area of his work when he has not yet fully mastered the shot and how he is to secure it, the machinery that surrounds him and the crew that is going to make the machinery work to serve his purpose, and the players and their interpretation. But with each additional film effort, experience develops insights. The subjective quality so necessary is arrived at by an objective handling of the tangibles that go to make up the film, from the emulsion of the raw stock to the intensity of the key light. However, experience alone is not the answer, because dismal failures have followed successful efforts. Coupled with experience is the need for a sustained and sincere attitude of questioning.

The film-maker cannot and must not compromise. It is far more important to breathe life into a film than to have it perfectly structured, perfectly set up, and perfectly shot. To be sure, this means taking chances may play havoc with the accepted way of doing things and may prove more expensive, but a film-maker dies if he has to craft-hack his way through life. What is even worse is that his films die before he does.

REALITY VERSUS THE IMAGE

Nothing is so excruciating to the beginner as that moment when, after having taken a few shots, he sits down to view them and finds that what he has on film is not what he thought he had photographed. To be sure the elements are the same, since one cannot photograph trees and get pictures of automobiles. Yet, the differences as seen on the screen between what was taken and what is there might, in a different way, be that marked. The feeling, the excitement, the intensity, and the mood that was so apparent during the filming has disappeared. In its place is a somewhat flat, uninspired, bedraggled series of shots that fail to come alive.

A number of things occur at this juncture. For one, the imagination, no matter how well controlled, insists on its flights of fancy. Once the film-maker sees the reality of what he had in his mind's eye, he has to overcome the initial shock of facing his brainchild. That first exposure forces the film-maker to see the shot for what it is. For another, inexperience coupled with the demanding work of preparation leads the beginner to expect the entire film, or at least a scene of it, magically to unfold before him. He has not yet oriented himself to the shock of the monumental task of realizing through application and sweat those wonderful visions he had before he started. In a sense, a film is made twice over: once when shooting and again when editing. There is no smooth development from the planning to the doing, as in theater.

But all of these conditions change considerably with added experience. By "experience" is meant a tangible set of checkpoints, all of which lead to the elimination of working from a preconceived point of view, so that the film-maker does not see what he wants to see, but what is actually there in his frame. When shooting in any setting, for example, it must be borne in mind that the film-maker is exposed to all of it. If he is shooting in a Greenwich Village beatnik apartment, he is at once exposed to all of the walls and the condition they are in, to the bits and pieces of furniture, and to the general disarray of the place. All of this creates a specific mood. Yet, when a shot is taken, it might be of a face in medium close-up in the foreground, with only a small part of the wall in the background, giving a neutral effect. The mood is different. The same could be true of any exterior location: a busy business section of a city and its mood can easily be lost when the camera moves in to take a piece of it. The point is that the film-maker must not judge from the full location or set there before him, but must look at the shot in the viewfinder of his camera. The shot must be seen through the camera eye to be judged.

Here, too, the neophyte is liable to make mistakes. He looks and is inclined to render a quick judgment without considering all four corners of the frame, because he is concentrating primarily on the subject. Therefore, he fails to see the shot as a complete unit having four sides, and considers it merely a medium shot, close-up, or whatever. Other values that could have been realized are allowed to fend for themselves, often neutralizing each other. The intensification of the shot is never achieved.

Still another oversight is not judging the light as seen in the viewfinder. So long as light is falling on the subject and in a general way is high or low key, the beginner forgets to examine its contribution in terms of nuance and shading. In addition, even the viewer can be deceptive in this respect, for it reveals the shot in natural colors, whereas on film these colors will be rendered in terms of blacks, whites, and grays. A seemingly warm scene as seen in the viewer can appear extremely cold on the screen because of harsh black-and-white contrasts. Exposing color film does not eliminate this problem, because it too has its mood-differentiating values in the way it registers the color. Color films today have as many color value differences as black and white and can render images from pastels to full primaries.

Another error might be in choice of film stock. Film manufacturers issue full specifications covering their stocks; and spectograms indicate the way colors are rendered in terms of black and white so that stocks, aside from their speed, can be selected according to degree of contrast. As important as the study of these specifications is, it leads at best to a general decision. Film tests should be made of the stock to be used under the conditions of shooting so that results can be judged on the screen. The laboratory where the processing is done should be visited so that the film-maker learns how it handles processing and what results it can achieve. In this way the film-maker and the laboratory work together toward a common goal. But it must be remembered that the laboratory men are not miracle workers. They cannot make good shots out of bad ones; but they can take good shots and render them correctly.

Another failure of the beginning film-maker is not to see his shots as parts of the whole, and consequently to lose consistency from shot to shot in movement, timing, and tone. The flow of shots, though out of sequence and seen through a viewfinder, still can be sensed. If cutting is in mind—as it should be—it makes itself apparent.

All told, the demands made on the film-maker during production are both broad and specific. As real as the medium may be and as realistic as the specific film is, reality is never a question of simply being on the spot and pushing the camera button. The reality of a set, a location, or actuality is not to be found ready-made in the viewfinder. It has to be worked for every step of the way.

SCREENING RUSHES

At stated periods during the shooting, the exposed footage is sent to a laboratory to be processed. Prints or copies are made immediately so that the work can be screened and checked. (The initial exposed footage, original reversal or negative, is usually stored in a vault held at specific temperatures.) The prints or copies are referred to as "rushes" or dailies, depending on the nature and scale of the operation. Where money and facilities permit, such screening is on a day-to-day basis; in other situations, the screenings can be anywhere from one to four days—

sometimes more—behind the shooting. And again, depending on the scale of the production, the screening may be attended by the producer, director, cameraman, and editor, along with other members responsible for key areas of work, or simply by one or two film-makers who are undertaking all of the work. Whatever the situation, and the variations are infinite, this matter of checking results is more than counting shots to see if everything is there prior to tearing down a set or moving to another location.

The beginning film-maker is often his own worst enemy at such times, because he is either quite dismayed by what he sees or loses all sense of objectivity and is ecstatic about the shots before him—here, too, the range of reaction is boundless. But more than anything else, screening rushes is not only a time to see whether specific values have been achieved, but also to assess the nature of the effort and draw further stimulation from it.

First, however, it must be remembered that final or release prints made from the negative or original reversal stock are timed, that is, each shot is graded and exposed to light in the printing so that the entire film is balanced. Since this process calls for additional time and money, rushes or dailies, which are used as work copies or work prints, are printed through one light (not graded) and on cheaper stock. Also, the laboratory should be consulted about work print stock because a number of kinds of stock can be had at varying cost. Selection is made on the basis of time and money available, and on the kind of information the film-maker seeks on examining his rushes. For example, if he is only interested in seeing the action and is not worried about the quality of photography, he could order an inexpensive copy that is given to high contrasts. On the other hand, if he wants some information about tone and shade, such stock would be useless.

The film-maker judges the action of the shot; the meaning of the shot, small as it may be within its own framework; the mood and tone, in terms of photography and lighting; and his coverage, in terms of how he plans to edit the film.

Despite the fact that shots are much like a jigsaw puzzle, in that the pieces have to be linked together to make a whole unit, the film-maker while examining rushes can take the general measure of his shots and foresee the flowing continuity that can be developed.

This process is a continuation of visualization. He applied it when he was shooting; he can further apply it when he has some of the material before him, and will apply it in editing. Although the bits are disjointed and out of arrangement, he actually can get a sense of timing, flow, and pattern. He learns to cut by visualizing the results. He may not be able to visualize the exact order and arrangement of shots as they will finally appear, but he can get a sense of continuity, and sometimes see many possibilities. He also develops a shot memory. Within the limits of his work he learns to recall shots and place them differently, much as one would fit together a jigsaw puzzle that has several possible variations.

Through this examination the film-maker can seize on the opportunity to gauge the effectiveness of his work and to consider the successive day's shooting. By constantly working over the film in an attempt to draw out the values in the mixture of the drama, the camera work, and the editing to take place, the film-maker develops the ability literally to read his shots and render judgments concerning the realization of his planning. These efforts are highly creative because the actors, the camera, and the shots are in a state of flux, and the reflective quality of screening provides a perspective whereby the film-maker can return to his work with renewed insight. The creative aspect of film-making has not ceased; the artist has done nothing more than step back from his canvas slightly for an objective look.

Such screenings are not a time for criticism or satisfaction, but rather a time when one idea leads to another in a state of constant development. It is not necessarily true that such an approach will play havoc with a film's budget, because the film-maker does not rewrite his story, change settings or locations, or arbitrarily throw out the work he has done and start anew. He works within his planned references. But his feeling of exploration never ceases. It is the difference between lines of dialogue, movement, a set and fixed camera, and a freer attitude toward the handling of them. This freedom not only introduces a first-time quality and catches something that has never been realized or seen before, but is a kind of controlled improvisation, which is what film-making is all about.

For an entire film to be alive, each and every individual shot that goes into it must have its own little spark. The meaning and value of the individual shot, the work it will do of itself, and the way in which it will relate to other units makes itself felt. If the finished film is going to have a sense of freshness and excitement, these same qualities will be apparent in the rushes from the very beginning, much as a broken high-tension wire that is spitting and bouncing in midair. The energy has to be contained, of course, and must go through all the units in order to avoid a short circuit, but the indications are there. Containing the energy is what editing is all about.

The film-maker looks to see that the shots come up with precise composition, motivated camera movement, correct balance in color or blacks and whites to set the specific mood, progressive value to create a sense of urgency—all technical elements leading to and supporting a feeling for humanity, whether it be serene or agitated, angry or calm, joyous or depressed—a vitality. A kind of perpetual motion is set up here as the film-maker, out of his own initial excitement, has the opportunity to examine a part of what he has made. He thereby stimulates within himself still more excitement, so that all of the shooting may achieve the same degree of intensity.

EDITING THE FILM

Almost everything that has been talked about up to this point has been film editing, for editing is the dynamic of film-making. It is a process continuing from the time a film is no more than an idea in the film-maker's mind to the time the answer print is returned from the laboratory—and often beyond that. Yet editing has come to mean many different things to many different people, all engaged in one way or another in some phase of film production, editing included.

To some, editing is no more than cementing two pieces of film together; to others it means securing a perfectly matched cut; while to still others it is the perfect synchronization of a piece of track and picture with a reaction insert coming in on an emphatic beat. Editing is all of this, of course, but obviously much more. Film editing is the selection, arrangement, and re-arrangement of pictured pieces of life, of sounds and music—all brought together in a rhythmic pattern to create both emotional satisfaction and beauty. From the successful coordination of these elements meaning is secured—which is not an end in itself —but reflects the film-maker's idea of life both explicit and implied. It is the art of film-making.

Much of the confusion, as well as the differences of interpretation, arises mostly because of the mixture, so common to film, of art, business, and technology. The artistic challenge often stimulates directors to do their own editing, or, where that is not allowed, to establish close and mutual understanding with an editor so that the two can act in concert.

The business aspect of film calls for mass production, which, in turn, calls for assembly line techniques. Hence the necessity for splicers, assemblers, cutters, editors, negative cutters, etc. Here the difference between the cutter and the editor is that the latter is usually a decision maker. Yet, since his range of choice is considerably restricted because so much of the work has been pre-edited, both on paper and in the shooting, he often merely supervises the assembly. The changes and alterations he might make are relatively light.

The technological requirements, which involve the handling of moviolas, sound readers, synchronizers, splicers, and the like, attract persons who are good at doing skillful mechanical work. Such ability, however, though important for editing, does not necessarily include the ability to make artistic decisions.

The result of these varied demands, therefore, is often that the art so natural to film is bottled up, held in check, and circumscribed. Thus it fails to prosper and grow as an art because it is used by people with different ability and varying talents to achieve an inartistic end.

Although many editors agree that editing has infinite possibilities for discovery, and although they enthusiastically endorse the ideas of relational editing, and smile warmly at the mere mention of Eisenstein and Pudovkin, they still return to their cutting tables to match the same tired cuts in the same worn way. This condition persists, however, not because editors are willfully arbitrary, but because the nature of the material being edited is such that no amount of juxtaposing or rearranging can break through the conceptual blindness that fettered the material from the start.

Because money talks and much of the film industry is controlled by its demands, financial interests have had a tremendous influence on Hollywood's products. In order to protect his investments, the average businessman would naturally prefer for the film to appeal to the largest possible number of customers. On the whole, the result has been to produce films that aim at the least specialized tastes, are as similar as possible to what has already been successful, and do not offend or disturb (i.e., challenge) anyone.

It is almost a cliché to say that a deliberate attempt has been made to find the common denominator for films. But the term is clarified by realizing that the common denominator is the lowest possible value that can be assigned to a series of fractions in order to express them all in the same terms. And, of course, this desire to express everything in the same terms (especially at a low level) is the very antithesis of good film-making. All freshness, spontaneity, artistic appeal, and creative stimulation are cut off by a fog of banality. Furthermore, not only are these characteristics vital to the growth and thriving of the film industry, but on them depends the industry's survival in its fierce competition for public attention.

No novelist would think of sending his manuscript off to be published only to find that sentences had been changed around, chapters shifted, or words struck out and others substituted. Nor would a painter rough out a sketch on canvas and send it to the lithographer to fill in the colors when he reproduces it. Absurd as this sounds, it points out the sharp line of responsibility that sets off the artist in other fields. In the film, idea, script, production, and editing blend so smoothly and are so interdependent that in the name of one, all can be tampered with; and thus the artist's function is usurped.

Many critics, and possibly film-makers too, assist in prolonging this condition by evaluating editing as if it existed in a vacuum. Traditionally edited films are usually discussed in terms of their story and character values alone; while dynamically edited films, which should involve the same values, elicit such comments as "a strong cinematic feeling," "exciting and arresting visuals," "a good film approach," "a sense of editing and an awareness of style," with little or nothing said of their story and character values. Unfortunately, such a view makes it appear as if the two (dynamic editing and a good story) were mutually exclusive, or as if one film-maker were ultraconservative and the other a wild-eyed devotee of the avant-garde.

Further, the implication is that the traditional approach and the dynamic approach to editing are styles in themselves; or even worse, that style in editing can be achieved through some specific assemblage of shots.

This kind of film cataloguing, which no doubt has a grain of truth in it somewhere, tends to cloud the film-maker's relationship to his material and to obscure not only the importance of editing, but the nature of style. Of course, there have been films with fine stories that were traditionally edited, and films with weak stories that have been somewhat enhanced by dynamic editing. But the new-found excitement that has caught the public imagination is not to be recaptured by superb editing (or even "modern" editing) of trite stories about unrequited love, violent action, or even week-ends of sex, whether European or American. Nor will it be found in presenting on screen the best of theater, novel, or short story within its original framework.

The excitement can only be renewed by appropriate editing and rich material. The source of the material is not important, whether from life or literature, so long as it is cinematically presented. When the successes of films based on the previously written word are examined, it is clear that the essence of the story has been abstracted, its meaning has been cherished with an almost religious fervor, and it has been presented anew in terms of the screen. This has been true over the years, as attested to by films from Lewis Milestone's *All Quiet on the Western Front* (1930) to Tony Richardson's *Tom Jones* (1963).

Editing's line of development has been clear and direct, from the crude efforts of Porter, who was the first to put together pieces of a scene to convey the sense of the whole, to the sophisticated editing of Fellini, for instance, who in *8½* uses flashbacks, flash-forwards, scenes in the present, make-believe, and reality to dramatize the confusion of a man's psyche. Underlying this development is the growth and exploitation of the principle of montage.

Montage is not a static technique of editing, a prescribed method for handling a few shots; it is the source of a film's power; it *is* editing. The understanding of montage has grown over the years, from the obvious symbol of arms caressing heaps of gold, treasures, and jewels in *Greed* (1924) to the more sophisticated symbol of a few gold pieces in *The Informer* (1935)—each dramatizing the inner forces that lead to a man's destruction; or from the simple picturing of a wheat tycoon who gains power only to destroy himself, as in D. W. Griffith's *A Corner in Wheat* (1909), to the subtle significance of a young easy-living man, standing by his sports car and looking up at a window framing a prim maid who has let down her neatly set hair, in Dino Risi's *The Easy Life* (1963)—each ironically pointing up through related shots a degree and kind of human isolation.

From this a number of observations can be made. First, the essence of all communication is based on the relationship of things and people to each other. The purpose of montage is to reveal this relationship through visual units. Second, to be effective, montage must be built on shots that contain both explicit and implicit values. Some of the experiments of the early Russian film-makers were criticized, and rightly so, for shots of flowing tears followed by rushing mountain streams. The effect was both banal and obscure at the same time. Nevertheless, they were on the right track, failing in some instances because they did not go far enough, but picked the trite and obvious connection. Through clear-sighted selection, shots bearing the right relationship to the tears undoubtedly could have heightened the total impact on the viewer.

The secret of montage lies in the stressing of meaning that grows out of shot relationships; but obviously, the shots themselves must contain perceptive bits of information and must work together cumulatively, not cancel one another out.

The process of getting implicit and explicit values in a shot can be likened to the use of symbols in literature. Thus, the shot must make literal sense and further the story while at the same time implying a deeper meaning. Such shots are well demonstrated in the closing unit of Roman Polanski's *Knife in the Water* (1963), in which a man and his wife (together again) are in a car approaching a crossroads: one road leads to the police station, the other back home. The car approaches the intersection, stops, the shot holds—and the film ends. How simple. Yet the very shot—cumulatively coming out of the final arrangement—contains the thematic punch, as the unfaithful wife and the self-centered, smug husband have no place left to go. If they return home they have to live without faith in each other. If they go to the police to confess a murder that never happened, the scandal will separate them. In every way, they have destroyed one another.

Naturally, such implication of meaning does not depend solely on the use of symbols. However, since film is expressly visual, it lends itself well to the use of symbols—the cross, a figure in black, a bowl of strawberries and milk. In this respect, every shot in the film is a symbol of the film-maker's meaning and must be handled as such.

Editing in its fullest sense, then, has to be accomplished in terms of what is being said and of what has been or is to be shot. The practice of editing cannot be arbitrarily superimposed on a story, but the story and the editing that points it must be developed simultaneously. It is thus that the film-maker reaches out to his audiences, struggles with his ideas, and seeks to throw more light on living. Such work cannot be accomplished on paper in advance and left at the end to cutters. Having captured the essence of his emotion and thought on film, the film-maker must enhance, heighten, and point up his creation by seizing on new flashes of insight that will reinforce his original aims. This he must do himself, or, if that is impossible, he must be in close and constant supervision of the editing.

THE EDITING KEY

By the "editing key" is meant the basic framework that is going to shape the editing operation. Because of its very nature, the film footage has in it a key, or indication of the way it can be handled. The shots can be about fishermen in a Portuguese coastal town, or about the intricate and delicate relationship existing between a man and a woman; but broad or narrow, objective or subjective, the material in the shots is the physical world and the shots themselves provide the working units. Form, movement, and rhythm are innately present and contained within these units. The film-maker must develop an ability to sense these elements in the film as it has been shot and to see them as they will relate to the finished whole. Thus, the footage must be looked at and studied again and again. Depending on the amount of footage at hand, it can be examined in terms of sequences, scenes, or even—if the film is a one-reeler—in whole units. After repeated viewing, the pattern of arrangement of shots begins to emerge from the haze and gives a clue to the proper editing key.

This pattern has been consciously or unconsciously set by the way the shots were looked on and seen during the shooting.

And as the film-maker refamiliarizes himself with the footage, the individual points of view of each shot begin to make themselves felt, and out of the accumulation comes a single directional force to indicate to the film-maker the way the scene can shape up. Through careful study of the footage, the film-maker also reacts to the raw, uncut shots and measures them against the intensity of his feelings. The ways and means for arranging and intensifying these pieces so that they support the over-all point grow out of the individual and cumulative values of each shot. Differences among the shots in terms of nature, level, and degree of contribution can be sensed and seen; and by controlling these differences—exploiting them or toning them down —a pattern for arrangement is developed. Thus the editing key depends on the nature of the material, the film-maker's view of it, and the kind of editing that will sustain that view effectively. Although the ability to pick out the key develops with experience and also depends on the clarity of the shooting, the footage, nevertheless, has to be looked at and studied over and over.

In one respect, planning is begun all over again at this moment, because the sizing up, measuring, and evaluating that takes place is a speculation as to the way the material will come together. And from this grows the extra values that montage, or relational editing as it is called here, can give. The emphasis, so far, has been on that relationship between shots that builds progressively so that the audience is given greater insight into the story, the people involved, and the film-maker. But this relationship is not the only one: as shot supports scene, and scene supports sequence, a relationship grows between the structure of the film and its content. True, this relationship has been thought about, planned, and held as a guide through the preparation and the shooting; but it is at this point that the film-maker finds out whether the relationship is the same, different, better, or worse than the one he had planned—and whether he can sharpen, clarify (or in some cases, even save) it.

When each shot has been so filmed that it carries its own little message, the underlying structural pattern serves as an approach to the cutting and is in no way mechanical because story elements are constantly available in all the shots. The long shots, medium shots, close-ups, and combinations of these, the limitless kind of movement that results, can be made to achieve an effect that is greater than the sum of all the shots and that communicates to the viewer highly specific and precise information.

To see this point clearly, a comparison can be made between traditional and relational editing. In traditional editing the scene is established, usually in a long shot, and as the action within the scene proceeds a number of medium shots and close-ups are taken to relate that action. This is a kind of theatrical staging with the camera used mostly to emphasize parts of the action. Editing in such an instance is pre-set and limited. In relational editing a series of long shots may be brought together, or a series of close-ups, or long shots interspersed with close-ups—unlimited combinations, all based on using the camera to relate shots and, in turn, to weave a pattern that is expressive within itself. As a result the film-maker in his editing can take the audience from a specific idea to a general one (close-up to long shot) and secure meaning out of this connection; he can take his audience from specific idea to specific idea (close-up to close-up) and secure meaning out of such a connection. Thus in the editing pattern the scene may be given to constant expansion by using shots that go from specific details to more general ones. Just as easily, through reversing this process, the audience is taken from general topics to specific related details.

These patterns are limitless, depending on the nature of the shots and the film-maker's intent. They are not possible in the editing unless they have been considered in the shooting. Traditional editing emerges from a script that is theatrical in scope, heavily controlled by dialogue. Relational editing emerges from a script that is developed in terms of camera and movement, with dialogue used to support these.

In brief, shots, as individual units, communicate; shots when brought together communicate further. Out of the combination of the two in an extended edited piece a pattern emerges, which can be handled and controlled, and which communicates even further. Out of such patterns grow idea, mood, and feeling.

Interestingly enough, in this aspect film appears to be related to the theater of Shakespeare's day and functions along similar, yet much broader, lines. Shakespearean scholars have pointed out that London's Globe Theatre, for example, was made up of inner and outer stages, upper stages (balconylike in effect), window stages at the sides, smaller stages above the balcony stages, trap doors and rope ladders, innumerable doors for entrances and exits, and a swinging curtain for quick change of scene. Broad patterns of movement were readily possible; shifts from place to place were immediate. The stage not only readily supported flow and movement in a sweeping manner, but represented the infinite characteristics of the real and outer world. Here was a vast canvas, given to broad perspectives. Yet, through the playing and speech, the opposite extreme was readily available through concentration on the fine details of action and character. In the full scope of this theater, richness was contained in the poetry of the word; but the significance and meaning of the word took on an even more telling quality through movement—movement related to a world that was limitless by suggestion.

It is no accident, for example, that the opening scene of *The Easy Life* (1963) shows a little sports car zooming around an empty, deserted St. Peter's Square early in the morning and slicing at the quiet with its noisy exhaust. The occupant of the car, Vittorio Gassman, is not seen for some time, until he pulls up to make a telephone call. Not being able to get his party, he once again zooms through the streets of Rome, the noise of his car shattering the quiet. The pattern of the cutting in this case supports character and theme. The vast empty square, solemn and dignified with its religious architecture and statuary, is contrasted with the blasé, free-and-easy spirit of the sports car and its occupant. This idea is maintained throughout the scene as long shots are slowly brought together, creating a tranquil quality against which is contrasted the interruptions of the action contained within the shots. Innumerable close-ups could have been shown of car wheels spinning, a steering wheel being spun frantically, a foot hitting the brake pedal, etc.; but by simply stressing speed, they would have destroyed the essential thematic pattern growing from the contrast of the solemn square and the jazzy little sports car.

It is no accident, either, that the opening of *Sundays and Cybele* (1962) introduces extreme close-ups of an airplane on its screaming bomber run, with audience orientation more a matter of agitation than acclimitation—one is not quite sure what is happening. Then, suddenly, in mounting close-ups, the face of a young girl appears in the bomber's sights. Thus the entire motivation for the central character's problem is sharply defined. The pattern of this cutting of close-up after close-up has clearly been planned to establish this motivation. Innumerable long shots—perhaps of the village where the girl lived, the plane a speck in the faraway sky, shots of it coming closer and closer—would have resulted in a pattern of totally different meaning. In fact, the audience would then never be subjected to the pilot's agitation, frenzy, shock, and mounting guilt.

Thus, the ability to control the cutting pattern as shots are brought together is an integral part of creative editing, and the uncut film must be studied carefully so that the shots can be measured against intent. Thus the editing pattern is discovered.

EDITING AND MOTIVATION

Editing as such has not changed as much as the point of view of the film-maker. But to achieve its end this new point of view in turn demands a kind of editing that is unfamiliar. Films today have taken on greater dimensions, and in some instances a worldliness and refinement that have not only strengthened the entire concept of editing, but have eliminated editing as a routine process. (Of course, this does not include those instances where film is turned out as a mass-produced product.) The new films are conceived in editing terms and so carried all the way through until completed, so that the editing is a continuous process instead of a final step in production. This view results from an ever-increasing awareness that image arrangement not only penetrates a scene to bring out its meaning, but calls for economy of dialogue. This in turn eliminates the clichéd and repetitious and emphasizes genuine attitudes and feelings on the part of the characters.

Until recent years, editing usually fell into one of two defined molds called empirical and theoretical editing, according to the way the film-maker approached his material. Empirical editing is based on shaping the film mainly during the cutting stage, as in the unscripted or outlined piece of work. Theoretical editing, on the other hand, applies to the scripted piece; it is planned according to the known ways and means for securing a film syntax.[1] But just as the methods of the documentary film-maker and the fiction film-maker have come closer and closer together, so have the various editing approaches.

Because editing is a result and not a cause and is shaped by the story itself, it appears new when a rule or two is broken and we are led to concentrate on values that previously have been alien to film in a general sense. Plot has been the Hollywood story mainstay from the very beginning, but plot is only one factor among a variety of others. When plot alone is emphasized, a certain kind of film becomes standard fare and sets up an example for all films to follow, thus providing built-in limitations. When a film comes along in which plot is not the main driving force, and when its editing rightly follows suit and takes a shape counter to hackneyed methods of the past, some movie sages wag their heads, desperately bemoaning the new development and failing to understand how anyone can cut a film in which the cuts fail to match.

[1] Reisz, *op. cit.*, p. 255.

The simple fact of editing is that each shot must move the story forward as the audience is taken from one point of reference to another. And the nature of those references, the way they affect one another, must be brought out by the editing. The value of the film, therefore, and of the editing, lies in the skill with which these shots are brought up and put together. Thus, shots and editing are intricately bound up—one cannot be completely successful without the other. The best editing cannot result in a good film if the shots are insipid, nor will superb shots carry a film that is poorly edited.

Plot, of course, is the simplest element to deal with in editing, because it involves the simplest form of dramatic action, exemplified by the proverbial Western or the mystery-suspense film. But emphasis solely on plot has limitations that dictate the nature of the cutting. Here there is a special need for inventiveness and a particular kind of imagination. Dramatically, the lack of depth (complex characterization and a theme of serious proportion) in a heavily plotted story calls for a rich development in breadth (one-dimensional characters and complexity of situation) by including different and fresh type-characters, unexpected and unusual situations, and highly motivated and believable entanglements to further suspense, excitement, and audience involvement. Cinematically, the shots should avoid hackneyed arrangements by providing sufficient information for the audience to grasp the goings-on and, at the same time, to be eager for the next scene, and the next.

Picture the traditional scenes in a film of the 1920's: the reading of the will at the stroke of midnight, the young heiress retiring for the night in a bed over which hangs a portrait, the eyes in the portrait move, alongside a panel slides open and a gloved hand emerges. Or, visualize a restaurant scene in the United Nations, a mistaken identity, a sneaky slaying, and stunned crowds. The former describes one of the many thrillers that featured Helen Twelvetrees and her bloodcurdling screams, while the latter marks the opening of Alfred Hitchcock's *North by Northwest* (1959). In the Ian Fleming stories—*From Russia with Love* (1964), for example—the clichés are recognized by the film-maker, but he secures freshness and a new point of view by refusing to take himself seriously. This is another way of solving the problem of securing breadth, until this idea wears thin with audiences and a substitute must be found. Editing in all these cases has a common denominator.

But story sophistication of a different kind introduces marked changes, and when the film-maker shifts from one kind of story to another that is radically different in genre, his need to communicate something different tells him that he must do it differently and thus guides his editing.

Editing today calls for a highly evaluative as well as creative point of view, because the advent of full-bodied literature challenges the sensitivity of the editor to subtle and varied story elements. Although the axiom is simple—select and arrange those shots that tell the story—the film-maker has to be familiar with those elements that go to make up his story. More than this, as editor, he has to react to the delicate balance among elements of plot, character, idea, and interplay to select those values he believes most in line with his intention.

In the early days, and in much of television today, editing was relatively simple because the bulk of the shots dealt with the mechanical arrangements to project the plot. One needed primarily to distinguish between a comic turn and a serious one, and beyond that to cut for the mounting action that the camera had captured. But when it comes to various shades of comedy or subtle nuances of level in serious pieces, obvious plots are not only of secondary consideration, but sometimes completely negligible. Michelangelo Antonioni's films would not be such mysterious, obscure epics to those who criticize them if they would but look at the screen without preconception, giving themselves to the images and emanating pulse of life. Films simply have had too much horse and cavalry, with the result that some viewers' sensitivity has been lulled into a coma.

One does not have to dig too deeply into his memory—for that matter he can look at some movie advertising today—to be aware of the sameness in film. Terms used to describe films were devised expressly to sell them, by fixing their location (the South Seas), indicating the action (a chiller-thriller), or describing a personal problem (the doctor who cannot choose between his practice and his wife). Actually there was no need for greater definition. The very sameness of theme and idea that made such generalized descriptions apt also led to prescribed methods for editing.

The values for which the editor must strive today—at least in those cases where artistic forces are in play—are more difficult to achieve. The editor must bring out both the over-all dramatic value that is the film's purpose, as well as the minor values from scene to scene as they work to support the whole.

One cannot get the sense and feel of editing except by having the film in his hand as he runs it through a moviola and places one shot against the next. But where formerly the editor would seek to join shots primarily so that the physical action was well matched, he now looks for linkages that will point up fresh and different intent. This is a far cry from the simple cutting of an action piece and calls for the editor to shift gears completely as he strives for totally new and meaningful values.

MOVEMENT

When the director in the theater stages a play, moving his actors about, arranging them in varying relationships, and composing them to form changing pictures, he does so in order to interpret the script. Although he relies on dialogue, he seeks support and interpretation of what is being said through what is being done. Therefore he uses movement to interpret every living moment of his story.

There is a good deal of similarity between this aspect of directing for the theater and directing for the film. But the film makes an immediate departure from such staging by breaking immediately from the fixed frame or proscenium—moving any-which-way—thus placing in the hands of the editor a most powerful means both for controlling the audience's attention and deriving implicit meaning from the movement among the shots.

Movement is the driving power that activates each scene and sequence, brings vitality and life to a film, and sharply defines the form of the edited unit. The movement is obtained by working and reworking the shots until they form a complete pattern. Already discussed is that movement that grows out of the character's action and reactions, as well as the movement of the camera and the combination of both. In properly edited shots, such movement is not only threaded and woven together, but given greater definition, subsequently proportioning the scene and conveying a meaning. For this reason movement is the foundation of editing, because it affects the technical, story-telling, rhythmic, and sensory values.

The very decision, for example, as to where to place a cut when joining two shots depends on the emphasis desired. An uninterrupted movement by a character in one shot, then cut and followed by a close-up, gives emphasis to the close-up (see Arrangement No. 1).

The audience has been brought closer to the subject, and the subject has been more prominently positioned in its relationship

Arrangement No. 1

to shot one. In addition, the two shots, placed as they are, sub-scribe to a tiny dramatic build.

The reverse of this arrangement (see Arrangement No. 2), in which the close-up precedes the medium long shot, still places the emphasis on the close-up, mostly because of the closeness to the subject. The action in the medium long shot would tend to decline in intensity.

Arrangement No. 2

Suppose the arrangement in this second instance were made even stronger; three close-ups were to be used at the beginning of the unit followed by the same medium long shot (see Arrangement No. 3).

Arrangement No. 3

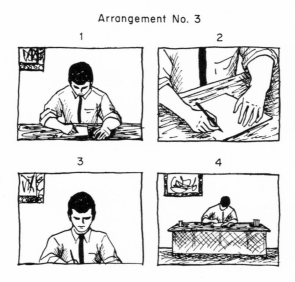

Here the close-ups, through repetition, take on even greater strength, with the medium long shot dropping considerably in intensity. The action within the long shot, however, could be of such a nature that alternate values would also be possible. Increased dramatic action on the part of the character, for example, could make the intensity of the unit rise in spite of the prominently positioned close-ups. In any unit of shots, therefore, emphasis can be secured by having shots rise in intensity,

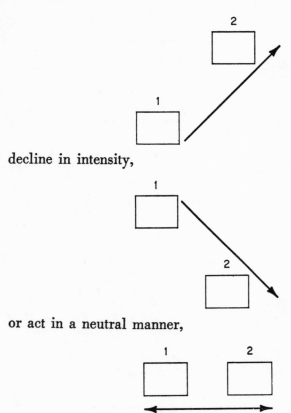

decline in intensity,

or act in a neutral manner,

all depending on the action within the shot, the point of view of the camera, and the method of arrangement.

By cutting constantly on movement, considerable excitement can be created, with the audience anticipating a climactic point to follow (see Arrangement No. 4).

Arrangement No. 4

By having each of these shots held in time on the screen (see Arrangement No. 5), presuming the content is slow moving, with cut moving slowly into cut, a reverse pattern would be established, supporting a soft, soothing, almost idyllic effect.

Arrangement No. 5

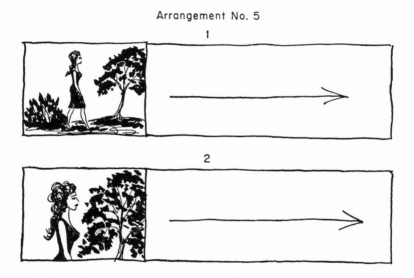

Not only can a shift of emphasis be secured repeatedly, but out of this shifting movement a pattern is being woven. Imagine the pattern being scribed in the air on the entrance of a ballerina who makes a sudden and electric leap and sweeps across the stage in huge spirals. Compare this with a reverse entrance: one in which the ballerina enters with mincing steps and small movements, comes center, and delicately begins to withdraw as if into a cocoon. Shots move constantly, and as they weave from point to point, first from one view, then from another, they are choreographed into a fluid design.

The examples given here are not meant as cutting examples —although they are quite possible and would achieve some stark effects—but are meant to point up that in the cutting, the shots themselves secure movement through placement and give rise to form and pattern. Rules are available to cover the effect of cutting before, during, or after movement; pictorial motivation through actors' movements (an actor looks toward the window, cut to the window); and the relative pictorial advantage of clarity gained by allowing an action to go uninterrupted and cutting at the point of rest (clarity is gained because the full action is seen and the audience, reaching the "rest," anticipates that they will be brought in for a closer look)—but all of these are purely mechanical.

Two points are evident even in the slight examples cited: first, cutting is impossible without full consideration of content. As oversimplified as this may seem, there are still editors who haggle over matching a shot and look for motivation in the cutting for a purely pictorial reason, rather than in the nature of the material. This is not a brief for a host of mismatched cuts, but an assertion that shot matching itself can be achieved in a number of different ways and in a number of places. Smoothness in flow, for instance, is not absolutely important for its own sake. Smoothness is one value among many that the editor can call on to achieve his effects. In some cases it may not be half as significant as the value that may be attained through a long series of static holds, abrupt agitational effects, counter-pointed shot arrangements with a constantly shifting emphasis, or a series of jumps taking the viewer from high point to high point for concentrated effect—any design pattern the film-maker can find to help him clarify his expression.

The variations of patterns that are to be found in editing are not arbitrary, but grow out of the fluid relationship between content, camera, and film-maker's intention. Even in a straightforward narrative progression, the editor is relinquishing opportunity when he fails to examine his material for the movement in it and the movement he can add through his cutting to bring about a more dynamic, dramatic, and telling design. Innumerable battle scenes have been portrayed on the screen, but those in Eisenstein's *Alexander Nevsky* (1938) and Sir Laurence Olivier's *Henry V* (1944) are unforgettable. A closer look at these scenes will reveal that the cutting brings about a movement that forms a most intricate design; and the audience not only understands what is going on, but reacts to it emotionally.

SENSORY VALUES

The value of film editing has usually been that it allows for selection, the accumulation of details, the guiding of audience reactions, a varying emphasis, the abridgment of time and space, and heightened emotional and intellectual effects through various kinds of montage arrangements (relational editing). Yet little mention is made of the point that any given series of shots, when cut together, will form a pattern or design linked by movement. This particular design not only conveys the story elements, but also appeals in a sensory manner. This quality makes a film unique and adds to its power to attract and hold attention.

Perhaps the reason why this quality is so seldom mentioned is that it is ignored by some film-makers, hardly understood, if at all, by others, and, because it is closely woven in with story values, cannot be explained simply. Story values are constantly talked about because they are reasonably obvious. One can explain a plot; a character can be described; an idea can be discussed; but an emotion is difficult to communicate directly and is not only fleeting, but extremely personal. However, sensory values project the mood, tone, and climate of the story in a well-established order that is both beautiful and satisfying.

Such values are abstract, of course, and appeal primarily to the eye and ear; but, through implication and shot connection, they take in the balance of the senses. Thus editing must be highly interpretive as it combines form, rhythm, and movement to appeal to the senses in many ways and on many different levels.

The elements that are at the editor's command to secure sensory values include movement within each shot, which may be of people or things moving from side to side, to and from the camera, up or down, or on the oblique. This movement, of course, is obtained primarily during the shooting; but during the editing its length, the juxtaposition of one movement to another, and the use of specific kinds of shots (long, medium, close) are the decision of the editor. Another element is composition, or form. Although by the time the cutting is done the composition of each shot is already fixed, the cumulative effect of a series of shots has a composition of its own. This comprises the relative tone qualities in black, white, or color, and whether they shade into one another or break abruptly; the individual patterns achieved in each shot through lighting, and the effect of these as shots come together. Sound, too, whether it be the spoken word, music, noises or all of these, works to support a pattern. But most important is that the joining of the shots in terms of the movement—how they relate to one another, at which point they make the transition, and the hardness or softness of the beat that forms the stress—can be built to provide a specific compositional design, fluid in nature yet with definite sensory appeal.

Carefully exercised control of these elements holds an audience and affects it in a number of ways. The kinds of shots selected and the way in which they are brought together to support a scene may create a feeling of looseness or release, or a feeling of tightness and constriction. Consider for a moment the scene at the Trevi Fountain in *La Dolce Vita* (1960), and the free-sailing pattern secured by the flow and movement of shots as the actress and her escort are followed through the streets and wind in and out of the fountain. The actress' movement, the sweep of the camera, and the way the shots have been combined all manage to convey strongly to the viewer a sense of freedom and lightness. Or consider the zany and ridiculously amusing hound and hunt scene in *Tom Jones* (1963). The fits-and-starts pattern created by shots that cough their way through the scene not only gives a feeling of the chase, but of the times and the exuberance of the people engaged in the chase. In contrast, take the final fight scene in *Champion* (1949), in which the fighter is in a vicious and savage exhibition; the projection of the tonal quality of this scene, shown in short, biting close-ups, expresses constant agitation and frustration. In all three instances the nature of the action, the backgrounds, and the ideas contribute directly to the tonal quality mentioned, but the arrangement and selection of the shots contribute equally. If any one of these scenes was rearranged in the pattern of the others, not only would a good part of the scene be lost, but what remained would be extremely bland, and lacking the original excitement; possibly it would be completely destroyed.

Design values fall into three general groups: they are regular or irregular (referring to a formal or informal arrangement of the compositional elements, a rigid and stern air as against a relaxed, fortuitous, or off-hand feeling); shallow or deep in perspective (the flat quality supporting a comic tone or at least lighter values, generally leaning toward the delicate and contrived overtones); and loosely or tightly arranged (the tight arrangements giving a feeling of being closed in, restricted, and the others a freer, pliant, flowing feeling). Although these designs have no true limitations since there are so many possible variations, some general patterns and their effects may still be cited. The cutting form of a series of shots in a scene, therefore, may be ordered or disordered, sprawling or condensed, rigid or relaxed, expanded or contracted, broad or restrained.

Though the content of the shots themselves defines the pattern specifically, the general tone and its connected emotional aura pulses from the arrangement. In addition, the emotional connotation is gained from a pattern that is not nebulous or obscure, but specific, as it is precisely planned. An ordered series of shots, for example, lends stiffness and formality. The degree to which such a pattern is extended can lead to a great sense of tension that may be shattered at any moment. A constantly expanding pattern introduces a sense of relief, as if deeper and deeper breaths were being taken. The reverse—the contracting pattern—suggests a gasping for air, a closing in, a choking off. Then again, either of these patterns may blend with an ordered or disordered array and thus secure further definition. A sprawling form is one that is relaxed and leisurely; it differs from a broad form in degree, in that it goes to an extreme. The same is true of condensed and restrained forms as they suggest retirement, withdrawal, frustration, and agitation.

Although the development of these forms as part of editing patterns comes under the film-maker's control during the editing, he does not attempt to force it by arbitrarily imposing the design on the unit being edited. First, the design is motivated by the story value of each particular unit. Second, the over-all statement of the piece, as well as the over-all pattern, is kept in mind, sensed, as it were, with the design shaping up within its framework.

If the film has been shot with both a creative and interpretive point of view, the pattern possibilities are increasingly vibrant and most definitely call for an awareness on the part of the film-maker to react to it and give it direction. With value in the shot and the power to control it through the editing, the film-maker is able to make a specific design quite consciously and deliberately. The extent of the deliberateness of the effort is so limitless that if it were possible to strip the film of all meaningful content, to see the pure abstraction of tone and mood and the way in which the shots veritably dance together, the pattern would be most clear.

More pronounced examples of such editing patterns are to be found in the opening shots of *The Last Laugh* (1924). Expansiveness and luxury are secured through a fluid camera and are punctuated by the restriction and closeness of static hold shots; concurrently, movement within each shot precipitates an emotional turmoil. In Antonioni's *The Eclipse* (1962), the medium close shots of the stock-market obsessed mother build to a frenzy and are set against the slow hold shots of an isolated daughter: busyness within a dispassionate atmosphere.

As the film-maker watches the film run through the moviola he gets a sense of this developing form. His decisions in many instances have to do with heightening it, making it stronger, clearer, more dynamic. When he succeeds in drawing the shots into their meaningful design, he begins to define the rhythm, and thus avoids imposing an arbitrary or limited one. When the design, rhythm, and movement reinforce one another to express an emotion or thought, the effect is so electric that the audience cannot for a moment keep its eyes away from the screen.

RHYTHM

In the over-all process of film-making, nowhere does the film-maker have the kind of opportunity to exercise the precise judgment and control required as when the film takes shape in the editing. It is then that the film begins to stir as if the incubation period were over, and to emerge from its cocoon to show itself for what it is. Its success will depend, to an extent impossible to assess, on its energy, its power to hold an audience, its rhythm.

Rhythm, however, is a value that is sensed, felt, and heard, and is somewhat easier to grasp in the older, established arts. It makes itself felt in the composition of a painting, and in the form of a piece of sculpture. Rhythm makes itself heard in spoken language, and, of course, in music. And because the film encompasses these areas—being made up of composition, design, form, movement, sound, dialogue, and music—it has in it their accompanying rhythms. These must be blended into a unified organization out of which grows the film's own total rhythm, based on that shifting on the screen from image to image that is commonly called cuts.

Yet, the simple change of images on the screen is not necessarily rhythmic, since rhythm involves a regularly recurring series of pulses containing periodic accents. The rhythm introduced by cuts can be quickly understood if one visualizes a white light hitting a film screen and alternating with darkness in a prescribed cadence. The cadence may be likened to that used by the army in marching: one-two-three-four, with the accent falling on the first beat. Such a pattern could be held constantly, but still could be speeded up or slowed down. The rate of speed of the rhythm is called "tempo." The film exists in time; the changes that can be effected by lengthening and shortening pieces, plus compounded movement brought by moving closer to or away from the screen, result in limitless rhythmic possibilities that are as complex, subtle, and fine as the rhythms of our finest prose, poetry, or music.

A film's rhythm, however, is not secured purely through the arrangement of cuts, but is also dependent on the rhythms inherent in the content. In some cases, the rhythm achieved through cuts is minor and subordinate to that coming from the movement within each shot; in other cases the rhythm of the cuts is most prominent. It all depends on the way the film-maker has approached his film, the way the elements relate to one another, the kind of scenes, and the values brought out. But before these relationships are looked into, it might be advantageous to list those sources from which the film draws its rhythmic quality.

First, if the shot has been composed and lighted properly, a rhythm pervades its composition. Closely linked with the mood and atmosphere of the shot, the design pattern, along with the amount of black and white even in a static shot, suggests movement. The rhythm of a composition made up of a series of flowing lines, for example, can quickly be distinguished from that of a design made up of straight angular bits. Should there

be movement within the shot in whatever is being photographed
—falling rain, turning wheels, birds flying, wheat bending to
the wind, flames of fire—such movement introduces an even
stronger rhythmic beat that must be taken into consideration.
With the addition of camera movement—panning, moving
closer to or away from, or trucking with—rhythms emerge from
both camera and subject. Movement within the frames and
camera movement can work together to make the rhythm even
stronger; they can counterpoint each other to make the rhythm
complex, or, if in opposition, can render the shots ineffective
and boring.

Second, there is the movement of people. The addition of
actual speech brings in the rhythm of language. A good part of
the film-maker's task is to observe his actors to see that the
rhythmic patterns of speech and movement are harmonious.
Sometimes, as in comedy, accented beats may be introduced
at places unexpected by the audience. One of the biggest problems in dealing with nonactors is that their sense of rhythm may
be interrupted through self-consciousness, or that the film-maker
in his zeal will arbitrarily force on them rhythms that are
foreign to their natural ways.

Third, a rhythm evolves during the selection and arrangement (or cutting) of the shots, and at this point any arbitrary
imposition of rhythms on those already existing could be disastrous. It is fairly evident, therefore, that the editor in a sense
enjoys the position of a symphonic conductor as he leads and
guides the various instruments to create the musical whole.
Similarly, the film's rhythm does not originate from any one
source, but from all of them together, now perhaps picked up
by one piece, now by another, and then another, but regardless
of the complexity, all in concert.

In some instances the cut itself serves as the basic rhythmic
pattern, whereas in other cases, it provides the accented stress
for dominant rhythms inherent in content. The cut, being the
hardest and sharpest transition from scene to scene, can be
varied so that the rhythmic pattern and its stress are projected

from related sources, depending on the cut's placement and the nature of the content. During the actual editing, the shots should be arranged loosely so that the footage can be viewed, and the rhythms felt and sensed. Then the cutting should be done, and the process repeated again and again, so that the rhythm is established and the tempo gradually fortified and sharpened. The dissolve from one shot to another prolongs the beat, like a held note, and softens the change even more. The fade-out is a rest note.

In those films where the entire emphasis during the shooting has been on theatrical rendering of the story, the film editor is left with little choice but to follow the rhythms set up by the actors' patterns and to allow his cuts to fall in line with them. But films should be considerably more than the theatrical projection of a story. The rhythm of editing, felt and carried through from the film's beginnings, serves to communicate to an audience on a sensuous level as part of the cutting pattern that is structured.

STYLE IN EDITING

When speaking about a piece of writing, a critic may refer to the author's prose, verse, or journalistic style; then again, he may speak of the style as being brilliant, colloquial, familiar, or realistic. In the first instance, style is being used to define the nature of the piece, while in the second, it describes a condition about it. Though somewhat loosely used, style describes all of these things and something more. Most certainly, style in writing hinges on and revolves around the way in which the author has assembled his words on paper; but although this is the way style becomes apparent, by itself it is not style. Style quite obviously has to include the ideas and subject matter contained in those words, along with what the writer has felt and thought in terms of his personal experiences and views.

By this definition, every piece of writing has a style. Nevertheless, style is usually coupled with distinction, so that the pieces credited with style are those that bear the author's "trademark," the stamp of his individuality. Those initiated in the arts can immediately distinguish the distinctive styles of Gauguin, Picasso, and Klee. The uninitiated, though unfamiliar with the artist, are captivated by the commanding individuality of his work. By the same token, the reader is able to distinguish the work of Hemingway, Steinbeck, Faulkner, and Saroyan. And in the theater, where style is achieved through dialogue, setting, direction, and acting, an O'Neill presentation is still immediately identifiable, as is a play by Tennessee Williams. Each of these artists sees the world in his special way and goes about describing it in a manner compatible with what he sees.

In the film, style lies in the way the film-maker has assembled his shots. Yet, editing by itself is a method, not a style. To speak of the rapid and precise cutting of Eisenstein's Odessa Steps sequence in *Potemkin* (1925), or the arrangement of the charge of the French knights in *Henry V* (1944) without regard for the qualitative values in the shots, as if they were separable from the editing, is to miss the crucial point. Worse, it is to presume that in film-making one can arbitrarily superimpose a style on his material. In spite of the fact that Eisenstein himself has spoken of the conscious manipulation of shots to secure effects through a series of shocks, the point is that he manipulated in order to achieve something that was germane to his material, not merely for the sake of the effects themselves.

Eisenstein's work demonstrates his theories of montage, but the nature of his work was his personal way of applying his insights about film. When similar theories were applied by innumerable other film-makers—from Josef von Sternberg, Pare Lorentz, and Willard Van Dyke to John Huston and Akira Kurosawa—they too expressed themselves through their personal points of view, and each man's films have a different style.

The constant growth and expansion of technique today has brought to the film a number of stylists—Bergman, Fellini,

Antonioni, Resnais, Truffaut, to name several—each of whose editing is as different from the others' as apples from oranges, and none of which can be fitted into any hard and fast formulas. The reason is that the editing patterns are too much a part of the individuals involved and are as infinite and varied in depth as are the men's personalities. The stylistic characteristics, therefore, are of the men themselves, and therefore cannot be safely tucked away and labeled as editing of one kind or another. However, among them there is a common fundamental: their films are motivated by their attitudes and philosophies toward life, and their editing in turn is shaped by that motivation.

Ingmar Bergman, for example, is said to have a strain of the mystic, as his stories take on meaning beyond the immediately apparent and deal with man as he relates to God.[2] Totally different in subject matter and interpretation, yet markedly similar in control exercised over that subject matter, is Federico Fellini. He hits at a decaying social order while dealing with the interwoven lives of people concerned with love, religion, art, and intellectualism. Equally different is Michelangelo Antonioni who, though criticized for obscurity, finds that "the relationship between an individual and his environment is less important than the individual himself in all his complex and disquieting reality and in his equally complex relations with others."[3] Thus, in seemingly formless storytelling, he hits at man's alienation and inability to contact others.

Still another factor common to all three film-makers is the degree of self-involvement and subjectivity toward their story material. This kind of film-making is quite different from that of earlier time or of television today. Here, there is no barrier between the film-maker and his material: to see the film is often to see the man. But a further point of clarification remains in

---

[2] Werner Wiskari, "Ingmar Bergman's Way with 'The Rake,'" *The New York Times*, May 7, 1961, Sec. 2, p. 11.

[3] Michelangelo Antonioni, "Direction Noted," *The New York Times*, February 18, 1962, Sec. 2, p. 9.

that self-involvement and subjectivity are not the same thing. Subjectivity is a way of approaching a body of material, while self-involvement indicates concern. Innumerable first-rate films have been made in which the film-maker's approach has been objective; that is to say, he is not part of the material, but stands to one side and shapes it. Even in such instances, the degree of the film's effectiveness or ineffectiveness is measured by the film-maker's feeling for his story and his people. Thus there is self-involvement within a highly objective framework.

Robert Flaherty is the foremost exponent of this approach, and his style is simple, direct, and warm. In fact, the documentary film in general calls for this kind of viewpoint because the material is that of the world around the film-maker, seen through his eyes, but not about himself. This world is around us all the time; it is indifferent, disinterested, and neutral. Yet underneath, it seethes with anguish, hope, despair, and aspiration. It is human life, and to bring out this quality the film-maker must involve himself, and reveal his concern and the nature of it through the camera. In this way he develops a film style.

The big difference between today's films and those of the past is primarily one of degree. Adventure and suspense for their own sake make escapist literature, which has its place. But today's audiences are restless, in a world of restlessness. They want to know more about themselves and that world. To satisfy this need calls for films of sizable artistic proportions, films with style.

SOME POINTS OF MECHANICS

For the beginning film-maker, creative editing is an addiction. Although surrender of this kind is both profitable and pleasurable, it does not lack its dangers. As previously pointed out, in addition to artistic ability film-making requires an aptitude for things both scientific and mechanical. Editing, perhaps more than any other aspect of film-making, is a gadgeteer's dream come true. An editing table needs to be stocked with a viewer, a splicer, a sound reader, a synchronizer, rewinds, reels, marking pencils, and a host of other units from expensive to seemingly trivial items like paper clips. Further complication is added by the host of manufacturers producing gadgets of individual design, and the constant improvement of existing designs, so that equipment often becomes obsolete unexpectedly. With electricity to be supplied to the readers, splicers, viewers, moviola, and bits and pieces of film leader, the editing table can look like a spaceman's nightmare. One of the cardinal requirements, therefore, is tidiness and order. Not only should things be kept in specific places and returned to these places, but, equally important, a prescribed order must be established for the steps to be undertaken. The editor, keeping clearly in mind the objective of the cutting, both for the over-all film as well as for the piece he is working on, must also visualize the steps he will take to arrive at that objective. The worst thing he can do is dive in among a mess of footage.

The planned routine should include a continuous examination of results to judge success. The great possibilities of editing lie in the different results that can be achieved by different arrangements. But the editor must have a keen imagination for spatial relations, the ability to visualize where he is, where he is going, where he has gone, and how he can get back. The process of editing is much like threading one's way through a maze. Should one reach a dead end, he must make his way back to the beginning to start again. In the broad sense, short cuts do not exist. Not being able to get back to the starting point could mean that shots have been overcut, cut into at the wrong places, or simply misplaced. Editing calls for an ordered mind. Interestingly enough, an ordered mind usually goes with busy hands. A good editor is usually very well coordinated, has a long memory and a longer patience, and can handle all sorts of small and precise instruments at one time. He can run film and sound tape through a synchronizer while the film passes through a viewer, mark changes, and even make the changes then and there by splicing either picture or tape.

Another possible pitfall for the beginning film-maker is that too much pleasure will be derived from the simple mechanics of making a splice, threading and running a machine, finding points of synchronization, and listening to the whack of the clapper board. A level of creative satisfaction is arrived at simply by mastering all the equipment. There is nothing wrong with this, except that the film is sometimes forgotten in the process. Many a beginner has spent countless hours on a cut or two, only to be chagrined when the audience remains indifferent to his film. Had the audience been witness to his performance, as he balanced a splicer on one knee, ran the sound through the head of the moviola with the left hand, and held the "sync" point of picture in his right hand, he would have received a thunderous ovation. However, the object remains the film, not a circus act in a cutting room. The physical act of editing is great fun, but the editor must never be sidetracked by the gadgetry that surrounds him.

On this count, it will pay the film-maker to fit his work to his tools. One cannot expect to cut complex dialogue tracks without a moviola, nor can one synchronize a number of tracks and a picture without a synchronizer. The beginner's greatest attribute is his enthusiasm, but this enthusiasm can also hurt him by clouding his judgment. Naturally, he is strongly influenced by the films he sees presented commercially. Furthermore, he strives to emulate them or even to go them one better in some of the effects they have achieved. However, he may forget that the most sophisticated equipment and the most experienced editors have been at work to achieve those ends. Unless he has similar resources, the tendency to compete is foolhardy.

There is a common area open for competition with the most costly of productions, however, and that is in idea. When it comes to the story being told, money is of no consequence, and the most expensive productions can be reduced in stature to the equal of the cheapest. One is judged by the film that appears on the screen, not by the money spent on it, or by the agony that went on in the cutting room. To accomplish specific operations specific types of equipment are needed; and if one is limited on this score, he must frame his work from the beginning in terms of these limitations, so that he can explore his material to the fullest within that framework.

It is not necessary to tie up sums of money in capital equipment. In large centers, such as New York, Washington, Chicago, and St. Louis, there are agencies that rent equipment as well as equipped cutting rooms that are available by the day or week. In New York, for example, there are innumerable recording studios, with the best type of recording equipment, which may be rented by the hour or day. However, considering the nature of budget and available equipment, the film-maker must be realistic in both production and editing. He must depend on his natural talent and ability to make his equipment, whatever it is, work for him.

It has been said that a film is the sum of its shots. This is literally true, because when shooting, individual pieces are taken; and in editing, individual pieces are brought together. Editing refuses to give itself to a mass operation. Even in the most streamlined studios, the work is funneled through one individual, perhaps two at the most. It remains a step-by-step building up of shots.

Certain phases of editing are purely routine physical operations calling for no judgment, while others are physical operations calling for constant judgments. It is more profitable and satisfactory to keep together those operations that go together. For example, actual splicing, though it must be cleanly done, is relatively unimportant. Therefore, it can be set aside so as not to intrude at those times when judgments have to be made.

When working on a viewer or moviola, a good way to get

the sense of flow and the effect of shots coming together is to outline one shot on the ground glass with a grease pencil and to pass the successive shot behind it. Constant manipulation of this kind points up the emerging patterns more quickly.

It is always easier to take out pieces of film than to put them back in. Hence the editor literally crawls up on his picture slowly and piece by piece, screening whenever possible to check the effect he is getting. The various steps such as rough cut, fine cut, and frozen cut refer to this process in which the material is roughly assembled and then trimmed away, until such time as it is deemed complete.

Timing and pacing can only be done when the film is viewed at the actual running speed, twenty-four frames per second. In a sense it is far simpler for a musician to get his timing than for a film editor to set the timing of his picture, because no matter how well the picture has been planned, there are too many contributing factors that have to be considered. These all come together when the film is being run; and again, slowly and cautiously, the timing is felt, the film trimmed, and the rhythms set, step by step.

When a film is in a rough-to-fine cut stage, it is both an exasperation and a pleasure to realize suddenly while watching it that a complete rearrangement, although it would change the story considerably, would make it more effective. This is more likely to occur in a voice-over documentary; but in dialogue films, the shifting of full scenes or even of an entire sequence from one position to another can suddenly bring the film into a focus. So the whole process starts all over again.

Finally, film-making is learned in the editing room. No matter what the budget, or how big or small a scale one works on, in understanding film it is imperative to handle it physically. Regardless of how well theorized artistically and mechanically, the frames of reference, the perspectives, and the relationships simply fail to take real hold until the film-maker has handled the shots.

7

POINTS IN
RETROSPECT

Some film-makers have spent a lifetime making films, but are
still not sure of their inclinations, may never be sure, and, what
is more, are not particularly concerned about it. This is not
necessarily a bad state and, if anything, may be quite positive,
for it is more important for the film-maker to be constantly making films than to be given to a kind of film-making yoga—talk,
study, and discuss the film, but not attempt it.

The problem of the film-maker, as the problem of other
artists, is his struggle for identification. At the center of this
struggle is the film-maker's need to know what he wants to say
and how he is going to say it. The problem is complex. Aside
from such obvious decisions as whether the film should be
documentary or dramatic, light or serious in tone, poetic or
social in tenor (matters that cannot be decided simply and
should not be decided prematurely because of the paralysis

that can result), the core of the matter rests with the film-maker's natural inclinations and the quality of his talent.

The film-maker needs, therefore, in addition to a solid technical foundation, an insight into those things involving ideas and values. He needs to know where his talents shape up best, with what kind of material he functions most effectively, in what way he can set up a frame of reference within which to explore his material, and how to clarify his point of view. How can he draw himself out to determine in the first place whether he wants to say anything, let alone decide the most effective way to say it?

To seek conscious and direct answers to these problems is next to impossible because they cannot be arrived at in the manner of a mathematical equation. Rather, the answers will emerge to one degree or another, through the actual making of the films. Through constant application, more and more becomes known about self, talent, and ways and means for becoming more effective in terms of the discovery of the nature of individual ability and in terms of a greater understanding of the craft in order to make the most of this talent. The film-maker has to constantly make films. The questions should be left to the critics, the scholars, and the analysts.

For all the direction that might be found through constant effort—with no real final answer forthcoming—it could very well be that the quest is not one of going from problem to solution but one of going from problem to artistic effort. The solution as such might not be worth the finding.

As important as the study of films may be, study itself should be clearly seen as being critical, on the one hand, and creative, on the other. Critical study is a springboard to an understanding of the craft and the medium. It also throws considerable light on what makes a piece of work good or bad. But it is also the intellectualization of a process that, from the very beginning, calls for emotion, drive, and spontaneity.

Learning is perhaps as much a subconscious effort as a

conscious one. And nothing could be more crippling to the beginner than to continue asking himself, to the exclusion of all else, what the values are of his film, or the meaning of the theme, or, for that matter, what theme itself is. He should arrive at a conviction fairly quickly, take camera in hand, and move into the midst of the dilemma, if dilemma it be. Nothing so quickly and precisely will reveal gaps and inadequacies as the work itself.

All this says is that a film-maker grows with his films, that he must be deeply concerned with value and with art, but that whatever learning and intellectual power he brings to bear on his work should be subjugated to the emotional and creative intensity that film-making requires. The best the beginning film-maker can do is to strive for honesty in his work, an idea far more simply said than achieved. To confront the young novice film-maker with the accusation that his effort does not ring true is to have the heavens fall and the earth stop dead in its spinning tracks. Yet to see truth in the literal sense is his fundamental task.

HOLLYWOOD VERSUS ANTIFORMULA

An "antiformula film" is a film that avoids the typical Hollywood boy-meets-girl pattern or, more specifically, a film that violates the ground rules of traditional scripting. In the established scheme, of course, a story's beginning, middle, climax, and end are precisely measured into a well-ordered plot in which all elements are neatly meshed, the whole thing as resplendent as a box of Valentine chocolates.

The antiformula film, on the other hand, has generally been defined in terms of what it is not: it has no formula. The implication is that it wanders formlessly or is given to an episodic

construction, or seeks to draw form through its thematic considerations as units of action are related to one another.

Interestingly enough, these differences between formula and
antiformula reflect the modern theater, for both kinds of play
have also appeared there. The realistic playwrights were icono-
clastic about well-made structure; much like today's film-
makers, they were motivated by stories truer to life and more
typical of it, and their plays dealt with problems that confronted
contemporary man both socially and philosophically. There
were a fair share of frothy escape dramas, too, enjoyable but
hardly challenging. This division in the theater, commencing
about the close of World War I, is still reflected in that both
types of fare are on the boards; witty, sparkling, well-made
comedy is found alongside the pertinent social drama, stabbing
at the ills of modern times. In addition, there is another movement, extremely strong and perhaps a reaction to the convention-
ality of the realistic theater, which calls itself the "theater of the
absurd." Robert W. Corrigan points out that

> this movement shares the conviction that the theater must express the
> senselessness and irrationality of all human actions . . . confront audi-
> ences with that sense of isolation—the sense of man's being encircled in
> a void—which is an irremediable part of the human condition . . .
> communication with others is almost impossible, and the language of
> these plays is symptomatic of their author's belief in man's inability to
> communicate his basic thoughts and feelings.[1]

The parallels between the developments in the theater and
those in the film are clear, and the changes in the film may more
readily be understood, at least in motivation, by being aware
of the diversity of thinking that has thus far marked the second
half of the twentieth century. For example, although the past
fifty years of theater growth is called "the realistic movement,"
it is questionable whether the term "realistic" could be universally applied to today's theater. "Individual" theater might be

---

[1] Robert Corrigan, ed., "Introduction: The Theatre in Search of a Fix,"
Theatre in the Twentieth Century (New York: Grove, 1963), p. 11.

249

a more appropriate label, for there are many variations in style, attitude, staging, acting pattern, and, of course, in the play itself. And the film appears, not only to have picked up its cue from the theater, but to be well ahead of it.

What this means to the beginning film-maker is that his task is both difficult and wonderfully challenging. In terms of his own film and material, he has many masters and yet—if he so chooses—none. Essentially, he can work to suit himself, handle his material formally or formlessly, traditionally or radically, subtlely or eruptively; his success is based primarily on what he has to say and how well he says it, both still effective criteria.

Yet as promising as this individuality may be, there are still pitfalls. Michelangelo Antonioni, perhaps the foremost exponent of antiformula, having clearly expressed himself on its behalf in several articles and interviews, retains a semblance of formula in the very free-flowing looseness of his stories. What is important to Antonioni, however, is not that he expressly avoids a formula, but that, in order to portray that in which he is interested, he finds the conventional formula inadequate.

The word "formula" is misleading. Formula implies structure, and no piece of work can be without that. But when any one structure is used often enough, by enough people, in the same way, and to get across the same things, it becomes worn and weary. Formula, therefore, implies a clichéd structure.

Antonioni structures his films so that episode spills into episode to give an impression of life being re-created in a most natural way. A close examination shows a building up of tension, incident being added to incident, leading to a climax with a very definite conclusion often coming from Antonioni himself as he places himself between his story and his audience and subsequently controls the flow of action. In the closing of *The Eclipse* (1962), for example, the shots recall the intent of previous scenes and serve to summarize the theme. Yet this is accomplished with such restraint, in an effort to emphasize the film's reality, that the structural qualities melt away. Structure seems effortless, and no one is aware of it. Thus, the key to the direction of a film can be found in the way in which the film-maker relates himself to his material.

Whether one is pro- or antiformula in one sense is a useless argument, because it matches triteness against structure, and the two do not align quite that simply. A work has to communicate, and communication calls for an integrated order, a structure. But a structure was never meant to be rigid and ironclad. If anything, a structure should give ground, bend this way and that, once the film-maker perceives his material sufficiently to allow it to flourish as its natural self.

It is true that some films call for greater structuring and others for less, but these are questions of different emphasis. The important factors are the film's vitality, freshness, and insight. Even an "old hat" structure takes on a new look when imaginatively dressed. It cannot help itself for the simple reason that it is no longer a "formula."

GIST OF MEANING

All too often, when reference is made to the meaning of a scene, a shot, or, for that matter, the film, the beginning film-maker may think that an intellectual statement is called for, that the purpose of scene, shot, or entire film is to point up a social or philosophical view that can be articulated in a quick, simple way. Such articulation is more the way of critics and scholars after the film is completed than of the film-maker engaged in making it.

The implication of meaning as used here is not that a moral conclusion is to be drawn, but simply that the scene, shot, or film is about something. The difference is vast. The film's direct line of appeal is emotional and in emotional patterns, and its progression of movement is similarly sparked with emotional surges. The meaning, therefore, may be that something beautiful is revealed, that someone has a desire, that someone is repulsed, or the like. Any sort of explanation of these feelings leads to their exploration, but not necessarily to their resolution.

The reason for something being beautiful may be sensed or felt; the depth of desire may be understood; the reason for being repulsed may be apparent; in short, one may feel, sense, or understand it all and yet not be able to add it up like a column of figures.

Meaning then, from the film-maker's point of view, is clearly connected with purpose and objective and not necessarily translated into intellectual conclusions. The reason for this is quite evident, for the film-maker has to approach his material artistically. He is neither political scientist, social worker, nor philosopher—armchair or otherwise. He may end by being all these things and much more, but his working method is unlike any of theirs. In the outstanding propaganda films of the past —*Potemkin* (1925), *Triumph of the Will* (1937), *Alexander Nevsky* (1938)—regardless of whether one agrees with the content, the material is set forth in emotional terms. *Potemkin*, for example, re-creates the Russian revolution of 1905 and is brought to the audience to show the tyranny of the system under the tsars and indirectly to convince them to be satisfied with their lot—the "you never had it so good" theme. Still, and in spite of, Eisenstein's mechanical and arithmetical approach to film-making, the scenes and shots have been handled, not only to support the theme, but also to project human relationships—the discontent, hopes, frustrations, and achievements of a people. Thus, the sailors' rebellion at the maggot-infested meat, the support given by the townspeople, the massacre, and, finally, the people joining together against tyranny rely entirely on emotion. And that is the artist's stock in trade.

Naturally, many experienced film-makers begin a piece of work from an intellectual premise and are successful in being able to translate their story into emotional terms, with a hard-core theme growing out of the story through implication. But the word "experience" in these cases means that the film-maker controls his material to the degree that his own natural inclinations and feelings are both clear to him and honestly presented. And even at that, there are innumerable times when the material itself emerges as something completely different from what the film-maker originally had in mind. This is the part of experience that leads to self-discovery, and it is profitable to allow the material to take shape and to evaluate it at a time when the film-maker can afford a critical approach.

To discuss this point from still another angle, a film has two levels of meaning, implied and explicit. That which is explicit is made up of each specific shot as it unfolds on the screen; when working with these shots the film-maker is concerned with their values in terms of themselves and not with some foreordained, preconceived world-saving truth. The film's implicit value is what the audience is left with: the sense of theme, or character, or excitement, the abstraction that the film-maker wanted to convey to others. Although the latter value is the mark of the significant work, it is highly doubtful that the film-maker consciously can instill it in his film. He works with those things close to him, on their own terms and within their own specific meanings, so that the result will reveal the film-maker for who and what he is.

STUDY APPROACHES

Because the narrative film apparently requires that the film-maker have considerable theatrical experience, it is often an issue whether theatrical training should precede learning how to make films. The question is difficult to answer for the simple reason that the would-be film-maker's individuality, talent, personal inclination, and way of seeing things all are relevant.

253

In addition, the limitless possibilities, both in style and content, available to film render such arguments academic. The one safe argument against such prior training, perhaps, that can be made is that the narrative film is so complex that to attempt to understand both cinematic principals and theatrical ones simultaneously is frustrating and futile.

From another point of view, the issue can be restated so that the difference in approach is, in the broadest and most general sense, between the narrative film and the documentary, the thought being that the material of the documentary deals with life as it is, that little—preferably no—staging will be required, and that the film-maker's entire concentration will be on reacting to, photographing, and editing his material. Theatrical experience would have no advantage here.

The issue has a history behind it. During the Hollywood heyday, there was a fairly direct learning route from the editing room to the film director's chair. The craft was learned in the practice of editing, and the person having such experience was better able to take command of the complicated floor work during shooting. It is true that during this time a few theatrical directors may have moved on into film-making, but mostly the men who moved on into the directing role were involved in editing and camera work. Conversely, when television began to flex its muscles in the early 1950's, few, if any, film-makers came in as directors. Rather, a host of theatrically trained talent from the college and university drama schools became the key people handling the directorial chores.

The backgrounds of the outstanding European film-makers, with the exception of Ingmar Bergman, who was theatrically trained, reveal that most of their early training was in the making of documentaries. Coupled with this experience, or shortly following it, there was usually a period of script writing and assistant directing, a kind of writing apprenticeship to a film-maker who also had been trained in the documentary.

All that this proves, however, is that film-making is perhaps the most difficult of all the arts to master and that there is no prescribed series of steps or courses one can undertake to master it. In the areas of painting, sculpture, dance, acting, and theater direction, for that matter, a fairly direct course of study and training can be pursued. But in film-making a line of development may suddenly reach a point where the student has to shift gears and undertake something totally new. On pursuing it, he may reach still another point where again he has to change and undertake the study of something calling for even less familiar types of knowledge. There is so much that can be involved in film-making: theater, dance, music, journalism, photographic art, cinematography, and graphics, to name a few. Film-making, in spite of all the mass-produced molds it has been forced into in the past, is a highly individualistic process, and the film-maker must either have a variety of talents or a single talent developed in a variety of ways.

In the most general way, however, one point of view is subscribed to here: theatrical training is such a strong discipline that the individual steeped in it has a difficult time surmounting it, that he sees the film as a play—which it is not—and puts it on in the most traditional fashion, thus making a visual recording of it. The theater is make-believe, but of a different kind than the film; it creates its quality indirectly through a penetration of actuality, even when it comes to dialogue. Jörn Donner, writing on Bergman, reports that "Bergman considers today that he can no longer write plays since his dialogue is entirely built according to the demands and specific possibilities of the film."[2] Here, then, is an outstanding film-maker, initially trained in the theater, who has absorbed film techniques to the point where he is highly sensitive to dialogue that serves (and combines with) a shot in order to communicate, as opposed to dialogue that performs the full function itself.

Although, recently, many men have successfully moved from

---

[2] Jörn Donner, *The Personal Vision of Ingmar Bergman* (Bloomington: Indiana University Press, 1964), p. 241.

theater into film-making, it appears relatively easier for the beginning film-maker to begin his study with the film proper. Because he plans to work in film, his frame of reference secured through editing and camera work keeps growing constantly. Bits and pieces of theater art as applied to film can be dovetailed as part of the growing process. A theatrical orientation requires that a good deal be unlearned, a task that relatively few achieve.

The most profitable way to undertake the study of film-making is through the documentary film. Not only does such training bring the beginner directly into camera work and editing principles, but also the wide range of the documentary itself has a common base with narrative storytelling, the attempt to tell a true-life story. However, the documentation uses real, not imagined or manufactured, life as material and thus plants the seeds of a good beginning.

TRANSCENDING TECHNIQUE

The beginning film-maker—and many old hands, too, for that matter—is constantly struggling between perfecting his technique, on the one hand, and clarifying what he is trying to say, on the other. It is the age-old artistic struggle, and, as he seeks help from critics, reviewers, teachers, film savants, and just about any source that will listen, he finds more and more that everyone has a lot to say about technique, but that few dare venture into content.

The Hollywood film-makers found the "solution" to this problem long ago: perfect the technique so that everything is clear to everyone and no toes are stepped on, have a rip-roaring story, and a first-rate picture will result. The problem now, however, is that television has commandeered this policy, and, in addition, offers its wares free of charge. The film people, therefore, have no choice but to turn out films that are pertinent, inspired reflections of life, rather than soporifics.

Talking about pertinency and inspiration is a great deal simpler than recognizing it, let alone achieving it. Technique, of course, cannot be separated from content; yet when the beginner discusses his work with others there is a most natural tendency on the part of his listeners to simplify the content so that the technique will hold up. In other words, suggestions are made to clear up the motivation in certain scenes; to cut, edit, and arrange shots to point up the scene or to simplify action and dialogue, so that the sense of the scene is immediately conveyed. Suggestions of this kind are absolutely valid, of course, for the piece of work must be clear and direct to be forceful. But the weakness of this type of criticism is that it can reduce a film to a cliché. This was the Hollywood method, and its intentions were quite sincere; but when there is a compromise that destroys subtle value so that everything is clear to everyone, the film is converted into a pot-boiling formula.

The solution is not to be slavishly devoted to accepted patterns and procedures. There are proved ways for assembling material, but the value of the material itself—in shaping the story, selecting and taking the shots, or in editing and arranging them—should not be sacrificed to method. On the other hand, one must not fall into an attitude common to many beginning film-makers. In his zeal to establish and identify himself, the beginner can easily be taken in by his own immaturity. Like the college sophomore who has read a book and gotten an idea from it, he suddenly discovers the world and smugly concludes that no one else could possibly have had the same thought. His material, therefore, is precious, sacrosanct, not to be tampered with in any way. Instead of giving way to a few genuine emotions, he fails to understand his own motives and wallows in a pseudo-intellectualism and obscurity that show up in his film from the very moment it hits the screen. And he is inclined to support his efforts with such statements as, "You don't under-

stand"; "You've missed the point"; "Don't you see the significance of the shot where the girl picks up the rose and pounds it
to death with a rock!" Could it be that she is making rose-petal
jam?

Film-making, then, as other arts, requires a balance in a piece
of work, a balance between what is being said and the way it is
said, so that the perfect union reaches and rewards the audience.
In the developing process, as the film-maker grows with his
films, it seems more profitable for him to concentrate on broad-
ening himself, on understanding how he relates to the world
about him, and the essence of his particular message, rather than
solely on perfecting his technique.

There are a number of cases in the past in which a conflict
between technique and material subtly underlies the screen presentation. Erich von Stroheim, for example, constantly battled
the studios to get into his films what he considered essential. He
had to fight uphill all the way and lost out, but whatever may be
said about *Greed* in terms of being overdone or obvious, even
today it possesses a raw power in its naturalistic presentation.
The well-known John Huston studio battle over *The Red Badge
of Courage*, in which Huston was not able to complete his work,
makes the same point. Yet, even here, though the film was finally
cut by others and Huston did not have the opportunity to compile
it, individual shots and scenes speak sincerely for Huston's
vision of war's mercilessness.

In television, during the 1950's, with *Studio One* and the
Goodyear and Philco playhouses, when a host of new writers
seemed to come from nowhere, there was a tangible excitement
in the presentations. Many faults were evident, and, although
many shows fell far short of their mark, the honest attempt on
the part of the writers and directors was constantly felt. That was
a time when television contributed heavily to the development of
new talent and the technical flaws were challenges for the audience. Most important, the writers obviously did not sacrifice

their feelings and intentions by writing such formulas as Gun-smoke and Wagon Train.

For the beginner, it is far more important to keep hammering away at substance than to worry about technique. Although it is true that both are essential, it is equally true that too much stress on technique means that substance is forgotten; a stress on substance means that technique can be acquired. A good portion of the movie audience today, young and old, shows signs of excitement and anticipation when a Jean-Luc Godard or John Schlesinger movie is released; the floating barges on the Nile go unnoticed.

MAKING A START

As in all other fields, one can begin shaping a film career by working at it, by studying for it, or by combining both. Each of these ways has its advantage, but a quick glance at recent developments as well as past trends points favorably toward beginning by study.

As previously pointed out, during the Hollywood Golden Age, the 1930's, the training route from editor to camerman or assistant director and finally to director was a well-established learning-and-training process. Its prime drawback, of course, was that the approach was mostly vocational. But, because the scripts of the time, in the main, called for little more than formula work, the system worked fairly well. But today, not only has the system disappeared, but the greater challenge set up by the world-wide movement toward films with greater artistic merit renders the mechanical approach to film-making inadequate.

The film can no longer be looked on as merely an industry product, in spite of the fact that it takes an industry to produce it. And this point, incidentally, is one of the most interesting aspects of a flourishing twentieth-century art, which is actually moving to a stability while being supported by a scientific complex in a mass-production system. Interestingly enough, the two are not mutually exclusive. At least, that seems to be the case as man increasingly finds that he alone is the master of his machine.

In addition, the lack of wherewithal for practice and the need for in-depth study of an art form guide the beginning filmmaker quite naturally to university training. An interesting parallel might well be drawn between the university film-teaching centers of the 1960's and the university theater-training centers of the 1920's. At the turn of the century, for example, university disciplines in theater art were not only frowned on, but also severely reproved by the classic scholars and academicians. But the theater required men of broad knowledge, depth, and keen perception. Theater art departments, offering a place to work, learn, experiment, and grow, attracted outstanding artists and teachers and, on the graduate and in many cases undergraduate levels, offered first-class professional study and training. Quite naturally did talented students gravitate to these universities. Today, the Broadway theater is almost exclusively commercial, with no genuine training ground for beginners, while university theater departments are actively engaged in the development of young talent. A few such departments not only serve as their communities' cultural centers, but also have attracted some enviable professional talent to assist with the programing; these are quite a few steps ahead of Broadway and its once-removed cousin, the off-Broadway theater. This pattern seems to be occurring among universities as courses in film study are being added to curricula. The more farsighted universities are even participating in the task of developing serious film-makers.

Ideally, the university film student works toward a degree and absorbs the classic disciplines, now more necessary than ever, while actively participating in film-making. Film-making is approached, not in traditional terms, but as a discipline with its own artistic requirements through which the student grows and develops self-expression. Such training is diametrically opposed to vocational practice, yet places at the student's disposal the technical and scientific machines that are his tools—still another reflection of the twentieth-century marriage of opposites.

But the development of film-making talent within the American university does not solve the beginner's problem any more than concentrated training in economics, history, fine arts, or the sciences prepares him for actual travail in these respective disciplines. On receiving his diploma, he is faced with the reality of earning a living. The problem, then, is for the young film-maker somehow to squeeze into the vast complex of the industry. One can no longer refer to the Hollywood industry as the home of the feature film and the place to start. The American feature-film industry has spread all over the world, and its leadership and proved talent are preoccupied with their personal film-making problems. It moves in high gear; it is based on experience, and it is in competition to produce films of genuine merit. Although this movement and expansion provide an opportunity, still it is a high-powered league and the chances of coming up through the ranks are slim.

In recent years, men have made their way to film by first becoming television directors; but although at one time this appeared to be a trend, so much of television programing is on film (which cuts out the television director) that this avenue has been considerably cut down. Furthermore, film-making for television is about the closest thing we have today to the old studio production methods. And such routine formula work is highly questionable as a training ground for the newly emerging type of feature film. In other words, learning how to manufacture a series of Westerns for television does not naturally enable one to understand the intricacies of such film expression as is found in the work of Karel Reisz, François Truffaut, Satyajit Ray, Arika Kurosawa, and many others.

The answer to the problem of where the student can continue to learn and grow is best found today in the documentary film field, particularly in the East, Middle States, and Southwest. This has been the pattern in Europe and appears to be the emerging pattern for the development of American talent. There are a number of reasons for this. First, there is a natural affinity between the realistic point of view of the documentarian and the vitality and pertinence of the feature film that is sought by today's audiences. Second, the documentary film-maker operates on a sensible and modest budget; mistakes, if made, cost considerably less, and experimentation is a part of his own growing process. Third, there are companies engaged in industrial and documentary production larger than some feature-film groups, as well as persons who make films on their own with one or two helpers. Apprenticeships are available on both levels, and the nature of the production in both instances is on such a scale that a beginner comes into contact with all phases of production on a highly skilled, professional level.

Most interesting of all is that many established documentary film-makers search for new talent, not necessarily for talent that has already arrived. They are not averse to student efforts, going out of their way to catch film showings and, on the basis of the potential they see on the screen, providing a work opportunity. If anything, student work is creating more interest, and the day seems close when film students will be interviewed on campus.

APPENDIX A

SAMPLE STUDENT EXERCISE

If anything has been proved thus far it is that there are no set routines or procedures for making a film. Aside from the vast artistic range possible in the film, the fact that operating budgets can be large or small—which has absolutely no bearing on artistic merit—in itself often dictates the way the film-maker must work. In addition, the subject matter itself practically demands that the film-maker make up new rules to fit his case as he goes along. This not only attests to the volatile and fluid nature of film, but amply supports Louis Kronenberger's statement that "in a final sense, there are never any rules in art; there are only risks."

The following example of student work, therefore, is not intended to prescribe a procedural pattern. Rather, it is to show that the one certainty of film-making is that it must be a labor of love. Beyond this, the exercise demonstrates a particular student's point of view as he took a short story he liked very much

263

through a number of steps, breaking down its literary characteristics and visualizing them in terms of film.

The short story, *Blue Silk and Tuesday*, by Oliver C. Grannis,
first appeared in the May 1959 issue of *Esquire* magazine.

Blue Silk and Tuesday[1]

Randolph leaned far far out over the window sill and gazed down at
the sidewalk, four stories below. He allowed a bit of saliva to form in the
top of his mouth, and then, slowly dropping his lower jaw and relaxing
his tongue, he let the saliva fall from his lips and splatter down on a
white cat that had been chalked on the sidewalk by a ten-year-old artist
who lived downstairs. The artist's name was Tuesday Reed, and she
was standing only three feet from her chalk cat when she heard the ball
of spit slap against its concrete fur. Tuesday didn't look up, because she
knew it was Randolph who had spit, and she didn't stop to scold or
even to think before ducking into the doorway of the apartment building, because she knew that Randolph had spit not at the cat but at her,
and that next time he would be sure to hit her.

At least a dozen times, Randolph had spit on Tuesday Reed, who had
moved to the neighborhood only nineteen days before. Randolph was
twelve, but since boys don't grow up as fast as girls the age difference
was just right. Tuesday's mother, who always looked ahead, thought
secretly that Randolph might someday want to marry her daughter, and
perhaps someday he might. Mrs. Reed had once been an artist too,
making beautiful pot holders from colored elastic bands, but she had
retired some time ago and preferred now to read mystery stories; and
when she read she told Tuesday to play outside, but not to leave the sidewalk in front of the building. So, whenever Tuesday's mother was reading a mystery story, Tuesday was running the considerable risk of being
spit upon by Randolph Horn.

Tuesday opened the hallway door just enough for her to squeeze
through and slip back outside, under the protective arch that extended
out about a foot over the doorway. She looked at her cat; it had a big
wet spot about three inches wide right on its stomach. Pressing back
against the door with the palms of her hands, she inched over to the
side of the arch and looked up at Randolph's window. She just had
time to pull her head back in before spit splashed down on the sidewalk,
right at her feet. That was discouraging. It was impossible to get out to

---

[1] Reprinted by permission of *Esquire* magazine; © 1959 by Esquire, Inc.

repair the damage that had been done to her chalk cat, to say nothing of taking the time to draw a new one. She scraped back along the wall to the door, opened it again and squeezed through into the foyer, where she pushed the second doorbell from the left in the next-to-top row. That was the Horns' doorbell, and ringing it was the only way she could think of at the moment to get back at Randolph. She waited for the harsh buzz which somehow unlocked the glass door at the end of the hallway, but it didn't come, and even if it had she probably wouldn't have gone in. She took a piece of blue chalk from her dress pocket and began drawing owls on all the mailboxes except the Horns'. She left that one blank.

Upstairs, Randolph was still leaning out the window, trying to catch a glimpse of Tuesday sneaking around underneath the arch. And then he looked at the sidewalk and felt a little sorry that he had missed Tuesday and hit her cat instead, sorry not because it was her cat but simply because it was *a* cat, and he liked cats very much. He had his own cat, a live one, named Silk. Silk was a girl. Her mother had been a black cat with a white ear, her father a gray Angora. When the kittens were born, they had all been black with one white ear or one white paw, all except for Silk. She was a gray Angora. Weeks after all the others had stopped sucking, Silk was still trying to get milk from her mother, eating only as a very last measure the chopped liver and tuna fish the others ate. And weeks after the others had learned to use the sandbox, Silk was still learning, putting her front feet into the sandbox and going all over the floor. But the others were all given away, and Silk stayed on, even after her mother had gone—after she ran away or was run over by a truck or fell victim to any one of the other fates that befall cats who live in cities.

Right now, while Randolph was leaning out the window, Silk was walking back and forth along the mantel in the living room. There was a false fireplace with glazed yellow tiles, and over the fireplace was a marble mantel on which stood a rather large blue vase. The vase was shaped like an imitation of a Greek vase would be shaped, colored like an imitation of Wedgwood would be colored, and contained the ashes, or at least a part of them, of Mrs. Horn's uncle. Mrs. Horn's uncle was called Bernie, even today, after being dead for seven years, and it was because of Bernie that the Horns were able to live as well as they did on, or in spite of, Mr. Horn's earnings as a drapery salesman. So the vase was very important, and no one was allowed to touch it, except to dust it. And no one ever did touch it, except for Silk, and she liked to rub her ribs against the white flowers on the side of the vase. That's what she was doing while Randolph was leaning out the window, trying to get a bead on Tuesday.

A blue uniform turned the corner and started down the row of apartment buildings in the direction of the doorway where Tuesday Reed crouched, drawing owls. Randolph ducked back into the room and grabbed something from the floor, something imaginary but nonetheless very heavy, something which caused him to grunt audibly when bending over to pick it up. He placed the heavy object on the window sill and waited for the policeman to walk directly beneath him. The uniform ambled along, pigeon-toed, swinging a stick, and stopped to admire the cat chalked on the sidewalk. The spit had long since dried. Randolph spread his feet apart to balance himself, put his hands squarely behind the weight he had placed on the window sill and pushed it out into space, throwing up his hands in a violent gesture of prayer. The weight hurtled down past four windows and struck him dead, but the policeman didn't notice. He gave the cat a final glance and continued his pigeon-toed beat, letting his night stick dangle from his wrist as he clasped his hands behind his blue back.

Randolph walked over to the mantel, picked up Silk and scratched her ears. He put her behind some books in the bookcase, watched her crawl out and then put her back again, doing this three or four times until Silk didn't bother coming out any more; then he went to the kitchen, got a cookie, and went back to the window. Tuesday had come out of hiding, had quickly drawn a bird, right on the cat's back, and had slipped back into the doorway again, all while Randolph was playing with Silk and getting a cookie. The bird was almost as big as the cat, and it had stripes running all the way from its head to the ends of its feathers. And the cat had been improved upon, getting a tail and a second eye. The tail was curved up and around, and the bird, which was riding backwards, could easily have reached out and pecked it. Randolph was quite angry. He was going to spit on the bird, but because he had just eaten a cookie, he couldn't get any spit; so he went to the bathroom and drank a glass of water.

When he got back, an umbrella had been drawn over the bird's head, and the umbrella had red stripes, which only made it worse. Randolph took careful aim. He wanted to hit the bird, but he missed and all he hit was a very empty space on the sidewalk about two feet away from either the bird or the cat; and, before he had time to get any more spit, Tuesday had run out from her doorway and drawn a blue circle around the spot on the sidewalk, marking his failure for the whole world to see. Randolph was still sucking in his cheeks and frantically pushing his tongue up against the top of his mouth when Tuesday was back in her haven.

Randolph had heard of men who lock themselves in apartments and then go berserk, shooting at men, women, policemen, and even children, shooting until they run out of ammunition or they're subdued by tear gas. It was a good idea. He went to the door of the apartment, locked it, and proceeded to pile up in front of the door every piece of furniture he could move. Finally, with a sofa, two armchairs, a coffee table and three telephone books, he quit and returned to the window. While he was gone, Tuesday had drawn two horses, three stars, a tree, and a heart with some initials in it, but he couldn't read the initials.

He took careful aim and hit one of the horses right in the head; he hit the tree, missed twice, hit the umbrella, missed again, hit the blue circle Tuesday had drawn around his other miss, and, finally, hit a woman who was walking down the street with a bag of groceries. He hit her on the head. The woman reached up and touched her head; she looked at her hand, touched her head again and looked at her hand again. She made a face and wiped her hand on her coat, and then she looked up and saw Randolph, his mouth working. She jumped in under the archway, beside Tuesday, and was again scored against, this time on the shoe. Tuesday scrambled out, ran in a quick circle around her art, and returned to the protection of her archway, all before Randolph could get off another one. She smiled smugly at the woman who was still wiping her hand on her coat. A man wearing a bowler and a pin-striped suit walked underneath the window and, when he looked up to see where whatever it was that had hit him on the shoulder had come from, he dropped the bowler. And when he picked it up, he noticed a large, round wet spot right on the crown. He too joined Tuesday under the archway. They were joined by a woman in a fox fur, and all of them waited for the policeman to come back, which he did.

The policeman stood back on the sidewalk and looked up at the window. Silk had joined Randolph at the window sill and they looked back at the policeman. Silk looked over at Randolph who worked his mouth for a moment and then hit the third button from the top on the policeman's tunic.

The policeman joined the others, and Tuesday was dispatched next door to get Randolph's mother, where she was visiting. Randolph's mother, the policeman, the man in the bowler, the woman with the fox fur, and Tuesday climbed the steps to the fourth floor. The woman wiping her hand on her coat stayed downstairs.

They knocked on the door. Mrs. Horn looked through the keyhole, and she saw Silk sitting on one of the armchairs, her eyes on the door-knob. The man in the bowler asked if he might look through the key-hole, but no one paid any attention to him. The policeman took a knife with a screwdriver from his pocket and began taking the lock apart. Silk stayed on the armchair, her head tilted to one side, watching the door, and Randolph kept his post at the window, managing to hit the chalk cat once more. He turned around and saw the furniture slowly giving away before the opening door. He took one last desperate shot, ran to the fireplace, grabbed the blue vase and ran back to the window. Silk jumped for the mantel as the policeman muscled his way into the room, Randolph's mother behind him. She emitted a muffled squeal when she saw the sacred blue vase in her son's hand, and as the police-man's arm gathered up the already limp Randolph and the vase dropped from sight, she rushed from the apartment.

Mrs. Horn stumbled down the four flights of steps, through the foyer and past the owls chalked on all the mailboxes but hers. She went out onto the sidewalk and looked, looked at the blue vase which was scat-tered for about ten yards in each direction, and looked for some sign of the last remains of Bernie, but it was impossible to distinguish between dust, ash and chalk. And nobody seemed to notice Tuesday as she skipped out wearing a bowler, drew a hasty circle around a frag-ment of blue pottery and disappeared around the corner.

The first draft of the story as a written-out film was dubbed a treatment.

Treatment

"Spittin' Image" (Possible title)

Titles are chalked in a child's scrawl on a city sidewalk. Under the titles music is sung by a little girl (Tuesday) to the accompaniment of a single instrument. The mood created by the titles and the singing is one of childish gaiety on a balmy summer day. As the camera progresses down the sidewalk to reveal all the titles, Tuesday Reed Loves Randolph Horn (in chalk), we eventually reach the hand of the artist—a child's hand, hard at work, drawing a large cat on the sidewalk. We finally see the artist herself—a ten-year-old girl diligently filling in the outline of the cat's body with white chalk.

The girl is in a summer dress—an attractive child. She has a lap full of colored chalks from which she selects artistically the implements for her creation.

We cut up to a long view from the street of a window on the fourth floor of the building in front of which the girl is working. A twelve-year-old boy is leaning out of the window, looking down at the girl drawing on the sidewalk.

A closer view of his face shows that he is ruminating like a mischievous camel, working his cheeks until he has a large ball of saliva in his mouth. He has an expression of conducting an interesting experiment. Taking aim, he lets the saliva drop to the sidewalk below. He watches with concern to see where it lands.

It splats on the cement cat. The little girl jumps up and with her hands over her head dashes to the protection of the doorway. The chalk that was in her lap has scattered all over the sidewalk.

She cautiously moves to the edge of the doorway and peeks up toward the boy in the fourth-floor window. The boy has let fly another ball of saliva. The girl jumps back just as the second missile hits on the top step near her foot. She pulls back her foot and inspects it distastefully. She is satisfied that he missed.

Randolph leans a little farther out the window, trying to see into the archway where Tuesday is hiding. He shows little or no expression except patiently waiting for his target to reappear.

Tuesday, standing in the doorway, looks out at her cat and the disarray of artist's materials with frustration. As the huge wad that Randolph had been saving for her is disgorged again on her chalk cat, she clenches her fists in anger and looks menacingly up in the direction of her enemy. She sticks her tongue out futilely.

Then she goes into the foyer to the row of mailboxes and door buzzers. Angrily she takes a piece of chalk from the pocket of her dress and begins writing on one of the mailboxes to extend on down the wall:

Tuesday Reed Hates Randolph Horn Hates Randolph Horn Hates Randolph Horn Hates Randolph Horn

Upstairs in the living room of his apartment, Randolph is leaning out the window. Randolph's mother walks into the room, sees the cat on the mantelpiece, rubbing against an ugly vase-like urn (or some other breakable monstrosity). The mother snatches the cat and hands her to Randolph. She scolds Randolph, pointing to the vase (or monstrosity), to show her concern for the safety of the object. Then she carefully, fastidiously wipes an imaginary speck of dust from it. She picks up a fantastic handbag, goes to Randolph, kisses him mushily, smoothes his hair in an overly protective manner. As soon as she turns her back, Randolph deliberately musses his hair up again. The mother waves goodbye to him at the door and goes out.

Randolph goes back to the window and looks down at the sidewalk. He is shocked at what he sees. Tuesday is furiously at work on her art again, which has now expanded. She has drawn a bird on the cat's back, and the cat has been improved upon, getting a tail and a second eye. She also has added two owls and a palm tree.

Randolph is working up another ball of spit and is about to let it fly, when his mother comes out of the doorway. She walks up to Tuesday, admires the art with broad gestures as if exclaiming, "Oh! how beautiful!" She pats the little girl on the head and moves off.

A policeman approaches. Mrs. Horn nods to the policeman, who salutes her with a smile. Mrs. Horn goes off down the street.

The policeman stops to admire Tuesday's art work. Randolph ducks back into the room in a blind rage. He grabs a heavy object from the floor—something completely imaginary but nonetheless very heavy. He pretends to be straining as he carries it to the window sill. He shoves it out into space. He turns back, his eyes closed with malicious glee, his hands held together in a wild prayer. He opens his eyes hopefully and peers out the window to see what his imaginary weight has done to his victims. He sighs as he sees the cop move on down the street, allowing Tuesday to resume her creation. The cop continues his pigeon-toed beat, letting his night stick dangle from his wrist, clasping his hands behind his back.

Randolph, dejected, works up some more saliva, lets it fly, and watches as it falls. It misses Tuesday's art work by a mile. Tuesday skips over to the blot which missed, draws a circle around it, and with a triumphant look up to Randolph, runs into the doorway before Randolph can retaliate.

Tuesday runs into the foyer, rings the buzzer to Randolph's apartment to signal her victory. Randolph listens to the bell with annoyance. He shrugs and takes a cookie from a bowl. It is crumbly and dries up his mouth. He picks up the cat and offers her a cookie. The cat sniffs and turns away. He puts the cat on top of the treasured vase (or monstrosity) and smiles as the cat nearly knocks it over by leaping off.

He wanders back to the window and looks down. Tuesday's art has now achieved its full-blown glory. Many animals and designs have been added, completely covering the area in front of the building. She has long since blotted out the heart which had said *Tuesday Reed Loves Randolph Horn* and in its place she has drawn a tombstone with the simple inscription, *Randolph*. The perpetrator of this infamy is nowhere in sight.

Randolph's mouth is constricted with cookie crumbs. He tries unsuccessfully to work up some saliva. Tuesday dances out suddenly and laughs at him. He is unable to do anything. He spits on his chin. He stares down in disgust for a moment and then becomes inspired. Tuesday touches up her art work nonchalantly. From out of nowhere a great spray of water rains down on the sidewalk. Alarmed, but untouched, Tuesday jumps up and looks up with disdain. Randolph holds an empty glass furiously. Tuesday begins to chant derisively, showing that she knows his aim has become wild with mounting rage.

Randolph disappears from the window. Tuesday gets a skiprope from the doorway and begins to skip happily.

In this first treatment two scenes are of key importance: one, in which Randolph's mother straightens his hair, which Randolph then musses; two, in which Randolph picks up an imaginary object and hurls it at the policeman below. Still, in spite of the flowing visual quality in the description of the incident, the importance of the two key scenes appears lessened as they fail to relate to the central situation.

The latter half of the story appears precipitously, as if the end had to come. The treatment had lost much of the subtle and underlying richness of the original story.

A second treatment was written, both to offset the weaknesses already mentioned and to include detail to flesh out the characters involved.

Treatment

(Second Draft—showing elaboration of ending)

Randolph takes the cookie out of his mouth, tries to spit on the art work below, then throws the cookie down in disgust at being unable to work up the necessary saliva. He tries desperately to spit again, and manages instead to spit on his chin. Tuesday sees his plight and stops skipping rope long enough to laugh hilariously as she points at him, then goes back to skipping rope. After a moment she glances up, stops skipping rope. She watches as Randolph's hand appears, holding a pan of water, which he turns over carefully, and lets the water deluge the art work. His face then appears, haughtily staring back at his foe.

*Tuesday bursts into a derisive chant, pointing down at her art work. Randolph, his aplomb momentarily shaken, peers over the window sill to see what his pan of water has done and is dismayed to see that there is a long streak of water down the front of the building and that none of it has damaged Tuesday's art work after all.

*Randolph, his fury mounting, disappears from the window. He snatches up the feather duster and wildly begins ripping feathers out of it until it is plucked bald, with feathers floating all over the room. The cat looks at him curiously. Then with the handle of the plucked feather duster, which he imaginatively converts into a machine gun tucked at his waist, he sprays everything in sight with a hail of bullets, his teeth chattering in imitative firing. He reserves the last of his imaginary ammunition for a special burst of fire at the door which slammed so rudely when his mother left.

Randolph decides to barricade that door. He drops his imaginary machine gun and pushes a piece of furniture against the door. He gets another piece of furniture and piles it on.

Then he goes to the kitchen, rummages around and gets out a dozen waxed bags which are used to put sandwiches in. He gets out a dishpan and as he fills each sandwich bag with the right amount of water from the faucet, he twists its top, and with a devilish smile arranges a neat grouping of these lovely missiles in place, in the dishpan. He now carries his dishpan full of ammunition to the window sill. Setting it down carefully, he looks out to find his foe.

Tuesday is now back on this side of the street, skipping rope not far from her art work. Randolph takes out his first sandwich bag of water. He holds it delicately and lets it drop. He hits a chalk horse. Another one, carefully aimed, hits a tree. Another one hits the umbrella, dangerously close to Tuesday herself, who dashes in alarm to the safety of the doorway, where she watches the devastating bombardment taking place.

Randolph continues with unerring accuracy. He hits an owl, misses once, hits the blue circle Tuesday had drawn around his earlier miss, hits a woman who unexpectedly appears from the corner with a bag of

---

* Designates scenes that were cut.

groceries. The woman drops the groceries with a smash onto the sidewalk and joins Tuesday in the doorway, looking up with consternation, then out to her oranges and tin cans rolling around the street. Tuesday waits until the next missile has splashed onto the sidewalk, then she scrambles out, sticks a thumb in each ear and wags her hands up at Randolph, scrambling back to safety as she sees the next bag of water descending. A man in a bowler rounds the corner just in time to receive the bag squarely on his proudly adorned head. The man takes off his bowler, examines it incredulously, looks up, and with a shriek, joins Tuesday and the woman in the doorway. A bag narrowly misses.

Randolph sees he is running low on ammunition. How to hold them off while he refills. He dashes to the kitchen, pulling a toy balloon out of his pocket. Slipping a rubber band looped around the end a couple of times, he stretches the neck of the balloon with a rubber band to hold it tightly onto the faucet; under it is a pan. He sets the water running into the balloon moderately.

Meanwhile, the man and woman and Tuesday are moving hesitantly out from the doorway. Should they make a run for it? No—they dash back as they see Randolph's face reappear at the window with a wax bag of water in his hand.

Randolph smiles grimly and runs back to see how his balloon is doing. Not ready yet. He dashes back, sees his besieged victims trying to explain to a woman in a fancy fur-piece that they cannot step aside to let her in and that she had better step aside herself. She ignores their pleas—to her sudden sorrow, for Randolph has let his last wax bag fly. Drenched, she tries to join the group in the safety of the doorway.

Randolph dashes back to the kitchen. The balloon has swelled with water until it fills the pan. Randolph shuts off the water, carefully removes the neck of the balloon, knots it, and lifts the pan in which it rests out of the sink.

The pigeon-toed cop is returning along his beat, oblivious to the mayhem ahead. Randolph is leaving the kitchen with his blockbuster cradled in his arms. The cop swings his night stick, carefree. Randolph approaches the window. The cop curiously looks at the debris littering the sidewalk ahead, then sees the people grouped in the doorway. Randolph is at the window. The cop says, "What the hell's going on. . . ." The people wave at him frantically. SPLASH!!!

The cop does a slow burn, then looks up. Randolph and the cat are looking down curiously at the people below—Randolph's face taking on a gradual realization of the enormity of his warfare.

The people in the doorway step aside for the cop, who enters just as Randolph's mother appears on the scene demanding to know what is going on. Everyone ascends the stairs in a chattering, gesticulating mass. The cop knocks on the door. No answer. Randolph's mother takes out her key and unlocks the door. It still won't open. She pushes the cop aside and peeks through the keyhole. She can't see anything. The man in the bowler asks if he can look through the keyhole. Nobody pays any attention to him. The cop takes a knife with a screwdriver from his pocket and begins taking the lock apart.

Inside, Randolph is frantic as he looks at the door. He sees the furniture gradually sliding as the people outside force their weight against the door. Desperately looking around for something else to weight down the door, he can find nothing. So he backs up and takes the urn containing Great-uncle Bernie. He holds the urn in his hands, threatening to drop it, as the people break into the room. The cop starts for Randolph, but the mother throws up her hands to her mouth and stops, frozen by seeing Uncle Bernie's remains about to go out the window. And out they go, just as the cop grabs Randolph. The urn crashes on the pavement below.

The mother makes her way through the people and furniture back down the stairs. The mother takes a look at the rubble in the area in front of the building. She stands there, staring with disbelief, and somehow doesn't even know what to do when Tuesday, wearing the bowler, comes skipping out of the doorway.

The mother watches Tuesday dazedly as she skips over to a piece of the broken urn, draws a circle around it, and skips off down the street, singing the same songs she sang in the beginning.

In reviewing the second treatment, the student decided that a number of scenes expanded the story to the point of dissipating it. These were cut. The ending, which appeared unnecessarily complex with the meaning of the scene lost in the shuffle of action, was rewritten.

The student, being generally satisfied now with his approach to the story, moved ahead to shot planning. Before the actual shots were laid out, however, the student found it helpful to outline the course of the action. These notes follow the treatment, but select key action only. Full meaning of the scenes would be found, of course, by referring to the treatment. After several starts, the final outline shaped up as follows:

OUTLINE[2]

Introduction

(The Game Begins)

1. Tuesday at work.
2. Randolph in window spits.
3. Tuesday surprised into doorway.
4. Randolph versus Tuesday—he spits again; she is helpless.
5. Randolph waits . . . spits, hits the cat.
6. Tuesday angry, reacts by writing on wall.

Development

(Game Interrupted)

7. Randolph in window waiting to continue game.
8. Mother enters, Randolph almost caught in act of spitting.
9. Mother scolds and puts him to work.
10. Mother removes cat, arranges room, leaves, re-enters, says goodbye to Randolph.
11. Randolph musses his hair, disposes of feather duster.
12. Randolph starts to work up spit for Tuesday, but Mother appears.
13. Mother compliments Tuesday and leaves.
14. Randolph starts to spit again, but cop appears.
15. Cop and Tuesday.
16. Randolph "shoots" cop.
17. Enters fantasy of barricading door (gangster, etc.).
18. Tired, he eats a cookie, and pets cat.

---

[2] The outline not only pulled out the essential points of the story treatment, but also introduced changes and refinements.

Complication, Exploitation

(Game Renews)

19. Tuesday, having filled pavement with art, is bored. Where's Randolph? Finally, she calls up to him.
20. He appears at the window, she taunts, he spits and misses.
21. She circles his miss and taunts him.
22. He tries to spit again, hits his chin. Picks up vase of flowers and dumps it.
23. She picks up flowers and ridicules him with a dance. (Water only went down side of building.)
24. Randolph disappears from the window.
25. Suspense. Tuesday wondering where he went. Arranges flowers. Keeps looking at empty window. Expands drawing around flowers.
26. Meanwhile, Randolph is unsuccessfully filling paper bag. Frustrated, finally discovers sandwich bags. Loads up arsenal.
27. Randolph appears at window and aims first bomb.
28. New weapon astonishes Tuesday. Another bomb scores hit, and dismays her. Barrage unexpectedly complicated by hitting lady with fur-piece (or fancy hat).

Crisis Development

(Movement toward Climax)

29. Lady joins Tuesday in the doorway. Tuesday laughing.
30. Man in bowler passes oblivious to situation, gets clobbered, looks up, screams, dives into doorway just as another missile hits where he stood.
31. Randolph, drunk with power now, waits patiently for a victim.
32. Wet group in doorway see lady with bags of groceries, they gesture frantically. She pauses in wonder; too late—she gets hit. Reaction. Joins group in doorway.
33. Cat and mouse game as hesitant group tries to escape and keeps returning to shelter when Randolph drops bomb.

34. Cop enters picture. Cop gets hit (work out details). Tuesday goes into hysterical laughter.

Denouement

35. Tuesday gasps as she sees Randolph's mother arrive; cop still reacting. The six of them go upstairs.
36. Randolph backing away from window, facing door. Frozen. Begins building up his barricade desperately. Phone books, etc.
37. Crowd arrives at the door; Randolph pushes against the opening door. Barricade gives way. The cop crashes in.
38. Randolph is at the point of no return, wraps his arm around vase. Mother seeing this attempts to restrain the cop. As cop grabs him, Randolph drops the vase out the window.
39. Mother shrieks and heads back downstairs. She arrives to see the ruined urn splattered all over the sidewalk.
40. The mother is incredulous as Tuesday comes out from behind her, wearing the bowler hat. She draws a chalk circle around one of the fragments of the urn, and skips off down the street.

The student next developed a shooting script: a visualization of the shots as he imagined them. After a conference with the instructor in charge, still another shooting script was prepared. Further discussion and evaluation led to yet another shooting script. And beyond this, still searching for refinement, came the last shooting script. Each time changes were made in order to control the camera work and in a sense to set the editing pattern, so that the character and theme values of the story would be brought into a favorable proportion.

The various shooting scripts, in progressive order, were labeled as follows: (1) Shooting Script, (2) First Final Shooting Script, (3) Second Final Shooting Script, (4) Third Final Shooting Script.

After the film had been shot and edited a log was made of the shots as they actually appeared in the film. Those changes that came about during the shooting, as well as the multiple changes brought about through cutting, may be spotted by comparing the log with the shooting script. Although these changes on the surface may seem purely technical, in that a pan may have been dropped for a direct cut, for example, the motivation is anything but technical. In the cutting the story has been intensified and proportioned, with shots relating to each other to reveal greater insight into character and motive. Note that the 76 planned shots worked out through shooting and editing to total 166.

Third Final Shooting Script	*Post-Production Script*
	1. FADE IN (40 frames): Title superimposed on an empty sidewalk. Title: The Motion Picture Workshop of New York University Presents 5 ft.
1. Title: based on an original story by Oliver C. Grannis	2. DISSOLVE TO: Super as above. Title: TUESDAY 5 ft.
2. Credits: Actors	3. DISSOLVE TO: Super as above. Title: based on a story by Oliver C. Grannis 4 ft.
3. Credit: Instructor	4. DISSOLVE TO: Super as above. Title: a film by Robert Guy Barrows Carlos M. Colon-Torres A. Robert Karl C. Kennon Robertson Hugh Rogers Gabriele Wunderlich 5 ft.

4. Credit: Instructor

FADE OUT

FADE IN:
5. EXTERIOR—CITY SIDE-
WALK—DAY—
CLOSE SHOT—PAN TO
GIRL'S HAND
A chalk heart drawn by the
child on the sidewalk with
the words:
TUESDAY REED
LOVES RANDOLPH
HORN
Pan slowly across sidewalk
to pick up Tuesday's hand,
drawing an animal with
chalk on the sidewalk.
6. CLOSE-UP—TUESDAY'S
FACE
She is totally absorbed in
her work, humming a tune
which we have heard from
the opening. She looks down
into her lap from time to
time as she selects from
there new pieces of chalk to
work with.

5. DISSOLVE TO:
Super as above.
Title: Instructor
Leo Hurwitz   4 ft.
FADE OUT (40 frames)

6. MEDIUM CLOSE—EXTE-
RIOR SIDEWALK: DAY
A chalk heart drawn on a
sidewalk with the childish
inscription inside the heart:
"TUESDAY LOVES RAN-
DOLPH." The camera pans
to the full figure of Tuesday
drawing a striped cat on the
sidewalk next to the heart.
6 ft. 25 frames

7. CLOSE-UP—TUESDAY'S
FACE—OBLIQUE ANGLE
She is absorbed in her
drawing.   1 ft. 36 frames

8. MEDIUM FULL SHOT
FROM ABOVE—TUESDAY
DRAWING
We see her working on the
cat. We can read the in-
scription in the heart again.
5 ft. 23 frames
9. CLOSE-UP—TUESDAY'S
FACE
Continuation of shot 7. She
blows dust off the drawing.
3 ft. 36 frames

279

Third Final Shooting Script	*Post-Production Script*
	10. LONG SHOT—FROM HIGH ABOVE—TUESDAY DRAWING From third-floor window. Much higher than shot 8. 2 ft. 7 frames
7. MEDIUM CLOSE SHOT—RANDOLPH IN WINDOW The boy is chewing from a stick of licorice, thoughtfully looking down on Tuesday. He thinks about it, then works up some saliva, takes aim—and spits.	11. LONG SHOT—FROM SIDEWALK—RANDOLPH IN WINDOW We see the small figure of a boy high up in the third floor window. He looks down without moving. 2 ft. 27 frames
	12. MEDIUM SHOT—TUESDAY DRAWING She draws unaware of the boy above. 2 ft. 22 frames
	13. FULL SHOT—TUESDAY As a man's legs pass by close to the camera, Tuesday turns and looks up at the window above. 1 ft. 24 frames
	14. LONG SHOT—FROM SIDEWALK—RANDOLPH IN WINDOW Similar to shot 11. 1 ft. 10 frames
	15. MEDIUM SHOT—RANDOLPH IN WINDOW He looks down. He seems about to do something. 2 ft. 7 frames
7A. TUESDAY DRAWING—FROM RANDOLPH'S POINT OF VIEW	16. LONG SHOT—FROM HIGH ABOVE—TUESDAY DRAWING Similar to shot 10. 2 ft. 17 frames

17. MEDIUM SHOT—RAN-
DOLPH IN WINDOW—
SIDE VIEW
He leans forward, works his
mouth and spits.
1 ft. 34 frames

8. CLOSE-UP—TUESDAY'S
HAND

18. CLOSE-UP—TUESDAY'S
HAND DRAWING HEAD OF
CHALK CAT   31 frames

9. CLOSE-UP—TUESDAY'S
FACE

19. CLOSE-UP—TUESDAY'S
FACE
With sudden disgust, she
jumps up.   19 frames

10. CLOSE-UP—TUESDAY'S
LAP—THEN PAN TO HER
FACE
As she rises the chalk falls
from her lap. The camera
pans up to her face, looking
up. She sees something
above and dashes out of
frame.

20. CLOSE-UP—TUESDAY'S
FEET NEAR THE CAT'S
HEAD
As she jumps up, the chalk
spills from her lap onto the
cat near where the glob of
spit landed.   30 frames

11. FULL SHOT—DOORWAY
Tuesday enters frame and
stands in doorway. She
peers up.

21. LONG SHOT—FROM RAN-
DOLPH'S POINT OF VIEW
—TUESDAY AT WALL
The little girl runs to the
building wall, directly under Randolph, but out of his
sight because of the window
ledges.   31 frames

22. FULL SHOT—FROM SIDE-
WALK—TUESDAY AT WALL
She runs and stands with
her back to the wall, looking
up.   2 ft. 1 frame

12. LONG SHOT—RANDOLPH
IN WINDOW (ALTERNATE:
PAN SLOWLY UP TO
RANDOLPH)
Randolph leans very far out
to peer down. He chews and
spits.

23. MEDIUM SHOT—RAN-
DOLPH
He looks down, trying to
find the girl. He spits again.
29 frames

Third Final *Shooting Script*	*Post-Production* *Script*
13. CLOSE SHOT—SPIT LANDS ON STEP NEAR TUESDAY'S FOOT Foot moves out, steps on blob and rubs it out angrily.	24. FULL SHOT—TUESDAY WITH HER BACK TO BUILDING She ducks.　28 frames
14. LONG SHOT—RANDOLPH'S POINT OF VIEW—PAN FROM TUESDAY TO DRAWING Tuesday's head peers out, then quickly withdraws. Pan to drawings.	25. MEDIUM SHOT—RANDOLPH IN WINDOW Still trying to sight the girl below.　2 ft. 38 frames
	26. CLOSE-UP—TUESDAY'S FACE AGAINST THE BUILDING She looks up—furious. 2 ft. 5 frames
15. CLOSE-UP—RANDOLPH IN WINDOW Calmly, he changes his aim, spitting at drawings instead of girl.	27. MEDIUM SHOT—RANDOLPH IN WINDOW He pulls a licorice stick from his back pocket and chews.　2 ft. 9 frames
	28. RANDOLPH CHEWS AND SPITS　1 ft. 32 frames
16. CLOSE-UP—CHALK ANIMAL ON SIDEWALK A blob of spit lands on the chalk animal.	29. CLOSE-UP—HEAD OF CHALK CAT—GLOB OF BLACK SPIT LANDS 1 ft. 33 frames
17. CLOSE-UP—TUESDAY'S FACE IN DOORWAY She looks out at her cat, and up toward Randolph angrily.	30. CLOSE-UP—TUESDAY'S FACE AGAINST BUILDING She looks out at cat and up at Randolph—furious. 2 ft. 7 frames
	31. FULL SHOT—RANDOLPH IN WINDOW He looks down, trying to see Tuesday, then spits again. 1 ft. 28 frames

18. FULL SHOT—TUESDAY IN
DOORWAY. PAN TO
ACTION
She runs out and with her
foot rubs out the spit on her
drawings, then runs back,
opens door and enters foyer.

32. GLOB OF SPIT HITS SIDE-
WALK   1 ft. 10 frames

33. FULL SHOT—TUESDAY
RUNS OUT
She runs from the wall,
picks up a piece of chalk,
and bends down to draw a
circle around the glob of
spit.   2 ft. 34 frames

34. CLOSE-UP TUESDAY'S
HAND
Circles the spit on the side-
walk.   31 frames

35. FULL SHOT—COMPLET-
ING THE ACTION
She finishes the circle,
drops the chalk and runs to
the doorway. Camera PANS
to follow her.   26 frames

36. FULL SHOT—NEW ANGLE
Tuesday arriving in door-
way.   2 ft. 21 frames

37. MEDIUM SHOT—RAN-
DOLPH IN WINDOW
Looking for Tuesday.
                2 ft. 26 frames

38. MEDIUM SHOT—TUES-
DAY IN DOORWAY
Looking up angrily at Ran-
dolph.   2 ft. 21 frames

39. MEDIUM SHOT—RAN-
DOLPH IN WINDOW
He spits again.   27 frames

40. CLOSE-UP—SIDEWALK
Spit lands on a different
chalk drawing.   37 frames

Third Final
Shooting Script

Post-Production
Script

41. FULL SHOT—TUESDAY
UNDER LEDGE
She runs out to the ledge to
look up.   2 ft. 15 frames

42. CLOSE-UP—TUESDAY
Full face as she looks up.
36 frames

43. FULL SHOT—TUESDAY
Tuesday runs out to her
chalk drawings again.
1 ft. 1 frame

44. FULL SHOT—FROM
ABOVE—RANDOLPH'S
POINT OF VIEW
Tuesday picks up a piece of
chalk and draws a big X
through the heart with the
inscription "Tuesday Loves
Randolph."   5 ft. 34 frames

45. MEDIUM SHOT—RAN-
DOLPH IN WINDOW
He watches Tuesday.
1 ft. 8 frames

19. INTERIOR FOYER
MEDIUM SHOT—
TUESDAY WRITING
ON WALL
The angry girl has taken a
piece of chalk from her dress
pocket and writes on the
wall: "Tuesday Hates Ran-
dolph." She draws an arrow
to his mailbox.

46. MEDIUM SHOT—TUES-
DAY BACK IN DOORWAY
—OPENS DOOR
She enters the vestibule,
takes out a piece of chalk
and begins to write on the
wall under the mailboxes,
"Tuesday Hates . . ."
15 ft. 33 frames

20. INTERIOR LIVING
ROOM—MEDIUM SHOT—
RANDOLPH'S BACK AT
THE WINDOW

Randolph is leaning far
out, trying to find Tuesday.

21. MEDIUM CLOSE SHOT—
MOTHER ENTERING
FROM ANOTHER
ROOM

The mother wears a hat,
dressed to go shopping. She
stops as she sees her son
and exclaims, "Randolph!"

22. MEDIUM SHOT—
RANDOLPH
AT WINDOW

The boy wheels to face his
mother; stuffs licorice in
pocket.

47. INTERIOR—LIVING ROOM
—RANDOLPH'S APART-
MENT—MEDIUM SHOT

The mother, hat on and
purse in hand to go shop-
ping, enters living room,
looks up, sees her son and
exclaims, "Randolph!" She
heads toward camera and
passes out of frame.

2 ft. 4 frames

48. REVERSE ANGLE—
MEDIUM SHOT—RAN-
DOLPH'S BACK

Randolph is leaning out the
window. He straightens up
and wheels to face his
mother who enters the
frame. We see her body and
arm and she takes the boy's
shoulder. He looks up at her
as she scolds.

4 ft. 19 frames

49. COMPLETION OF SHOT 46
—TUESDAY IN VESTIBULE

The girl finishes writing
"Tuesday Hates Randolph,"
then draws an arrow to one
of the mailboxes, discovers
it is the wrong mailbox,
rubs out the first arrow and
draws a second one.

5 ft. 39 frames

Third Final Shooting Script	*Post-Production Script*
23. MEDIUM TWO-SHOT— RANDOLPH, THEN MOTHER	50. MEDIUM TWO-SHOT— RANDOLPH AND MOTHER
The mother comes up to Randolph and points to a cleaning implement nearby. He nods and possibly picks it up.	The mother reaches out of frame to take a carpet sweeper by the handle and demonstrate to Randolph how to use it. 2 ft. 24 frames
	51. CLOSE-UP—RANDOLPH AND MOTHER'S FEET
	The carpet sweeper moves to and fro. 1 ft. 23 frames
	52. COMPLETION OF SHOT 50 —RANDOLPH AND MOTHER
	She finishes the demonstration and hands him the sweeper. 3 ft. 7 frames
24. CLOSE SHOT—TABLE (IN BACKGROUND OF PREVIOUS SHOT)	53. CLOSE-UP—VERY LOW ANGLE UP TO TABLE WITH URN
Randolph's cat jumps onto the table containing an urn on which is inscribed, "R.I.P. BELOVED UNCLE BERNARD HORN—1883– 1932." Next to the urn is a framed photograph of Uncle Bernie.	The cat jumps onto the table next to the urn. 1 ft. 11 frames
	54. MEDIUM TWO-SHOT— RANDOLPH AND MOTHER
	The cat is on the table behind the mother. 2 ft. 3 frames

25. CLOSE-UP—MOTHER'S
FACE

> She sees the cat on the table, and moves out of frame to get it.

26. FULL SHOT—RANDOLPH
AND MOTHER

> Mother grabs cat on table and hands it to Randolph, scolding him.

27. MEDIUM CLOSE-UP—
HIGH ANGLE—MOTHER'S
POINT OF VIEW

> Randolph looks up with the cat in one hand and the cleaning implement in the other. He nods that he understands her orders.

28. MEDIUM CLOSE-UP—LOW
ANGLE—FROM
RANDOLPH'S POINT
OF VIEW

> The mother bends down to kiss him, smiling sweetly.

29. MEDIUM SHOT—
RANDOLPH AND MOTHER

> She kisses his forehead and smoothes his hair. She turns head past camera toward the door.

55. CLOSE-UP—VERY LOW
ANGLE—CAT, THEN
MOTHER'S FACE

> The mother's face swoops down as she picks up the cat.
> 1 ft. 24 frames

56. MEDIUM TWO-SHOT—
OVER MOTHER'S SHOUL-
DER—RANDOLPH

> The mother hands the cat to Randolph, who looks up at her. Mother then walks out of frame. Randolph's face turns to watch her as she leaves.   7 ft. 17 frames

57. FULL SHOT—MOTHER
WALKING AWAY FROM
CAMERA TOWARD DOOR

> When she gets to the door, she turns and looks back at Randolph.   4 ft. 14 frames

58. MEDIUM SHOT—RAN-
DOLPH HOLDING CAT

> He forces a smile to his mother at the door.
> 1 ft. 10 frames

59. FULL SHOT—MOTHER AT
DOOR

> She smiles at Randolph, then turns and goes out the door.   4 ft. 35 frames

Third Final
Shooting Script

Post-Production
Script

30. MEDIUM CLOSE SHOT—RANDOLPH

He watches her go. Sound effect: door slam. (May need 30-A: shot of mother turning back at door to blow kiss, then slam door.) Randolph deliberately musses up his hair, then lets the cat down on the forbidden table. He tosses aside the cleaning implement and smiles as he watches the cat. Intercut shot 24: taking licorice out of his pocket.

60. MEDIUM SHOT—RANDOLPH WITH CAT

He puts the cat on table which urn stands on.

2 ft. 14 frames

61. CLOSE-UP—PHOTO

Photo is of Uncle Bernie, on the wall above the table.

1 ft. 20 frames

62. MEDIUM SHOT—RANDOLPH AND CAT

At the table with the urn, Randolph pets the cat, then pushes the sweeper across the room. 6 ft. 24 frames

63. CLOSE-UP—PHOTO OF UNCLE BERNIE

Tighter close-up than shot 61. 1 ft. 37 frames

64. FULL SHOT—RANDOLPH GOING TO WINDOW

He pulls out a stick of licorice from his back pocket, jerks a bite out of it, and goes away from camera to window to look out.

2 ft. 34 frames

31. LONG SHOT—STREET
BELOW—RANDOLPH'S
POINT OF VIEW

Tuesday is again drawing
on sidewalk—a drawing has
been added. The mother
comes out of the doorway
below and stops to admire
Tuesday's art, exclaiming,
"Oh, how beautiful!" Tuesday looks up and smiles.
The mother starts to leave.

31A. TUESDAY—CLOSE-UP—
SMILING AT MOTHER

31B. CLOSE-UP IN WINDOW—
WATCHING, FRUS-
TRATED, THEN ABOUT
TO SPIT BUT STOPS,
THEN SWALLOWING
SPIT

32. MEDIUM CLOSE—COP'S
FACE—FROM TUESDAY'S
POINT OF VIEW

The cop gives official ap-
proval of Tuesday's art
work.

65. LONG SHOT—FROM RAN-
DOLPH'S POINT OF VIEW
—TUESDAY ON SIDE-
WALK—THEN MOTHER—
THEN COP

Tuesday sits on sidewalk,
drawing; Mother comes out
of building; goes to Tuesday, pats her on the head,
and walks away; as mother
walks away, she meets cop
who salutes her, then cop
walks over to look at Tuesday's drawings.

7 ft. 3 frames

66. CLOSE-UP—TUESDAY'S
FACE

She smiles up at the cop.

37 frames

67. MEDIUM LONG SHOT—
FROM SIDEWALK—RAN-
DOLPH LOOKING DOWN
FROM WINDOW

He looks down without
moving; he seems angry.

1 ft. 38 frames

289

Third Final
Shooting Script

Post-Production
Script

33. CLOSE-UP—TUESDAY—
FROM COP'S POINT OF
VIEW

She smiles up at cop. Intercut Randolph about to spit
(31B). Tuesday looks past
the cop to see Randolph,
then quickly ducks behind
the cop's legs. She draws an
outline around each of the
cop's shoes. Intercut cop's
face smiling down (32).
The cop's feet step out of
the outlines, leaving new
designs.

33A. LONG SHOT—
RANDOLPH IN WINDOW
—FROM TUESDAY'S
POINT OF VIEW

He points his thumb and
forefinger, making a pis-
tol.

68. LONG SHOT—FROM RAN-
DOLPH'S POINT OF VIEW
—COP AND TUESDAY
BELOW

Continuation of shot 65.
Cop walks around behind
Tuesday.   3 ft. 1 frame

69. INTERIOR—MEDIUM
SHOT—RANDOLPH LOOK-
ING OUT WINDOW

The boy straightens up as
he sees cop walk behind
Tuesday.   2 ft. 37 frames

70. FULL SHOT—EXTERIOR—
COP'S LEGS—FULL FIG-
URE OF TUESDAY

The girl turns around on the
sidewalk and draws a chalk
circle around each of the
cop's feet, then looks up at
him, smiling.
6 ft. 9 frames

71. CLOSE-UP—COP'S FACE

He grins down at the girl
and lifts his cap slightly.
1 ft. 31 frames

34. INTERIOR—LIVING ROOM
—RANDOLPH AT
WINDOW—MEDIUM SHOT

Randolph, his thumb and forefinger making a pistol, aiming at the cop, mouths "Pow! Pow!" Then he wheels toward camera and fires a few more shots, pulling a second imaginary pistol from an imaginary holster. (Try using the "weight" from original story.)

35. NEW ANGLE—RANDOLPH
BEHIND A CHAIR

He keeps firing his imaginary revolvers toward the door, crouching behind a chair. He jumps up and races toward the door.

36. NEW ANGLE—RANDOLPH
BARRICADING THE DOOR

At the door, he takes a piece of furniture, barricades the door, then backs away, covering door with his "pistols." Then he blows smoke out of each barrel and pockets each of his "guns" in the holsters, victoriously, the grim cowboy.

72. INTERIOR—RANDOLPH
LOOKING OUT WINDOW

Continuation of shot 69. Randolph makes a "pistol" with his forefinger and shoots down at the cop below, then wheels into the room and fires at something outside the frame.
4 ft. 39 frames

73. MEDIUM SHOT—RAN-
DOLPH AT COUCH
"SHOOTING"—CAT ON
BACK OF COUCH

Randolph continues to "shoot" at something imaginary, then ducks at the foot of the couch as if being fired upon.   8 ft. 11 frames

74. MEDIUM SHOT—PAN TO
FULL SHOT—RANDOLPH
RUNNING TO DOOR

Randolph, "shooting," runs past couch to chair, then to door, opens it, shoots out into hall, closes door, barricades it with a chair, turns back into room and fires toward window, then blows the "smoke" from his "pistol."   7 ft. 17 frames

75. EXTERIOR—CLOSE-UP—
TUESDAY'S FACE

She is drawing on sidewalk again.   3 ft. 4 frames

Third Final Shooting Script

Post-Production Script

37. NEW ANGLE—RANDOLPH GETTING COOKIE

He gets a cookie from a bowl, picks up the cat, and squats on the floor with cat in his lap.

76. INTERIOR—MEDIUM SHOT—GETTING COOKIE FROM CUPBOARD

He looks for and finds a cookie, then walks past camera, eating.

10 ft. 17 frames

38. EXTERIOR—TUESDAY ON SIDEWALK

Tuesday at work, looks up toward window. Where's Randolph? She stops drawing and just sits there, looking up plaintively. She sighs, watching the empty window.

77. FULL SHOT—PAN TO FOLLOW ACTION—RANDOLPH GETS CAT

Randolph comes from hallway into living room, picks up cat from couch, gives cat a bite of cookie, then sits on floor with cat. The boy looks idly across the room.

13 ft. 27 frames

78. CLOSE-UP—UNCLE BERNIE—PHOTO ON WALL

Photo of Bernie, austere.

2 ft. 1 frame

79. CLOSE-UP—URN

Urn of Bernie's ashes on table.   2 ft. 13 frames

80. CLOSE-UP—TIGHTER THAN 78

Photo of uncle on wall.

2 ft. 21 frames

81. MEDIUM SHOT—RANDOLPH GETS UP AND GOES TO WINDOW—PAN TO FOLLOW

Randolph still holding cat, and with cookie in mouth, gets up and goes to window to look out.   6 ft. 18 frames

39. EXTERIOR—RANDOLPH COMES TO WINDOW

Randolph looks down at Tuesday, cookie in mouth, cat in arms.

82. EXTERIOR—MEDIUM SHOT—RANDOLPH WITH CAT—STANDING IN WINDOW LOOKING OUT

Petting the cat, Randolph looks down at the sidewalk. He lets the cat out of his hands.   3 ft. 28 frames

83. CLOSE-UP—TUESDAY— LOOKING AT RANDOLPH

Her hand to her mouth, the girl anticipates something.
2 ft. 33 frames

84. LONG SHOT—FROM SIDEWALK UP—RANDOLPH IN WINDOW

Randolph blows out the cookie crumbs from his mouth angrily.
1 ft. 7 frames

85. CLOSE-UP—TUESDAY'S FACE

She giggles.
1 ft. 12 frames

86. LONG SHOT—FROM SIDEWALK UP—RANDOLPH IN WINDOW

He spits some more crumbs.
1 ft. 37 frames

87. CLOSE-UP—TUESDAY'S FACE

She laughs up at him.
1 ft. 19 frames

88. MEDIUM SHOT—RANDOLPH IN WINDOW

He wipes his mouth with his arm.   2 ft. 9 frames

Third Final
Shooting Script

Post-Production
Script

89. LONG SHOT—FROM SIDE-
    WALK UP
    Randolph wipes mouth
    again.   2 ft. 9 frames

40. MEDIUM CLOSE—
    TUESDAY
    She sticks out her tongue
    and stands, moving out of
    frame.

90. MEDIUM SHOT—TUESDAY
    She stands up, coming into
    frame, and makes an ugly
    face with her tongue stick-
    ing out at Randolph.
         1 ft. 25 frames

41. CLOSER SHOT—
    RANDOLPH AT WINDOW
    He lets cat go, takes cookie
    out of mouth, and tries to
    spit. It dribbles over his
    chin. He is humiliated. He
    disappears from window
    for a moment (or simply
    reaches into room) and re-
    turns with a vase of flowers.
    Dumps contents out the
    window.

91. CLOSE-UP—EMPTY
    WINDOW   3 ft. 30 frames

    DISSOLVE TO:

41A. FOLLOW FLOWERS
     FROM VASE TO SIDE-
     WALK

92. FULL SHOT—TUESDAY
    SITTING ON SIDEWALK
    DRAWING
    She stops drawing, turns
    and leans back so that she
    can look up at window.
         4 ft. 15 frames

41B. INTERCUT: TUESDAY—
     MEDIUM SHOT—LAUGH-
     ING AT RANDOLPH

93. CLOSE-UP—EMPTY
    WINDOW   1 ft. 31 frames

42. FULL SHOT—TUESDAY IN DOORWAY—PAN TO FOLLOW ACTION

She runs to get one of the flowers, which she sticks in her hair; looks up defiantly at Randolph. Intercut the empty window (part of 38). She puts her hands on hips and waits.

43. NEW ANGLE—TUESDAY ON SIDEWALK—CLOSE SHOT—PAN TO DRAWING

Tuesday moves into frame by sitting down to draw some more. Pan slowly to the animal she begins to draw.

44. CLOSE-UP—THE SAME DRAWING LATER—IT IS NEARLY COMPLETE

A water bomb lands smack in the drawing near Tuesday's hand. The hand moves quickly out of frame.

94. COMPLETION OF SHOT 92

Tuesday sighs and returns to her drawing.

2 ft. 12 frames

95. CLOSE-UP—EMPTY WINDOW   1 ft. 34 frames

96. FULL SHOT—TUESDAY PAN TO FOLLOW ACTION

She is arranging her various colored chalks by one of her drawings. Picks up her chalk, moves to a new spot and begins to draw a rabbit.

4 ft. 10 frames

97. LONG SHOT—FROM SIDE-WALK UP—THE EMPTY WINDOW   1 ft. 4 frames

98. CLOSE-UP—TUESDAY'S HAND

Drawing the rabbit.

13 ft. 25 frames

99. CLOSE-UP—FROM EX-TERIOR—LOOKING PROFILE AT RANDOLPH'S WINDOW

Hand extended holding a bag of water.   36 frames

100. CLOSE-UP—COMPLE-TION OF SHOT 98

Hand drawing rabbit. Bag of water lands.   39 frames

295

Third Final Shooting Script	*Post-Production Script*
45. FULL SHOT—TUESDAY DASHING INTO DOOR-WAY—MOVES INTO FRAME She looks up and sees: shot 46. She quickly withdraws.	101. FULL SHOT—TUESDAY RUNNING TO DOOR—PAN TO FOLLOW HER The girl jumps up and runs to the steps leading down to the door of the apartment building. As she runs, a second water bag lands on the sidewalk. She jumps up and down angrily. 2 ft. 18 frames
	102. LONG SHOT—FROM RANDOLPH'S POINT OF VIEW—TUESDAY ON STEPS The girl looks up, then disappears out of bottom of frame to safety of doorway. 2 ft. 17 frames
46. MEDIUM CLOSE-UP—RANDOLPH AT WINDOW Randolph holds a dishpan from which he takes a water bomb and delicately lets it drop. Intercut Tuesday in doorway looking out, watching bombs land (more of 45).	103. LONG SHOT—FROM SIDEWALK UP—RANDOLPH IN WINDOW The boy has a dishpan from which he takes a bag of water 1 ft. 4 frames
	104. MEDIUM CLOSE-UP—INTERIOR—LOOKING AT RANDOLPH IN WINDOW Randolph takes a bag of water from dishpan. 1 ft. 10 frames
	105. LONG SHOT—RANDOLPH'S POINT OF VIEW Bag falling toward sidewalk. 33 frames

46. A, B, C. CLOSE-UPS—
BOMBS LANDING

46D. BOMBS FALLING—FROM
RANDOLPH'S POINT
OF VIEW

47. MEDIUM CLOSE—TUES-
DAY IN DOORWAY—
WOMAN WITH HAT
COMES INTO FRAME
Tuesday watches.

48. MEDIUM CLOSE—
RANDOLPH AT WINDOW,
THEN LEAVES
Randolph sees he has run
out of ammunition. He
leaves window.

48A. CLOSE-UP—EMPTY
DISHPAN

106. CLOSE-UP—BAG SPLAT-
TERING
Hits next to circle around
spit.   1 ft. 29 frames

107. MEDIUM SHOT—EX-
TERIOR—RANDOLPH IN
WINDOW
Takes bag from dishpan.
2 ft. 35 frames

108. LONG SHOT—RAN-
DOLPH'S POINT OF VIEW
One bag, then a second
lands on the chalk heart
below.   3 ft. 3 frames

109. MEDIUM SHOT—EX-
TERIOR—RANDOLPH IN
WINDOW
Dropping more bags.
11 ft. 38 frames

110. MEDIUM SHOT—TUES-
DAY IN DOORWAY
Looks up at Randolph.
1 ft. 25 frames

111. FULL SHOT—A NEW
DOORWAY NEARBY
A lady in a big hat comes
up the three steps to the
sidewalk, taking a hand-
kerchief from her purse
and touching it to her lips.
2 ft. 33 frames

*Third Final
Shooting Script*

*Post-Production
Script*

49. CLOSE TWO SHOT—TUES-
DAY, THEN WOMAN INTO
FRAME

Tuesday frantically beckons
the woman in the fancy hat,
who comes into frame, asking what is wrong. Tuesday
points. The woman looks
up. Intercut the empty
window (part of 38). The
woman sympathizes with
Tuesday, then starts to
move out. Intercut Ran-
dolph arriving at window
with dishpan of bombs. As
Randolph drops a bomb,
the woman is saying good-
bye to Tuesday, waving as
she walks from the door.
The bomb lands on her
fancy hat.

112. MEDIUM SHOT—TUES-
DAY IN DOORWAY—
MORE OF SHOT 110

The girl sees the lady coming and puts her hand to
her face as she anticipates
the lady getting hit by a
water bag.   29 frames

113. MEDIUM SHOT—LADY
IN HAT

The lady sees Tuesday and
waves to her. A water bag
hits her on the big hat. The
lady runs out of frame.
1 ft. 11 frames

114. FULL SHOT—LADY RUNS
TO JOIN TUESDAY—PAN
TO FOLLOW

The lady is galvanized into
running to join Tuesday
in the doorway, where she
tries to brush the water off
her dress.   4 ft.

50. CLOSE-UP—RANDOLPH IN WINDOW

He claps his hand over his mouth, realizing what he's done.

51. NEW ANGLE—TUESDAY AND WOMAN IN DOOR-WAY

The woman runs back into frame, angrily trying to dry herself.

52. INTERIOR TO STREET—RANDOLPH'S POINT OF VIEW (SEE 50)

We can see a man in a bowler hat coming into range. Intercut Randolph's face taking on a new look (more of 50), as he decides this time it might be fun to hit that bowler hat on purpose instead of acciden-tally. He aims a water bomb.

53. CLOSE-UP—WATER BOMB —RANDOLPH'S FACE IN BACKGROUND

He holds the bomb deli-cately. Intercut more of the

115. MEDIUM SHOT—RAN-DOLPH IN WINDOW

Dropping bags of water.
2 ft. 24 frames

116. FULL SHOT—A MAN IN BOWLER HAT APPROACHES

The man walks along read-ing a book, unaware of what he is walking into. He walks right up to the cam-era to a full close-up. Book title: *Catcher in the Rye*.
3 ft. 35 frames

117. MEDIUM SHOT—NEW ANGLE—MAN IN BOWLER

Continues walking to bull's-eye area.
1 ft. 10 frames

118. CLOSE-UP—FACE OF MAN IN BOWLER

The man stops and smiles at something he is reading.
1 ft. 11 frames

119. MEDIUM SHOT—NEW ANGLE—MAN IN BOWLER

As he pauses, smiling at the book, a water bag hits

*Third Final
Shooting Script*

*Post-Production
Script*

man approaching from Randolph's point of view (52). The bomb is released. Intercut more of 51; Tuesday and the woman look up as they see the man approaching. The woman starts to say something. But the bomb hits the man squarely on the bowler. He freezes, takes off his hat, looks up, lets out a shriek and joins the woman and Tuesday in the doorway. A new bomb narrowly misses.

his bowler hat, knocking it askew and crushing in the top.   2 ft. 7 frames

120. MEDIUM SHOT—
RANDOLPH AT WINDOW
He laughs and takes another water bag from the dishpan.   1 ft. 3 frames

121. CLOSE-UP—MAN
TAKING OFF HAT
The surprised man takes off his hat, now crushed. He looks at it, looks up, sees Randolph, and hastily runs out of frame.
3 ft. 32 frames

122. MEDIUM SHOT—SIDE
ANGLE—RANDOLPH
IN WINDOW
He drops another water bag.   37 frames

123. CLOSE-UP—WATER BAG
LANDING
Lands on sidewalk next to iron cellar plate.
1 ft. 40 frames

124. MEDIUM SHOT—SIDE
ANGLE—RANDOLPH
IN WINDOW

Laughing, enjoying himself.   1 ft. 33 frames

54. NEW ANGLE—MAN, WOMAN, TUESDAY IN DOORWAY, THEN COP

The woman sympathizes with the man who is trying to regain his dignity. Tuesday is trying to keep from laughing. The cop comes up to them.

125. MEDIUM THREE SHOT—MAN, LADY, TUESDAY IN DOORWAY

The man and lady angrily look up at Randolph. Tuesday watches, crouching behind the lady.
                    6 ft. 32 frames

126. LONG SHOT—FROM RANDOLPH'S POINT OF VIEW—THE THREE COME UP TO THE STEPS

The man, the lady, and Tuesday cautiously go up the steps to the sidewalk. A bomb sails down and lands in front of them on the sidewalk. The three turn and descend again to the safety of the doorway.
                    7 ft. 19 frames

127. INTERIOR—MEDIUM SHOT—RANDOLPH AT WINDOW LOOKING OUT

He sees that his dishpan is empty of water bombs. He dumps the remaining water in the dishpan out the window, turns into the room and heads out of the frame toward the kitchen.
                    2 ft. 10 frames

301

Third Final
Shooting Script

Post-Production
Script

128. MEDIUM THREE-SHOT—
MAN, LADY, TUESDAY IN
DOORWAY
Continuation of shot 125.
The angry people see
someone coming.
1 ft. 2 frames

129. LONG SHOT—FROM
RANDOLPH'S WINDOW—
COP APPROACHING
As the cop approaches
from far down the side-
walk, the camera tilts with
his approach to bring him
nearer to the building. He
sees something is wrong
and quickens his pace.
5 ft. 24 frames

55. CLOSE-UP—COP
He asks what's going on.

130. MEDIUM THREE SHOT—
MAN, LADY, TUESDAY,
THEN THE COP
The man anxiously beck-
ons the cop to hurry to
them. The cop's back en-
ters the frame as he goes
down the steps to face

56. REVERSE—MEDIUM SHOT
—MAN, WOMAN, TUES-
DAY
They all talk at once, point-
ing and complaining.

them in the doorway to
listen to their anxious
story. The man points up
to the window. The cop
looks up. 9 ft. 3 frames

57. CLOSE-UP—BROKEN
WATER BAGS ON DRAW-
INGS ON SIDEWALK, ETC.

131. CLOSE-UP—RANDOLPH'S
WINDOW
Only the cat is seen there
on the window sill.
2 ft. 5 frames

58. NEW ANGLE—TO IN-
CLUDE COP, WOMAN,
MAN, TUESDAY

The cop steps into the doorway and looks at the mailboxes to read the names. He
gets out his book to write
some notes as the others step
on the sidewalk to point up
at Randolph. Intercut Randolph looking down at
people, taking aim (Shot
46). They scurry for shelter. The cop steps out from
the doorway to look up.

59. CLOSE-UP—COP LOOKING
UP

He sees a bomb coming
down and tries to duck—too
late. It splashes on his shoulder (or some part of body).

60. SHOT OF ADULTS ENTER-
ING DOORWAY

60A. MEDIUM SHOT—RAN-
DOLPH'S MOTHER AP-
PROACHING

60B. SHOT OF MOTHER FROM
RANDOLPH'S POINT OF
VIEW

132. FULL SHOT—COP, MAN,
LADY, TUESDAY

The cop gestures that no
one is up there. The others
come up the steps toward
the sidewalk to see for
themselves.

2 ft. 25 frames

133. SIDE VIEW—MEDIUM
SHOT—RANDOLPH
AT WINDOW

First the empty window;
then Randolph suddenly
appears with the dishpan
and sails a fresh water bag
out without looking down.

1 ft.

134. LONG SHOT—
RANDOLPH'S POINT OF
VIEW—THREE ADULTS
AND TUESDAY BELOW

The bag sails down. The
cop ducks—too late—it
hits his back. The three
adults and Tuesday head
back down steps to door-
way   2 ft. 6 frames

135. LONG SHOT—MOTHER

She is seen coming up the
street toward the camera.

4 ft. 14 frames

303

Third Final *Shooting Script*	*Post-Production* *Script*
61. FULL SHOT—FOUR ADULTS AND TUESDAY The mother pushes her way through the others, and with cop, they all enter the doorway of the building. The mother carries a hat box or some other luxury item; her shopping was trivial.	
62. CLOSE-UP—RANDOLPH'S FACE IN WINDOW He is absolutely horrified.	**136. INTERIOR—RANDOLPH AT WINDOW LOOKING OUT** He claps his hand to his mouth, turns into the room, sets the dishpan on the floor and runs out of frame toward door. 4 ft. 15 frames
63. INTERIOR LIVING ROOM —MEDIUM SHOT—RANDOLPH AT WINDOW Randolph turns into the room, looking at door he barricaded. He sets down the dishpan, looks right and left, wildly trying to figure a way out of this mess.	
	137. CLOSE-UP—THE DOORKNOB WITH CHAIR BARRICADING—THEN RANDOLPH'S FACE Randolph's face and hands come into frame as he presses against the door to keep anyone from entering. 1 ft. 23 frames

304

138. FULL SHOT—MOTHER

She is standing on the sidewalk looking at the watery mess.

2 ft. 18 frames

139. MEDIUM SHOT—THE SIDEWALK

Bags and water splashed all over.   1 ft. 23 frames

140. CLOSE-UP—RANDOLPH PUSHING AGAINST DOORKNOB

Continuation of shot 137. The boy pushes, then turns, going out of frame for a second, returns and sits in the chair with his back to the door, eyes tightly closed, mouth screwed up.

2 ft. 26 frames

141. FULL SHOT—MOTHER

She runs down the steps and into the door of the building.   2 ft. 15 frames

142. INTERIOR FULL SHOT— ADULTS COMING UP THE STAIRS IN HALLWAY— PAN TO FOLLOW

From above looking down into the stairwell, we see the adults running up the stairs toward the apartment: first comes the cop, then the lady, then the man in the hat, then the mother, who passes the man and knocks his hat off with a package she has. The man stops, is torn between his

*Third Final
Shooting Script*

*Post-Production
Script*

lost hat and the boy up-
stairs. Camera holds on
him. He forgets the hat
and runs out of frame.

7 ft. 18 frames

64. NEW ANGLE—RANDOLPH
ADDING TO BARRICADE

He pushes a chair into place
at the door, then looks
around desperately. All he
can find handy are two
phone books which he adds
to the barricade.

143. FULL SHOT—RANDOLPH
IN CHAIR WITH BACK TO
DOOR

The boy opens his eyes,
decides to get something,
runs out of frame; camera
holds on empty chair; boy
runs back into frame with
a flimsy little table which
he piles onto the chair;
then he runs out of other
side of frame and returns
with a phone book which
he adds to the barricade,
hesitates, goes back out of
frame.   6 ft. 25 frames

65. NEW ANGLE—RANDOLPH
BACKING TOWARD WIN-
DOW

As he backs away, he sees
the urn (insert shot 24,
without cat), and impul-
sively grabs the urn, hug-
ging it to his bosom.

66. INTERIOR—LANDING OUTSIDE APARTMENT—FULL SHOT

The four adults and Tuesday arrive, puffing. The man in the bowler loses his hat in the rush. He tries to recover it. They rush past the camera toward the door. Intercut 65; Randolph with the urn.

144. CLOSE-UP—COP'S FACE FOLLOWED BY LADY'S FACE AS THEY APPROACH DOOR

They are outside and just reach the door.

1 ft. 2 frames

145. MEDIUM SHOT—BARRICADE AT DOOR

Randolph returns with a second phone book; finally he backs toward camera and out of frame.

5 ft. 16 frames

146. FULL SHOT TOWARD WINDOW

Randolph runs into frame, across room toward table, picks up urn and clutches it to his breast.

2 ft. 33 frames

147. CLOSE-UP—COP'S FACE, THEN LADY'S

Mother pushes lady aside to come up by cop.

1 ft. 2 frames

67. MEDIUM SHOT—FROM RANDOLPH'S POINT OF VIEW—COP AND MOTHER ENTERING

The cop pushes the barricade aside, forcing door open. Mother is right behind him; others in background. Cop starts toward Randolph; Mother grabs

148. FULL SHOT—THE BARRICADE

The cop pushes the barricade aside as he opens the door. He enters room, followed by mother, lady, and man. They all head into the room toward camera. Mother grabs cop's arm.   3 ft. 18 frames

*Third Final
Shooting Script*

*Post-Production
Script*

cop's arm as she sees: cut of shot 65—the boy at window with urn. Randolph in desperation holds the urn out the window, threatening to drop it. The cop, dragging the mother, continues toward Randolph. Out the window goes the urn as the cop grabs Randolph.

149. FULL SHOT—RANDOLPH
Randolph holding the urn steps toward the window.
1 ft. 6 frames

150. MEDIUM TWO-SHOT—
COP AND MOTHER
The mother looks horrified and drops her package.
1 ft. 26 frames

151. EXTERIOR—LONG SHOT
—FROM SIDEWALK
LOOKING UP
Randolph in the window, and holding the urn, looks out.   21 frames

152. MEDIUM TWO-SHOT—
COP AND MOTHER (MAN
AND LADY IN BACK-
GROUND)
The mother turns, runs back out the apartment and down the steps.
2 ft. 11 frames

68. EXTERIOR LONG SHOT
FROM STREET LOOKING
UP AT WINDOW
The urn comes hurtling
down until it blacks out the
frame.

69. CLOSE-UP—URN
CRASHES ON PAVEMENT

153. EXTERIOR LONG SHOT—
CONTINUATION OF
SHOT 151
Randolph heaves the urn
out the window. Camera
pans down with it.
1 ft. 12 frames

154. CLOSE-UP—URN
Crashes on the sidewalk.
16 frames

155. CLOSE-UP—URN
FRAGMENTS
These fly across the sidewalk.
14 frames

156. CLOSE-UP—URN
FRAGMENT
Another fragment goes
skidding.   20 frames

157. CLOSE-UP—URN
FRAGMENTS
More fragments go skid-
ding.   31 frames

70. INTERIOR MEDIUM
CLOSE SHOT—MOTHER
MAKING EXIT
Crowding her way through
heads and shoulders, she
gets out door.

158. INTERIOR—MEDIUM
SHOT—COP RUNS AND
GRABS RANDOLPH—
PAN TO FOLLOW
The cop runs across the
room and grabs Randolph
in his arms. The boy kicks
and flails in cop's arms.
2 ft. 27 frames

159. EXTERIOR—CLOSE-UP—
FRAGMENT
A final fragment skids and
rocks to rest.
1 ft. 25 frames

309

Third Final *Shooting Script*	*Post-Production* *Script*
71. EXTERIOR—MEDIUM SHOT—MOTHER IN DOOR-WAY Mother appears in doorway and surveys the sidewalk.	160. FULL SHOT—DOORWAY —MOTHER COMES OUT AND UP STEPS TO LOOK She stops on the steps and her hands come to her face as she takes in the horror of the broken urn. 5 ft. 21 frames
72. PAN SLOWLY ACROSS DEBRIS ON SIDEWALK	161. CLOSE-UP—THE BROKEN URN FADE IN: Superimposed photo of Uncle Bernie over the urn fragments. FADE OUT. 6 ft. 25 frames
73. NEW ANGLE—TUESDAY APPEARS BEHIND THE MOTHER With bowler hat on her head, Tuesday pops out from behind dazed mother and skips out to the broken pottery.	162. MEDIUM SHOT— MOTHER ON STEPS LOOKING AT URN Tuesday comes out from behind the mother; wearing bowler hat, she comes up the steps. 4 ft. 9 frames
74. CLOSE-UP—TUESDAY'S HAND DRAWING CIRCLE AROUND BROKEN FRAG-MENT	163. CLOSE-UP—FRAGMENT WITH LETTERS: "R.I.P." Girl's hand draws chalk circle around this frag-ment. 1 ft. 15 frames
75. FULL SHOT—TUESDAY SKIPPING DOWN THE STREET Camera holds on the little girl wearing the bowler, skipping off happily down the street until she is almost out of sight. We can faintly hear the tune she was hum-ming in the beginning.	164. FULL SHOT—TUESDAY— PAN TO FOLLOW—ENDS IN LONG SHOT Tuesday finishes the cir-cle, stands up and skips off down the street to the corner, where she takes off her bowler hat and waves with it as she continues to skip around the corner out of sight. 8 ft. 20 frames

FADE OUT
FADE IN

76. THE END. A project of
N.Y.U. Workshop, etc.

165. TITLE: SUPERIMPOSED
ON SIDEWALK AS FOR
BEGINNING TITLES
cast
Tuesday
Patty D'Arbanville
Randolph
Noah Lamy
Mother
Elizabeth White
Cop
James Anderson
Lady in Hat
Terry Heyl
Man
Lou Cutelli   6 ft.

166. DISSOLVE TO:
TITLE:
The End
A project of
The Motion Picture Work-
shop of New York Univer-
sity
1960   3 ft.
FADE OUT

The shooting was well handled, as some extremely fine shots were taken, particularly of Randolph. This was accomplished by shooting from a rooftop across the street (using telephoto lenses), from windows above Randolph, and from still another window adjacent to Randolph's.

The directing of the players was equally well done; the performances of the boy and girl were strikingly good. They were neighborhood children with no professional training of any kind. The production was scripted, planned, shot, edited, and completed in six weeks' time, so that the pressures were often greater than in a professional production.

Although in some places dialogue could have been used to advantage, the shots were so self-descriptive that there was no real need for it. Also, the students had their hands full working out and securing the visualization. The elimination of complicated sound equipment to some extent simplified the field work. A full musical track was added in the sound studio.

The film was shot on 16-mm black-and-white reversal stock, set up on A and B rolls in the printing.

APPENDIX B

TECHNICAL FUNDAMENTALS
OF PRODUCTION

The basic technical steps in making a film are usually the same whether the film be elaborate or simple, big budget or small, with a cast and crew of thousands or a film-maker acting as his own cameraman and accompanied by an assistant. To be sure there are differences, but these more often are variations of the basic steps. Once these are understood, then changes brought about by specific conditions and needs are readily grasped.

STEPS IN PRODUCTION

A. *Preparation and Planning*
      1. An *outline, treatment* or *script* is prepared of the original idea. (See pages 51–55.)
      2. *Research* is conducted.
      3. A *shooting script* is drawn up.

313

4. A shooting *breakdown* is prepared.

5. A *shooting schedule* is prepared.

6. Decisions are made about the *raw stock* to be used: black and white or color, *negative* or *reversal* film. *Emulsion speeds* and *film characteristics* (*properties*) are considered.

7. Usually, a *double system* shooting operation is planned as against *single system*.

8. Lighting is considered: sources and power available and types of *lighting units* to be brought in.

B. *Production*

1. Shooting gets underway: considered are *lenses* in terms of *focal length, light meters, filters, reflectors, barn doors, scrims, silks, cookies.*

2. If there is *live sound,* selection is made as to the type of *recorder, microphone, fish pole* or *boom; microphone placement* is decided.

3. At the same time discussions are held and initial plans are made for:

   a. music

   b. art work (*titles* and *animation*).

4. As the shooting continues, the *exposed footage* is developed daily.

5. From the developed footage, a *work print* is made.

6. Before any editing is done, the *work print* and *original footage* are *edge numbered.*

7. If there is *live sound* (initially taken on ¼ inch tape and now transferred to *magnetic sprocketed tape*), it is synchronized with its corresponding picture and also *edge numbered.* In such instances the *magnetic tape, work print,* and *original footage* all carry corresponding *edge numbers.*

C. *Post-Production*

1. The *original footage* is stored away safely.

2. The *work print* is edited either on a viewer set up

between *rewinds* or on a *moviola*. If *live sound* is being edited, a moviola is imperative, for the *live sound* on *sprocketed tape* and film picture are handled together.

3. As editing continues, damaged places in the *work print* are replaced with pieces of *leader* called *slugs*. Smaller tears and ripped sprocket holes are repaired with a *transparent film tape*.

4. A separate *sound effects magnetic track* is prepared and *laid in* on a *synchronizer* with the picture *work print*.

5. A *music magnetic track* is prepared and *laid in* on a *synchronizer* with the picture *work print*.

6. The *sound effects track* and *music tracks* are checked for effectiveness by *playback* on a *moviola* or an *interlock* system.

7. Further corrections or changes to the music and effects tracks are made either on a *moviola* or *synchronizer*, more often on both.

8. If needed, a separate *narrated track* is made by screening the *work print* and having the narrator speak to the picture while he is being recorded.

9. The music and sound effects tracks are *mixed* with the *dialogue (live sound) track* and/or the narrated track.

10. All of these tracks mixed on one track are called a *composite sound track*.

11. The *composite* track (magnetic) is transferred to an optical track, so that it can be printed with picture.

12. At this point the sound track is complete, and since all of the work has been done in conjunction with the picture *work print*, the picture is complete—except that the *original footage* now has to be prepared for printing.

13. The *original footage,* which had been stored, is now *matched* to the *frozen work print* through corresponding *edge numbers* on a *synchronizer.*

14. *Slugs* placed in the *work print* to denote titles, art work, and/or torn or damaged places designate the actual and precise spots to be matched with *original footage.*

15. The *original footage* if in 16-mm gauge is usually set up on A and B rolls during the *matching* process. In the 35-mm gauge it may or may not be set up on A and B rolls, depending on effects desired.

16. The completed *original A and B footage* along with the composite optical track is *timed* and printed on one strip of film, called a *composite.* Prior to printing the track is advanced twenty-six frames.

17. This first *composite print* is generally referred to as the *answer print.*

18. Subsequent prints are called *release prints.*

Note: In all such matters as transfer of magnetic tracks to optical tracks and preparation of A and B rolls, the particular laboratory doing the printing should be consulted for its particular requirements.

GLOSSARY

A and B Rolls   A method of preparing the original film into two strips rather than one in a checkerboard pattern (picture alternating with black leader) so that splices will not show and special effects, such as title superimposures and dissolves, can be achieved. Although absolutely necessary in 16-mm printing, its use in 35-mm printing depends on the number of effects needed.

Ace   A thousand-watt spotlight, generally equipped with a Fresnel lens.

Animation   A general term used to designate apparent movement of inanimate objects or drawings. There are innumerable ways of achieving such movement as drawing directly on the film or preparing drawings on celluloid sheets to be photographed.

Answer Print   The first print made of the completed film showing the balance achieved by the laboratory *timer*. Each shot has been graded so that there is evenness throughout the entire film.

Aperture   The opening through which light is admitted to a lens and passes onto the film.

ASA   Used generally in reference to the system for rating speed characteristics of film emulsion as set up by the American Standards Association.

Assembly   Roughly putting shots in order; linked with the term *Rough Cut*, indicating an assembly of shots.

Astigmatism   A defect of lenses where rays of light from horizontal and vertical lines in a plane in the object are not focused in the same plane on the edges of the image. This defect is corrected by using anastigmatic elements in a lens.

Barn Doors   Hinged flaps mounted on sides of lighting units to keep light from falling on unwanted areas; a device used to control light spill.

Base (Film)   Refers to transparent material coated with light-sensitive emulsion that makes up film; it has a shine and is distinguished from the emulsion, which is dull.

Blimp   A camera housing to deaden the sound of the camera and to prevent it from being picked up by the microphone when recording sound.

Bloop   The sound caused by a splice in an optical track.

Blooping Ink (or Patch)   A black ink used to paint over the splice in an optical track to eliminate the splice sound. The patch is a specially shaped opaque piece of material used for the same purpose.

Boom   A mount used to extend the microphone over the players; it has built-in controls for turning the microphone in different directions.

Booster Light   Any heavy-duty light, usually an arc, used to supplement daylight when shooting outdoor scenes.

Breakdown   In the cutting process, prior to an assembly, the separation of the various shots of a roll of film; applied to original footage as well as work print.

Chromatic Aberration   A defect of lenses in which light is refracted, causing the spectral colors to be separated. The lens will focus the different colors in different planes.

Circle of Confusion   That point where rays of light passing through a lens converge. The circle of confusion is created by spherical aberration. Therefore, the diameter of the circle of confusion is directly indicative of the amount of spherical aberration of a lens system, and is the permissible blur that is accepted as being in focus, or sharp, according to standard vision.

Clapper Board (*Slate*)   A set of hinged sticks, painted in black and white stripes, and clapped together at the beginning of a *take* when shooting synchronous sound. In the editing, the picture of the sticks coming together is lined up with the sound modulation on the track, thus lining up picture and sound in synchronization.

Code Numbers (*Edge Numbers*)   Numbers placed on original stock by the manufacturer at intervals of one foot. These are printed through to the *work print* to simplify the process of *matching*. Also placed on *track, work print,* and *original footage* to simplify sound cutting. In 16-mm work, coding machines are frequently used for this purpose because the printed edge numbers are often too difficult to read.

Composite Print   A positive film containing both picture images and sound track, sometimes referred to as a *married* print.

Contact Printing   A method of printing in which emulsion comes in contact with emulsion. Printing through the *base* results in a soft image.

Contrast   The difference in intensity between tones of black and white. The final contrast of a film is controlled to a great extent by the degree of development. Short development times yield less contrast than do longer periods. However, contrast also depends on the quality of the emulsion itself, known as gamma-infinity.

Cookie   It is a cut-out of variegated patterns placed in front of a light unit to cast a shadow to break up a dull or monotonous surface.

Depth of Field   When a lens is focused on a plane, the definition both in front of and behind that plane will gradually fall off, until the lack of sharpness becomes so apparent that the eye will no longer tolerate it. Between these limits definition will be acceptable, the distance between the nearest and farthest sharp planes in the subject being called *depth of field*.

Deuce   A two-thousand-watt spotlight, generally equipped with a Fresnel lens.

Development   The process of treating exposed original footage in order to make visible the *latent image*.

318

Dinky-Inky   A small one-hundred-fifty-watt spotlight used for special highlighting effects.

Dissolve   An optical effect in which one shot disappears while another appears, achieved by superimposing a fade-out of one shot on a fade-in of another.

Double System   A synchronous sound shooting system in which the picture is taken on one strip of film while the track is made separately, usually on tape.

Edge Numbers   See *code numbers* or *footage numbers*.

Effects   Also referred to as opticals. An inconclusive term referring to dissolves, fades, wipes, and other patterns whereby one shot replaces the next through an effect.

Effects Track   A sound track containing sounds other than music, dialogue, or narration.

Emulsion   Mixture of light-sensitive silver salts and gelatin, coated on transparent base to make film. Sometimes it is referred to as the dull side of the film.

Emulsion Speed   The degree of light sensitivity of the emulsion expressed in numbers as set by the American Standards Association. The higher the rating, the more sensitive the emulsion. Also called *film speed* and *exposure index*.

Exposed Footage   Film that has been exposed in a camera and holds a latent image not yet developed.

Exposure   Any given intensity of light allowed to reach a film emulsion to produce a latent image.

Exposure Index   See *emulsion speed*.

Exposure Meter   An instrument used to measure light intensity incident upon or reflected by a subject being photographed. Hence there are two types of light meters: incident light meters, and reflected light meters.

Fade In or *Fade Out*   An optical effect of a shot in which the shot gradually appears (fade in) out of blackness or gradually disappears (fade out) into blackness.

Film Characteristics (or Properties)   An inconclusive phrase taking in general properties, exposure index, color sensitivity, processing, etc. Data sheets are obtained by writing directly to the film manufacturer.

Filter Factor   A number designating how much exposure should be increased to allow for the light loss caused by the filter being used.

Filters   Pieces of colored gelatin or glass placed in front of a lens to correct tonal coloring in terms of black-and-white photography or to increase the contrast. These are called correction and contrast filters. Other filters cut down the amount of light that reaches the lens and are called neutral density filters. Still others, called polascreens, or polarizing filters, eliminate unwanted reflections.

Fine Cut When editing of the work print has reached a stage near completion, it is referred to as a *fine cut*.

Fishpole Usually a bamboo pole from which a microphone can be suspended. Used in those instances where a boom would be inconvenient.

Flip A kind of wipe in which one shot appears to turn over to show a second shot on the back.

Focal Length The distance between the principal focus of a lens and its optical center or vortex, expressed either in inches or millimeters. The shorter the focal length, the more area will be seen from any given point; the longer the focal length, the less area will be seen from any given point; but that area seen will be magnified. The focal length of a lens is inversely proportional to the depth of field of a lens. Normal, wide-angle, and telephoto lenses are of different focal lengths.

Focus The point on the optical axis behind the lens at which a sharp image point is formed.

Frame One picture unit on a strip of motion picture film.

Fresnel Lens A specially devised lens used in lighting units and identified by concentric ridges in its face. It throws a soft edge spot and is good for blending light.

Frozen Work Print A work print that has been fine cut and is considered so complete that no further work is to be done on it.

f. stop A geometrically calculated measure of the light that enters a lens, secured by dividing the *focal length* of the lens by its diaphragm.

Gaffer The chief electrician in a studio who is responsible for lighting the sets, and answers to the cameraman.

Gamma-Infinity The maximum gamma, or development contrast, that a given emulsion can attain.

Gobo Black wooden screens, usually held by stands, used primarily to cut light from entering the camera lens. Smaller goboes are called *flags, teasers, targets*, each of different size and shape.

Grain Small silver halide particles made up of bromide, chloride, and iodide within the emulsion of a film. In any type of emulsion, the exposure activates the largest grains first. If visible upon screening, the film is said to be *grainy*.

Head The beginning of the film. The end of the film is called the *tail*. When a film is ready for projection, it is said to be *heads up*.

The term also refers to the moving portion of a tripod on which a camera is mounted.

High-Key Lighting Lighting that results in a picture having gradations from gray to white primarily; dark grays and blacks are present, but in very limited areas.

Hot Spot An area in a picture that has been overlighted. Intense and unacceptable brilliance caused by a metallic reflection or mirror reflection also is called a *hot spot*.

Hyperfocal Distance That distance at and beyond which all objects are in focus when sharp focus is secured at infinity. Should the lens be focused on the hyperfocal distance, however, then everything from one half the hyperfocal distance to infinity will be sharp.

Incident Light Meter An instrument that measures the intensity of light falling on a subject. See *exposure meter*.

Interlock A system in which a projector and tape or film playback machines all turn at the same speed. Each unit is equipped with a synchronous motor and then tied together with *selsyn* motors, which keep them together. Insures absolute synchronization on playback.

Intermittent Movement The action of the film through the camera or projector gate in which each individual frame of picture stops and goes. Lack of such movement would cause a blur of picture on the screen. Such movement is to be differentiated from the movement of the sound track, which is continuous. For this reason picture (moving intermittently) is in advance of the sound track by twenty-six frames. This separation allows for the track to move continuously, all within the prescribed area in a projector.

Keg (or Keg Light) A seven-hundred-fifty-watt spotlight, so named because of its keglike shape.

Key Light The apparent principal source of directional illumination falling on a subject or area.

Latent Image The image registered on a photographic emulsion that becomes visible after development.

Latitude The amount by which a film may be overexposed or underexposed without appreciable loss of image quality. The latitude of a film is its ability to provide satisfactory results over a range of exposures.

Lay In Refers to a number of editing operations in which film is put together, usually on a synchronizer, i.e., *lay in* the track, *lay in* original, etc.

Leader   Black film having a coated or uncoated base and placed at the head and tail of a film for threading purposes. There are also a variety of kinds of leaders for different purposes, i.e., *academy leader*, placed at the head of the projection prints for cueing; *black leader* used for *checkerboarding* original in the preparation of 16-mm *A and B rolls*.

Lens   A piece or pieces of glass or other transparent substances called elements and having two opposite regular surfaces, either both curved or one curved and the other plane, for forming an image by changing the direction of rays of light.

Lenses, Complement of   A full set of lenses to include a short focal length lens (wide-angle), a medium focal length (normal) lens, and a variety of long focal length lenses (telephotos).

Lighting   The illumination of a scene set up before a camera. It includes *key light, fill light, cross light, back light, high light, eye light, set light*—all or some of it to make up either *low-key* or *high-key* lighting.

Lighting Units   The variety of fixtures available for lighting purposes. The two broad categories are *spotlights* and *floodlights*, which include *dinky-inkies, kegs, aces, deuces, heavies* or *brutes*, and *arcs*.

Light Meter   See *exposure meter*.

Live Sound   Recording of actual sound at the time of shooting, usually in reference to dialogue.

Low-Key Lighting   A type of lighting which, applied to a scene, results in a picture having gradations from middle gray to black with comparatively limited areas of light grays and whites.

Luminance   Unit of measurement of reflected light as distinguished from illumination, the unit of measurement of incident light, measured in foot candles.

Magnetic Recording   A recording system in which a ferromagnetic medium is subjected to magnetic variations; most popular are quarter-inch synchronous tape recorders.

Married Print   Print made by having sound track and picture on one strip of film.

Matching   The cutting of original negative or reversal where the original is *matched* shot for shot to the *frozen work print;* also known as *negative cutting, conforming*.

Microphone   An instrument for transmitting sound; a variety of kinds are available for specific purposes, i.e., unidirectional, directional, lavalier, shotgun, etc.

Microphone Placement   The positioning of the microphone for satisfactory pickup, normally said to be two feet in front of the speaker and one foot above him during a shooting setup.

Mix or Mixing   Usually refers to the process where two or more sound tracks are played back and *mixed* so that a composite sound track is made of music, sound effects, and voice.

Moviola   Trade name of a machine that permits picture and sound tracks to be run separately or together so that editing can be done.

Music Track   A specially prepared sound track carrying music, usually on tape and to be *mixed* with other tracks.

Narrated Track   A specially prepared sound track carrying *voice-over* narration, separate from a *dialogue track*, usually on tape and to be *mixed* with other tracks.

Negative   Original film exposed in the camera, and in which black and white values are opposite to those in the print. Term also applies to *negative sound track*, an optical track containing sound that is lined up with *picture negative* to make a *composite print* for projection purposes.

Optical Printing   A method of printing by projecting the image to be duplicated through a lens system; the image may be reduced, enlarged, or copied the same size.

Optical Recording   A recording method different from magnetic recording in that sound modulations are placed on film. As in picture, either positive or negative optical tracks may be secured.

Opticals   An inclusive term referring to special picture effects such as dissolves, fades, wipes, etc.

Original Footage   The initial footage or *raw stock* used in the camera. It may be *negative* or *reversal* (positive).

Outline   A general sketch of the way the film-maker intends to handle his story content.

Parallax   The difference between what is seen by the camera viewfinder and the camera lens as a result of the viewfinder being placed beside the lens; corrections are made by adjusting the viewfinder.

Perforations   The precise and evenly spaced holes found on the side of motion picture film that are engaged by claw, sprockets, or pin as the film passes through a camera or projector.

Playback   The replay of a sound recording. Magnetic recording may be played back immediately; optical recording would have to be developed.

Positive   The print made from a negative.

Post-Synchronization   Recording speech, music, or sound effects to a picture after the picture has been filmed. In the case of speech it is referred to as *dubbing*.

Push-Off   A type of wipe in which the visible line of the second shot is perpendicular as it moves across the screen.

Raw Stock   Film that has neither been exposed nor processed; it may be either *negative* or *reversal* (positive).

Recorder   An instrument for recording sound, available both for magnetic and optical recording.

Reflector   Aluminum foil placed on a hard backing to direct sunlight onto actors. There are hard and soft reflectors, depending on the intensity of light to be reflected.

Release Prints   A print of a completed film, containing picture and sound with the sound in projection synchronism.

Research   An inclusive term that covers such pre-production tasks as checking of facts and story background, visiting and selecting locations to be used for shooting.

Reversal Film   A film stock that after exposure is processed to produce a positive image instead of a negative one.

Rewinds   A geared device for winding film up on reels or flanges.

Rough Cut   After the *workprint* has been *assembled* the very first tightening and trimming of it is called the *rough cut*. In editing the steps are from *assembly* to *rough cut* and gradually to *fine cut*.

Scrim   Similar to a *gobo*, except that it is made of translucent material and its purpose is partly to diffuse the light and partly to cut it off.

Selsyn Motor   A type of self-synchronizing motor that provides an *interlock* when connected to other motors. Selsyns make the armatures of synchronous motors rotate similarly.

Sensitometry   The science that measures the effect of light on film and the effect of developers on film as latent images are made visible.

Shooting Breakdown   A separation of the shots in a script into an order for shooting and in terms of a day-to-day schedule. Also, breakdowns may separate sound shots from silent ones, depending on amount of each, so that sound crews will not wait while silent shots are taken.

Shooting Script   The film script broken down into a shot by shot presentation and in its continuity.

Silks   Translucent material set within a holder and placed in front of a lighting unit for softening and diffusing the light.

Single System   A sound shooting system in which the picture and the sound track are placed on one strip of film so that a composite is secured after development. Track here may be either magnetic or optical. Used primarily for newsreel work where interviews or speeches are to be quickly recorded. Not practical for regular production because the track in single system is in projection synchronization.

Slugs Pieces of leader placed in the work print to replace torn or damaged areas; also, to denote position of titles or other art work.

Sound Effects Track A special track made up of sound effects to be *mixed* with music and voice.

Sound Reader Sometimes called a *squawk box*, it is a device set up between rewinds, is operated manually, and plays back sound track. Used for spotting speeches, sound effects, pieces of music.

Spectogram A graph that shows the response of film emulsion to color in terms of black-and-white scale.

Speed May refer to film speed, meaning ASA rating, operation of the camera (usually twenty-four frames per second), or the cry *"speed"* of the sound man as his recorder comes up to running speed.

Spherical Aberration A defect of a spherical lens whereby rays of light passing through parts of the lens nearer its edge do not focus at exactly the same point as the rays passing through the center of the lens.

Spin A kind of optical effect in which the entire shot, or part of the shot, is rotated quickly.

Sprocketed Magnetic Tape Magnetic tape that has perforations along one edge similar to film. In synchronous work these sprocket holes mark off frames that are in direct line with frames of picture.

Synchronizer An instrument through which two or more lengths of film or sprocketed magnetic tape can be moved along in step with one another for the purpose of editing or laying-in film or sound track.

Synchronous motor A motor that insures constant speed, used on cameras and recorders for synchronous sound shooting.

Sync Pulse An electrical pulse system whereby quarter-inch tape is kept in synchronous operation with a camera. A number of such systems are now on the market and have been the basis for portable, lightweight field-recording equipment. A pulse is placed on the quarter-inch tape, which during rerecording is checked through an oscilloscope so that adjustments can be made on the recorder to maintain synchronization.

Take The individual photographed shot; when many of these are made repeatedly they are referred to as "Take 1," "Take 2," etc.

Timing The act of examining original footage, determining its density and the corresponding printing light to be used to make the print, to balance the different densities found in the original footage so that the print will be visually satisfactory.

Timing Card A card that carries the notations of the various printing lights used. It is prepared by the laboratory *timer,* the man who judges the shot density, and is referred to when corrections or changes have to be made.

Transparent Film Tape A specially designed transparent material that can be placed directly onto torn or ripped pieces of workprint. If the torn places are beyond this minimal repair, then *slugs* have to be used.

Trims The pieces of shots left over as the editor moves from a *rough assembly* to a *fine cut.* Shots not used are called *out takes;* pieces left from shots used are the *trims.*

Turn A kind of wipe similar to a flip in which the axis of the turn is vertical rather than horizontal.

Turret A revolving mount, held in front of a camera, carrying two or more lenses that can be swung around to be brought before the aperture.

Twenty-six Frame Advance Also called *projection sync.* Because the picture runs intermittently while the sound runs continuously, the two cannot begin at the same point in a *composite print.* Hence, before printing, the sound is advanced. In 35-mm this difference of space is *twenty* frames. During editing, of course, sound and picture are handled from a common starting point. This is referred to as *editorial sync.*

Viewer An instrument, usually manually operated, for viewing film; used a good deal in cutting silent footage to which sound is yet to be added.

Wild Sound The nonsynchronous recording of sounds that later may be laid in on a synchronizer against specific portions of picture.

Wild Track A sound track that does not have a synchronous relationship to picture; it may contain general background noise, voices, etc.

Wipe An optical effect occurring between two successive shots in which the second shot replaces the first. Distinctions in terminology come about because of the various methods used to achieve varying effects. (See wipe-off.)

Wipe-Off An optical effect of two successive shots in which the second shot appears along a visible line and wipes away the first shot.

Workprint A positive print, usually untimed and printed with one light, used exclusively for editing purposes. It is made up of the accumulation of the prints drawn from daily shooting and comes into being with the first *assembly.*

ANNOTATED SELECTED BIBLIOGRAPHY

In little more than half a century a great deal has been written about the film, both in book and periodical. Some of these books are either outdated or written in a ponderous style that is often obscure; others comprehensively treat specific or highly specialized aspects of the film industry.

The following book list, therefore, is not in any way meant to be a complete one, nor is it of wide scope as far as the many aspects of both film art and industry are concerned. Rather, it is a select list recommended for the beginning film-maker to serve as the basis for a personal library. In addition, the books have been selected primarily with an eye toward providing the beginner with a knowledge of historical trends and traditions, techniques and approaches, and recent insights into film as expressed by critics, theorists, and film-makers.

HISTORY AND BACKGROUND

A. R. Fulton, *Motion Pictures, The Development of an Art from Silent Film to the Age of Television* (Norman, Okla.: University of Oklahoma Press, 1960).

327

Although familiar historical ground is covered here, the author selects highlights, and his research has taken him into interesting and seldom-mentioned occurrences, events, incidents, and attitudes of the film pioneers. In addition, a number of chapters are devoted to other literary forms and their adaptation to film: a basis is established for film aesthetics.

Penelope Houston, *The Contemporary Cinema* (Baltimore: Penguin Books, 1963).

Covering that period from World War II to the present, Miss Houston provides a thorough picture of the trends and development of film during a complex and volatile period, with film passing through an international revolution. The author deftly places things in perspective and gives a clear account of what to the uninitiated may seem utter confusion, all the while seeing justification for the variety in films that is available today.

Lewis Jacobs, *The Rise of the American Film* (New York: Harcourt, Brace & Company, 1939).

Still one of the most detailed and lucid accounts of film from its beginnings until World War II, Mr. Jacobs' work remains the classic reference for the serious student and film-maker. The book's value lies not only in its documentation, but also in the author's love and enthusiasm for the film medium.

Arthur Knight, *The Liveliest Art* (New York: The Macmillan Company, 1957).

Beginning with the nickelodeon days and tracing film development up through the middle 1950's, the author stresses this development in terms of the growing art. This work is extremely helpful in understanding artistic motivation, the role of the film-maker, and the manner in which the particular film is affected by the man, the times, and his ideas.

CRAFT AND THEORY

W. Hugh Baddeley, *The Technique of Documentary Film Production* (New York: Hastings House, 1963).

The author provides the benefit of his personal experience and knowledge in the making of documentary films. Much of the book is given to technical matters in a clear and comprehensible way. As the book covers film-making from the script to distribution, the latest practices, trends, methods, and equipment are covered in detail.

Ernest Lindgren, *The Art of the Film* (New York: The Macmillan Company, 1963).

Given more to aesthetics and theory, this book forms a good companion piece to Karel Reisz' *The Technique of Film Editing*. Statements and ideas of early film-makers are analyzed and placed in correct perspective, and film theory is discussed in the light of film classics.

Karel Reisz, *The Technique of Film Editing* (New York: Hastings House, 1963).

In its seventh printing, this compilation of the thoughts and ideas of England's foremost film-makers, brought into sharp focus by Karel Reisz, is far and away the best working manual on both craft and theory. Beginning with a precise and clear analysis of the work of D. W. Griffith, Pudovkin, and Eisenstein, the text covers craft and editing, with the stress on the ways in which artistic expression is achieved.

Paul Rotha, *Documentary Film* (New York: Faber and Faber, 1952).

Here is both a history of the documentary and a discussion of the artistic principles involved in its production. Although much has happened to the documentary and the short subject since the book was written, Mr. Rotha's theory of the documentary as applied to the British movement is of particular interest because of the theory's likeness in a number of ways to many current feature films.

Raymond Spottiswoode, *Film and Its Techniques* (Berkeley and Los Angeles: University of California Press, 1951).

Touching on theory slightly, the book in the main explains the complex technical processes in film-making. Both equipment and practices are examined, from camera and lighting to laboratory printing procedures. Although recent advances, particularly in portable quarter-inch tape recording, are beyond this text, it is still invaluable as a basic reference.

TECHNICAL AREAS

Arthur Clarke, *Professional Cinematography* (Hollywood, Calif.: American Society of Cinematographers, 1964).

A detailed and highly technical explanation of cameras, lighting, and related subjects, this text is for the skilled technician. Particularly when challenged by special problems having to do with technical phases of film-making, the film-maker will find a valuable reference here.

Joseph Mascelli, *American Cinematographer Manual* (Hollywood, Calif: American Society of Cinematographers, 1960).

An extremely necessary book for the film-maker actively engaged in camera work. It is divided into ten sections, each providing immediate working information on cameras, film, lenses, exposure, black-and-white filters, color, lighting, background process, television, and sound and special techniques.

William Offenhauser, *Sound Motion Pictures* (New York: Interscience Publishers, 1949).

Referred to as "A Manual for the Professional and the Amateur," it is still for the highly skilled technician with a leaning toward engineering. It is an excellent reference work describing in minute detail cameras, printing apparatus, sound recorders, and sound systems.

SPECIALIZED AREAS

Vincent J. R. Kehoe, *The Technique of Film and Television Make-up* (New York: Hastings House, 1958).

Although the film-maker in general may not be interested in the specialized details of make-up, the book can serve as a general reference. Early sections dealing with make-up, light, and facial anatomy are of broad interest.

Roger Manvell and John Huntley, *The Technique of Film Music* (London: Focal Press, 1957).

This book is essential reading for every film-maker. Beginning with a discussion of music as it relates to drama and the film, the authors go on to discuss music in the days of the silent film and its function with sound film. Included are a number of discussions with film-makers in which they explain reasons for their decisions. There are numerous examples of pieces of music, lined up with shots and analyzed to show relationship and function.

PERSONALITIES AND
POINTS OF VIEW

Jörn Donner, *The Personal Vision of Ingmar Bergman* (Bloomington: Indiana University Press, 1964).

The author, a critic and film-maker himself, discusses Bergman's relationship to modern cinema as he analyzes his films. The book is given mostly to a philosophical evaluation of the films in an attempt to discover Bergman, the film-maker.

Peter Cowie, *Antonioni, Bergman, Resnais* (New York: Barnes and Company, 1963).

The author provides an account of each of the film-makers' early years and then gives an analysis of those films that brought them widespread recognition. An effort is made to discuss the material in terms of the individual techniques of the men.

Robert Hughes, ed., *Film: Book I* (New York: Grove Press, 1959).

The author has compiled a series of interesting articles by critics and film-makers, among them Arthur Knight and George Stoney, and has included replies to a questionnaire answered by such men as Luis Buñuel, René Clement, Elia Kazan, David Lean, Sidney Meyers and Satyajit Ray.

Lewis Jacobs, *Introduction to the Art of the Movies* (New York: The Noonday Press, 1960).

An anthology in which the author updates his earlier work, *The Rise of the American Film,* and offers thoughtful articles by the leading critics, scholars, and film-makers of each decade from 1910 through 1960.

Ado Kyrou, *Luis Buñuel* (New York: Simon and Schuster, 1963).

An attempt to understand Buñuel the film-maker by examining his early years, his experiments and successes, and, finally, by bringing together select criticism.

Pierre Leprohon, *Michelangelo Antonioni* (New York: Simon and Schuster, 1963).

This book provides an account of Antonioni's early years, quotes from articles he has written, and gives a critical comment on his films drawn from many sources in order to provide insight.

331

PERIODICALS

Film Comment, a quarterly edited by Gordon Hitchens, 11 St. Luke's Place, New York.

A relatively new journal, *Film Comment* has proved its value by covering a variety of film subjects from new schools of film-making around the world to new film-making equipment. Articles include legal aspects, film festivals, new films, new books, as well as film-making ideas of outstanding directors, writers, actors.

Film Quarterly, University of California Press, Berkeley, 4, Cal.

Must reading for the film-maker and serious student. Edited by Ernest Callenbach, and assisted by a host of people long associated with film, the *Quarterly* provides articles, interviews, and reviews of current film topics and trends, without any hoop-la—a serious and sober journal.

Sight and Sound, published by the British Film Institute, London.

Usually covering features, articles, film reviews and book reviews, this English quarterly represents the latest and perhaps best of British thinking on film. Although published by the British Film Institute, this magazine is independent and does not express official policy.

INDEX

INDEX

budget, control of shots and, 190–191
Buñuel, Luis, 125

Cabinet of Dr. Caligari, The, 9
Cacoyannis, Michael, 125
Caesar, Sid, 179
call sheet, 160
camera, freedom of, 200; hand-held, 195; movement of, 117–118, 187; moving or panning, 92, 195, 200; range and flexibility of, 15–19; reverse angle and, 94–97; saturation coverage with, 196; versus television, 200; timing and, 187
camera angle, 23, 114–118
cameraman, 195–196
camera report sheet, 160
Cannes prizes, 125
Captain Jinks of the Horse Marines, 46
Caron, Leslie, 177
Carra, Lawrence, 18 n.
cartoon, animated, 149
Cercle du MacMahon, 176
Champion, 233
Chaplin, Charles, 154
Chatterjee, Soumitra, 176
cinematic story-telling, 125
cinema vérité, 203
Citizen Kane, 8, 114
City, The, 7, 40 n., 195
Clair, René, 155
Clément, René, 101, 105
climax, as beginning point, 198; crisis and, 64–66; defined, 44
close-up, 171, 221; camera angle and, 117; editing and, 219; intensification of detail through, 143; movement through, 226–228; use of, 78–89
Clurman, Harold, 179
Cocteau, Jean, 125
coherence, 31
color, editing and, 232; value of, 11
Columbia Pictures, 123
communication, verbal to visual, 134–138
complication, defined, 43
composition, 11
compromise, mediocrity and, 203

concept, defined, 60; structure and, 59–61
conflict, defined, 44
Contemporary Cinema, The, 181
content, as controlling element, 18; form and, 3, 129; technique and, 1, 257
continuity, defined, 79; physical, 79–85
Corner in Wheat, A, 215
Corrigan, Robert W., 249
Courtenay, Tom, 176
craft, defined, 3, 72; as film technique, 72–121; progress to art, 74–79
creativity, story-telling and, 127
crisis, 44; climax and, 64–66
Crosby, John, 176
cross-cutting, 76, 102; reverse angle and, 95
cross plot, 160
Crowther, Bosley, 124
cutaway, 97–102
cutback, 97
cutting, medium shots in, 90; movement through, 229–230; "rough" and "fine" types, 245; tempo and, 10–11; *see also* cross-cutting; editing
cutting room, 244

dance, film and, 10
Darwin, Charles, 27
Dean, Alexander, 18
Defenders, The, 200
delays, production, 160
depth of field, 154–156
design values, 233
detail, identification through, 141–144
deus ex machina, 44
dialogue, 16; editing and, 183; filmic versus theatrical, 255; use of, 25–26
Dickens, Charles, 191
Dietrich, Marlene, 20
direction of movement, 102–106
director, 14–15; self-involvement of, 240–241; squabbles with, 175–176; style of, 239–240; *see also* film-maker
director-cameraman, 196
director-writer, 123
discovery, defined, 43
dissolves, 111–112

334

INDEX